THE MAKING OF
JEWISH AND CHRISTIAN WORSHIP

TWO LITURGICAL TRADITIONS

Volume 1

The Making of
Jewish and Christian Worship

Edited by

PAUL F. BRADSHAW
and
LAWRENCE A. HOFFMAN

University of Notre Dame Press
Notre Dame   London

BV
169.5
.M35
1991

Library of Congress Cataloging-in-Publication Data

The Making of Jewish and Christian worship / edited by Paul
F. Bradshaw and Lawrence A. Hoffman.
    v. cm. — (Two liturgical traditions ; v. 1)
    Papers delivered at a conference on liturgy held at the
University of Notre Dame, June 1988.
    Includes bibliographical references and index.
    ISBN 0-268-01206-7
    1. Liturgics—Congresses. 2. Judaism—Liturgy—
Congresses. 3. Christianity and other religions—Judaism—
Congresses. 4. Judaism—Relations—Christianity—
Congresses. I. Bradshaw, Paul F. II. Hoffman, Lawrence
A., 1942-   . III. Series.
BV169.5.M35   1991   90-70856
264'.009—dc20   CIP

Contents

Abbreviations   vii

Preface   ix

PART I: ORIGINS AND METHODS

Ten Principles for Interpreting Early Christian
Liturgical Evidence • *Paul F. Bradshaw*   3

Reconstructing Ritual as Identity and Culture
• *Lawrence A. Hoffman*   22

The Politics of Piety: Social Conflict and the Emergence
of Rabbinic Liturgy • *Tzvee Zahavy*   42

Using Archeological Sources • *Marilyn J. S. Chiat
and Marchita B. Mauck*   69

PART II: EVOLUTION AND CHANGE

The Early History of Jewish Worship
• *Stefan C. Reif*   109

Jewish Worship since the Period of Its Canonization
• *Eric L. Friedland*   137

Christian Worship to the Eve of the Reformation
• *John F. Baldovin*   156

Christian Worship since the Reformation
• *Susan J. White*   184

Index   207

Abbreviations

GLS   Grove Liturgical Study

HTR   Harvard Theological Review

HUCA   Hebrew Union College Annual

JJS   Journal of Jewish Studies

JLS   Alcuin/GROW Joint Liturgical Study

JQR   Jewish Quarterly Review

SL   Studia Liturgica

Preface

This volume is the first of a series celebrating the liturgical and ecumenical breakthrough that has marked the past several decades. Both Jews and Christians have come to new, even revolutionary, views of worship: not only how it began, but also what it is today. This dual focus on both past and present is not accidental. From a liturgical point of view, there is no such thing as purely academic scholarship. In an age that values tradition even as it criticizes it, a novel reconstruction of yesterday's origins has an impact upon today's spirituality.

This first volume describes how the worship of synagogue and church were born and how they evolved through the ages. Part 1, "Origins and Methods," describes the evidence—both textual and archeological—that allows us to reconstruct early Jewish and Christian worship and delineates the advances in recent scholarship that affect what we think those sources mean. Part 2, "Evolution and Change," traces Jewish and Christian liturgical traditions from the time they were conceived to the twentieth century, indicating along the way the major shifts in form and character that they underwent at significant points in their history and that, to a large extent, continue to affect the shape of worship today.

The idea for the series which this book inaugurates came from what we believe was the first-ever joint Jewish and Christian conference on liturgy, held at the University of Notre Dame, Indiana, in June 1988 and made possible by the Crown-Minow Endowment of the Department of Theology there. The first two volumes of this series contain papers delivered at the conference itself and other contributions specially written to complement them.

The essays were originally envisaged as a way of introducing members of each tradition to the history and current situation of the worship of the other. It soon became clear, however, that we had more than a digest of information that was well known to members of one of the traditions but unknown to members of the other. The authors provided instead the most up-to-date analysis, in nontechnical form, of the state of liturgical scholarship today. The chapters which follow are therefore important scholarly contributions to Christian and Jewish self-understanding of their own liturgical traditions as well. It is hoped that Jewish and Christian readers will not only learn much from the parts that speak about the other tradition but also from those which deal with their own, and that they will find striking parallels as well as some significant differences in the past and present of both.

Paul F. Bradshaw
Lawrence A. Hoffman

PART I

Origins and Methods

Ten Principles for Interpreting
Early Christian Liturgical Evidence[1]

PAUL F. BRADSHAW

[Editors' note: Paul F. Bradshaw, Professor of Liturgy at the University of Notre Dame, here challenges some traditional assumptions about how to handle the complex evidence for the evolution of liturgical practice in the first few centuries of Christianity's existence and sets out some principles to guide students in this field.]

As is the case with Jewish liturgy, extant liturgical manuscripts from the Christian tradition are nearly all of relatively recent date, beginning around the eighth century c.e. Sources for a knowledge of the practice of worship prior to that time are fragmentary, consisting chiefly of brief, and often partial, descriptions of rites in letters and sermons; of even briefer, and less easily interpreted, allusions that appear in writings dealing with some quite different subject; of pieces of legislation affecting liturgical matters that occur among the canons produced by various councils and synods; of some fragments of what seem to be the texts of individual prayers; and, last but not least, of the prescriptions concerning worship in an extremely enigmatic genre of early Christian literature, the pseudoapostolic church orders.

All these are, in effect, little more than a series of dots of varying sizes and density on a large sheet of plain paper. To the liturgical historian, therefore, falls the task of attempting to join up those dots and so creating a plausible picture that explains how, and more importantly why, Christian worship evolved in the way that it did. Because, however, the dots on this sheet of paper are not prenumbered and so the connections which should be made between them are by no means obvious, the assumptions and presuppositions with which one begins such an operation are vitally important in determining its outcome. If one adopts, for example, the axiom that the primary connections must always run between the dots that lie closest to one another on the paper, then one will get a very different picture than if one starts by joining up all the largest dots first and then proceeding to the smaller ones in relative order, no matter how many times one's pencil has to crisscross the page.

What follows, then, is a brief critique of certain methodological presuppositions that have tended to be followed in traditional study of the origins of Christian worship, some indications as to how these are already changing—or in some cases ought to be changing, even if they are as yet not doing so—and the effect that this altered perspective has on our picture of early liturgical practice. Quite fortuitously, it turns out to be a decalogue of proposed principles for the interpretation of early Christian liturgical evidence.

1. What is most common is not necessarily most ancient, and what is least common is not necessarily least ancient.

As I have indicated elsewhere,[2] the dominant view of liturgical scholars concerning the origins of Christian liturgy has traditionally been that the many varied forms of the celebration of the eucharist, of baptism, and perhaps also of other rites that we find in different geographical regions in later centuries can all be traced back to a single common root in their institution by Jesus; and that variety tended to increase in the course of time as the Church developed and these practices were subject to differing local influences and emphases. Thus, it has been thought, what is common to most or all of these later forms must represent the very earliest stratum of Christian worship, while what is found in just a few instances, or merely one, is a later development.[3]

Such a view cannot really be sustained any longer in the light of recent scholarship. Not only has the theory always had considerable difficulty in demonstrating how such very diverse later practices can all arise from a single source, but it now has to take into account both the fact that Jewish worship of the first century C.E., from which Christian worship took its departure, was not nearly so fixed or uniform as was once supposed, and also the conclusion that New Testament Christianity was itself essentially pluriform in doctrine and practice.

Thus, what is common in later Christian liturgical practice is not necessarily what is most primitive. It certainly may be so, but it is equally possible that similarities that exist between customs in different parts of the ancient world are the result of a conscious movement towards conformity. Similarly, what is unusual or unique is not necessarily a late development. Once again it may be so, but it is equally possible that the unusual is the vestigial remains of what was once a much greater variety of forms of worship than we can now see in the surviving evidence, an ancient local custom that somehow managed to escape—or at least avoid the full effect of—a later process that caused liturgical diversity to contract its horizons.

For the true story of the development of Christian worship seems to have been a movement from considerable differences over quite fundamental elements to an increasing amalgamation and standardization of local customs. This can already be seen in the second century C.E., but it gathered much greater momentum in the fourth, as the Church expanded, as communication—and hence awareness of differences—between different regional centers increased, and above all as orthodox Christianity tried to define itself over against what were perceived as heretical movements, for in such a situation any tendency to persist in what appeared to be idiosyncratic liturgical observances was likely to have been interpreted as a mark of heterodoxy. As Robert F. Taft has written,

> This is the period of the unification of rites, when worship, like church government, not only evolved new forms, but also let the weaker variants of the species die out, as the Church developed, via the creation of intermediate unities, into a federation of federations of local churches, with ever-increasing unity of practice

within each federation, and ever-increasing diversity of practice from federation to federation. In other words what was once one loose collection of individual local churches each with its own liturgical uses, evolved into a series of intermediate structures or federations (later called patriarchates) grouped around certain major sees. This process stimulated a corresponding unification and standardizing of church practice, liturgical and otherwise. Hence, the process of formation of rites is not one of diversification, as is usually held, but of unification. And what one finds in extant rites today is not a synthesis of all that went before, but rather the result of a selective evolution: the survival of the fittest—of the fittest, not necessarily of the best.[4]

2. *The so-called Constantinian revolution served as much to intensify existing trends as it did to initiate new ones.*

The conversion to Christianity of the emperor Constantine early in the fourth century is usually portrayed as marking a crucial turning-point in the evolution of forms of worship; and it is undoubtedly true that a very marked contrast can be observed between the form and character of liturgical practices in the pre-Constantinian and post-Constantinian periods. For example, whereas the first Christians saw themselves as set over against the world and were careful to avoid any compromise with paganism and its customs, stressing rather what distinguished Christianity from other religions, in the fourth century the Church emerged as a public institution within the world, with its liturgy functioning as a *cultus publicus,* seeking the divine favor to secure the well-being of the state, and it was now quite willing to absorb and Christianize pagan religious ideas and practices, seeing itself as the fulfillment to which earlier religions had dimly pointed.

On the other hand, scholars are now beginning to realize that one must be careful not to overstate this contrast between the two periods of ecclesiastical history. A number of developments, the genesis of which has traditionally been ascribed to the changed situation of the Church after the Peace of Constantine, are now shown as having roots that reach back into the third century, and in some cases even earlier still. Hence, in these respects at least, the so-called Constantinian revolution did not so much inaugurate new liturgical practices and attitudes as create conditions in which some preexistent customs could achieve a greater measure of preeminence than others that were no longer considered appropriate to the changed situation of the Church.

The pattern of daily worship, for example, practiced in the monastic communities that began to emerge in the early fourth century was not entirely a new creation of this movement. In some respects the monastic pattern was simply a conservative preservation of a very traditional style of prayer and spirituality. There are certainly some new features—as for example the regular recitation of the book of Psalms in its entirety and in its biblical order as the cornerstone of the spiritual life—but in other ways the monks and nuns of the fourth century were simply continuing to do what ordinary Christians of earlier centuries had once done. The customs only appear peculiarly monastic because they had now been abandoned by other Christians, who, in the more relaxed atmosphere of the Constantinian era, tended to be more lukewarm about their religious commitment than their predecessors in the age of persecution.[5]

Similarly, the interest in time and history that comes to the fore during this period is not something to which the Constantinian world gave birth, though it certainly suckled and nurtured it. It is simply not true, as earlier generations of liturgical scholars tended to conclude, that the first Christians could not possibly have been interested in discovering and commemorating the precise dates and times of the events of the life of Jesus or in establishing a rhythmical pattern of hours of prayer because they expected the end of this world to come at any moment with the return of their Lord. On the contrary, an interest in time and eternity, history and eschatology, can coexist, and indeed the one can be an expression of the other: the early Christians established regular patterns of daily prayer times not because they thought that the Church was here to stay for a long while but precisely so that they might practice eschatological vigilance and be ready and watchful in prayer for the return of Christ and the consummation of God's kingdom.

Hence, the interest in eschatology, which certainly declined when it appeared less and less likely that the world was going to end soon, was not simply replaced by a new interest in time and history. Rather, a preexistent interest took on a new vigor in a new situation, and a multiplicity of feasts and commemorations began to emerge in the fourth century in a way they had not done earlier. This development was generated at least in part by apologetic factors. The Church now needed to communicate the tenets of its faith to a barbarian world which was willing to listen, and to defend its doctrinal positions against a variety of heretical attacks; and what better means could be found than the promotion of occasions that publicly celebrated aspects of what the Church believed?[6]

3. Authoritative-sounding statements are not always genuinely authoritative.

Many ancient Christian writers in their allusions to liturgical practices make very emphatic statements about what is or is not the case, and traditional liturgical scholarship has been inclined to accept such remarks as truly authoritative declarations of the established doctrine and practice of the Church at the time that they were written, especially as many of those making these apparently *ex cathedra* pronouncements did actually occupy the office of a bishop. So, to cite two early examples which actually concern the development of the ordained ministry rather than liturgy itself, the First Epistle of Clement, usually thought to have originated from the church at Rome c. 96 C.E., is a long and impassioned denunciation of the church at Corinth for dismissing its presbyters and replacing them with others; and the letters of Ignatius of Antioch, conventionally dated early in the second century, repeatedly insist on the necessity of obedience to the bishop and his fellow ministers. Both have generally been understood as expressing the agreed position of the Church on these issues—that ministers were always appointed for life and that episcopal government was the norm early in the second century. Recent study, however, has suggested that, since they were apparently having to argue the case at considerable length and with great vigor against opponents who seemingly did not share their conclusions, they must, on the contrary, represent only one view among others at the time, a view which ultimately came to triumph but which did not achieve supremacy without a considerable struggle against alternative positions and practices.[7]

Hence the development of ecclesiastical structures and liturgical practices seems to have been much slower than has traditionally been supposed. Many things did emerge quite early in the life of the Church but did not immediately achieve normative or universal status, however strongly some individuals might have thought that they should. Authoritative-sounding statements, therefore, need to be taken with a pinch of salt. When some early Christian author proudly proclaims, for example, that a certain psalm or canticle is sung "throughout the world," it probably means at the most that he knows it to be used in the particular regions he has visited or heard about: it remains an open question whether a similar usage obtained in other parts of the world.[8] Similarly, when some ancient bishop solemnly affirms that a certain liturgical custom is "unheard of" in any church, he is almost certainly excluding from his definition of *church* those groups of Christians whom he judges to be heretical, among whom the practice might well still be flourishing as it once had done in many other places in earlier times, in spite of our bishop's confident (though ignorant) assertion to the contrary.[9]

4. Legislation is better evidence for what it proposes to prohibit than for what it seeks to promote.

When attention is directed toward the decrees of ecclesiastical councils and synods in the search for information about the practice of worship in the early Church, there is a natural

tendency to focus on the things that it is said shall or shall not
be done. Thus, to cite a simple example, when the Council of
Braga in 561 C.E. insists that "one and the same order of
psalmody is to be observed in the morning and evening services; and neither individual variations nor monastic uses are
to be interpolated into the ecclesiastical rule," one might be
tempted to conclude that liturgical practices in Spain must
have been uniform thereafter. Such a conclusion, however,
can be shown to be false by the fact that synods held in later
years found it necessary to repeat over and over again this
demand for a standardization in usage.[10] Just because an
authoritative body makes a liturgical regulation does not mean
that it was observed everywhere or ever put into practice anywhere at all. Conservatism in matters liturgical is notoriously
intractable, and, as we all know well, canonical legislation
from even the highest level is frequently unable to dislodge a
well-established and much-loved local custom.

This does not mean, however, that such pieces of legislation
are entirely valueless in the search for clues to the liturgical
customs of the early Church. Indeed, quite the opposite is the
case: regulations provide excellent evidence for what was actually happening in local congregations, not by what is decreed
should be done but by what is either directly prohibited or
indirectly implied should cease to be done. The fact that such
regulations were made at all shows that the very opposite of
what they were trying to promote must have been a widespread
custom at that period. Synodal assemblies do not usually waste
their time either condemning something that is not actually
going on or insisting on the firm adherence to some rule that
everyone is already observing. Thus, for example, the fact
that the Council of Vaison in 529 C.E. decreed that the response *Kyrie eleison* should be used does not prove that this
foreign innovation was quickly accepted in that part of Gaul—
and indeed we have virtually no trace of its subsequent adoption there—but it does show that prior to this time that response was not a common part of the worship of that region.

The same is true of the liturgical comments that are found

in many of the writings and homilies of early Christian theologians and bishops. We generally cannot know whether the practices and customs that they advocated were ever adopted by their congregations, or just politely listened to and then ignored, as the pleas of preachers often are; but we can conclude that there must have been some real foundation to the contrary custom or practice that is either directly criticized or implicitly acknowledged in the advice being given. Such writers may sometimes be suspected of hyperbole in the things they say, but they do not usually tilt at nonexistent windmills. So, for example, when John Chrysostom describes those who fail to stay for the reception of communion at the celebration of the eucharist as resembling Judas Iscariot at the Last Supper,[11] we do not know if he had any success in reforming the behavior of his congregation, but we can safely assume that what he is complaining about was an observable feature at that time.

5. *When a variety of explanations is advanced for the origin of a liturgical custom, its true source has almost certainly been forgotten.*

One frequently encounters in early Christian writings not only a partial description of some liturgical practice but also an explanation as to how it originated. Sometimes it is very easy to detect when such an explanation seems to be no more than the product of a pious imagination. When one reads, for example, in Coptic tradition that it was Theophilus, patriarch of Alexandria in the fourth century, who introduced baptismal chrism into Christian usage in response to the instruction of an angel to bring balsam trees from Jericho, plant them, extract the balsam, and cook the spices,[12] one may well have serious doubts about the veracity of the claim. But in other cases it is less clear whether the author has access to a reliable source of information or not. Sometimes several writers will allude to the same custom but offer widely differing stories as to its true meaning or origin. This is the case, to cite just two examples, with regard to the times of daily prayer commonly observed in the third century, and with regard to the custom, first evidenced in Syria in the late fourth century, of placing the book of the Gospels on the head of a bishop during his ordination.

It is tempting in such instances to opt for the explanation that one finds most congenial to one's point of view and to discount the rest. This is in fact what scholars have generally done with respect to the explanations for the customs just mentioned,[13] but there seems no particular reason to suppose that any one of the ancient commentators had access to a more authoritative source of information than the others. Indeed, the very existence of multiple explanations and interpretations is itself a very good indication that no authoritative tradition with regard to the original purpose and meaning of the custom had survived, and hence writers and preachers felt free to use their imaginations. This is not to say that the real origin can never be unearthed by modern scholarship, with its access to sources and methods not known to the ancients, or that sometimes one of those early writers may not accidentally have hit upon the right solution, but it does suggest that in such situations it may often be necessary to look for the real answer in a quite different direction from that of the conventional accounts.

6. Ancient church orders are not what they seem.

Within early Christian literature is a group of documents that look very like real, authoritative liturgical texts, containing both directions for the conduct of worship and also the words of prayers and other formularies to be used in this activity. Since they claim in one way or another to be apostolic, they have generally been referred to as apostolic church orders. But they are not what they seem. Not only is their claim to apostolic authorship spurious—a judgment that has been universally accepted since at least the beginning of the twentieth century—but they are not even the official liturgical manuals of any third- or fourth-century local church, masquerading in apostolic dress to lend themselves added authority—a judgment that is still not always fully appreciated by all contemporary scholars.

It is usually recognized that at least some of them, especially those dated later in the sequence, were in part the products of the imagination and aspirations of their compilers, armchair liturgists dreaming up what the perfect liturgy might be like if only they had the freedom to put into practice what their idiosyncratic tastes and personal convictions longed for. But there has still been a tendency to want to hold on to at least one or two of them as reliable descriptions of the real liturgy of the local church from which they seem to derive. Indeed, the prayers contained in one of them, the so-called *Apostolic Tradition* of Hippolytus,[14] have been reproduced for use in the modern service books of a considerable number of Christian churches in the last few years, so convinced have the revisers been that here we are in touch with the authentic liturgy of the early Church and so we can now say the same words that ancient Christians once did when we celebrate the eucharist, ordain a bishop, or initiate a new convert.

There is, however, no reason to suppose that this document is a more, or less, reliable guide to what early Christians were really doing in their worship than any of the other church orders, especially as there is also some uncertainty as to what part of the ancient world it comes from and what its original text actually said, since all we have extant are translations and reworkings of it. This does not mean that these church orders are of no value in attempting to recover the liturgical practices of the early Church. They may indeed present evidence for what was actually going on in the churches from which they come, but that evidence can only be disentangled with difficulty and caution from both the idiosyncratic idealizing of the individual authors and the corrections and updating to which the documents tend to have been subjected in the course of their subsequent transmission. Without corroborative evidence from another source it is dangerous to claim that any particular prayer text in them was typical of the worship of the period, and it is still more unwise, on the doubtful presumption of its once-authoritative status, to ask twentieth-century congregations to make it their own.[15]

7. *Liturgical manuscripts are more prone to emendation than literary manuscripts.*

F. L. Cross once observed:

Liturgical and literary texts, as they have come down to us, have a specious similarity. They are written in similar scripts and on similar writing materials. They are now shelved shoulder to shoulder in our libraries and classified within the same system of shelfmarking. . . . But these similarities mask a radical difference. In the first place, unlike literary manuscripts, liturgical manuscripts were not written to satisfy an historical interest. They were written to serve a severely practical end. Their primary purpose was the needs of the services of the Church. Like timetables and other books for use, liturgical texts were compiled with the immediate future in view. Their intent was not to make an accurate reproduction of an existing model.[16]

In other words, copyists or translators of ancient liturgical material did not normally expend considerable time and energy on their work merely out of a general desire to preserve antiquity for its own sake but because they believed that the document legitimized as traditional the liturgical practices of their own day. What were they to do then, for example, when they encountered in a text the apparent omission of some element that was regarded as important or essential in their own tradition? They could only conclude that it ought to be in the text before them, that it must have been practiced in ancient times and had simply been omitted by accident from the document or had fallen out in the course of its transmission. It was then only the work of a few moments to restore what they thought was the original reading and bring it into line with current practice.

This is a very different situation from, say, the copying of the works of Augustine or some other patristic writer, when the desire was precisely to preserve antiquity and make an accurate reproduction of the original. Although such literary manuscripts might also be subject to occasional attempts to correct what were perceived as lapses from doctrinal orthodoxy in the text, these emendations are relatively rare and much easier to detect than in liturgical manuscripts, where the risk of a passage being updated and modified to fit a changed situation is far greater. The latter constitute "living texts," and hence one should not easily assume that the received text of any liturgical document necessarily represents what the author originally wrote, especially when it has been subsequently translated from one language to another. This is the case with regard to the *Apostolic Tradition* of Hippolytus mentioned earlier, where unfortunately such caution is all too rarely exercised. The careful disentangling of the various strata present in such texts can often not only point to a very different reading in the original but also tell a fascinating story of how later liturgical practice evolved.

8. *Liturgical texts can go on being copied long after they have ceased to be used.*

This principle serves as an important counterbalance to the last, in that we should be cautious about concluding that everything that appears in an ancient source must have been in active use in the communities through which that document is thought to have passed. We are all doubtless familiar in our own experience with certain prayer texts, or hymns, or complete orders of service that go on appearing in successive editions of an official book of liturgies for years and years without ever being used by anyone. They were appropriate or fashionable in some earlier generation, perhaps at a particularly sensitive point in the history of that religious tradition, but have since become out-of-date. Yet nobody has the courage to say, "Let's drop this from our formularies," since to do so would appear to be somehow a betrayal of our heritage, a reneging on our ancestors in the faith, or a wanton disregard for tradition. So it goes on appearing in the book, and everyone knows that when you reach it in the order of worship, you simply turn the page and pass over it to the next prayer or whatever.

Thus, while it is true that liturgical manuscripts were generally copied in order to be used, yet Christians of earlier generations were quite as capable as we are of carrying some excess liturgical baggage along with them, of copying out primitive and venerable texts into later collections of material just because they were primitive and venerable and not because of any real intention of putting them into practice. The problem is that they knew which of their texts were to be used and which passed over, while we are left to guess at it with whatever assistance other sources can give us. So, for example, while all who have studied the matter are agreed that a number of the prayers in book 7 of the fourth-century church order, the *Apostolic Constitutions*, have a strongly Jewish character, nobody can be sure what conclusions should be drawn from it. Does it mean that Judaism was still exercising a strong influence on Christian worship at this late date, or it is just another piece of what Robert F. Taft has called "liturgical debris" carried down by the tide of tradition from former times?[17]

9. *Only particularly significant, novel, or controverted practices will tend to be mentioned, and others will probably be passed over in silence; but the first time something is mentioned is not necessarily the first time it was practiced.*

It is dangerous to read any ancient source as though it were a verbatim account of any liturgical act. This is obviously so in the case of the brief allusions to Christian worship that crop up in writings dealing with some quite different topic. We cannot there expect the authors to be describing in exact and full detail all the aspects of the custom to which they are referring, but they are naturally only choosing to mention what is germane to the point they are making. It is important to remember, however, that the same is also true of other early sources. Even those fourth-century sets of homilies that were delivered to new converts to Christianity and were intended to instruct them in the meaning of the liturgies of baptism and the eucharist cannot be presumed to be mentioning everything that was said or done in those services. The authors will have highlighted those parts of the liturgy which seemed to them to be especially significant or to contain something of which they judged it important for the neophytes to be conscious, but they probably will have passed over other parts that they thought less significant or out of which a relevant lesson could not be drawn.

What is more, the same selectivity can be expected even in sets of directions for the conduct of worship, such as we find in the ancient church orders, in conciliar decrees, or in early monastic rules. At first sight, they may look like a complete list of instructions, but one has only to consider for a moment the twentieth-century equivalents of these texts to realize how much is always left unsaid because it is presumed to be familiar to the readers. Indeed, many amusing stories can be told of groups attempting to replicate liturgical rites that they have never seen solely on the basis of the printed rubrics, for even the clearest of instructions always contain an element of ambiguity for those unfamiliar with the tradition. Thus, directions do not generally deal with accepted and customary things but only with new, uncertain, or controverted points: everything else will tend either to be passed over in silence or to receive the briefest of allusions. What is most infuriating, therefore, for the liturgical scholar are passages that give the reader an instruction like "say the customary psalms" or "do what is usual everywhere on this day," since it is precisely those things that were known to everyone of the period and so were never written down that are consequently unknown to us and of greatest interest in our efforts to comprehend the shape and character of early Christian worship.

On the other hand, we ought not to rush to draw the opposite conclusion and assume that the first time something is mentioned was the first time it had ever occurred. As Joachim Jeremias has said, "In investigating a form of address used in prayer we must not limit ourselves to dating the prayers in which it occurs; we must also take into account the fact that forms of address in prayer stand in a liturgical tradition and can therefore be older than the particular prayer in which they appear."[18]

All this naturally makes the task more difficult. We cannot assume that just because something is not mentioned, it was not being practiced. Equally, arguments from silence are notoriously unreliable. Earlier generations of liturgical scholars frequently attempted to reconstruct the worship of the first and second centuries by reading back customs which were described for the first time only in the fourth century, especially if they bore the slightest resemblance to Jewish customs which were, rightly or wrongly, thought to have been current in the first century C.E., for it was concluded that the one was directly descended from the other and so must have been practiced by Christians in unbroken continuity in the intervening years. In many cases, more recent investigation of either the Christian or the Jewish custom has often shown such conclusions to be mistaken.

10. Texts must always be studied in context.

This principle is in effect a summary of many of the others, for knowledge of the true nature of a document is vital to its correct interpretation, and the temptation to "proof-text" sources must be resisted as much here as in biblical study. For example, whether or not it is significant that something is mentioned or omitted will depend to a considerable extent upon the type of material with which one is dealing: the same treatment of a subject should not be expected in, say, a mystagogical catechesis as in monastic directions for reciting the divine office. Even historically inaccurate statements, like the Theophilus story referred to in principle 5 above, can continue to yield useful evidence for the period in which they originated, once their *Sitz im Leben* is properly appreciated.[19] Contextual study, however, involves more than just source- or form-criticism. It also requires the search for another point of reference besides the text itself, whether this is a further docu-

ment or archaeological remains or whatever, so that any conclusion drawn may be based not upon the unsubstantiated testimony of one witness but upon some form of "triangulation."

Conclusion

These, then, are ten principles or guides that may be of
assistance in the task I described at the beginning as that of
"joining up the dots," the scattered pieces of possible evidence
for the ways in which Christians were worshiping in the early
centuries of the Church's existence. I make no claim that these
ten constitute a definitive or comprehensive set of such principles, and more could doubtless be added to them.[20] But
perhaps my ten will suffice as a starting point for the operation.

On the other hand, in the light of all the caution and uncertainty that I have stressed in the course of my journey through
them, you may feel that the whole attempt to reconstruct patterns of ancient Christian worship is doomed to failure, that it
is not simply a matter of joining up dots on a sheet of plain
paper as I advertised at the beginning, but rather of finding the
dots in the first place, buried as they are among countless
others of different shades and hues, and of doing so with a
blindfold over one's eyes. I share some of that trepidation: the
task is certainly not as easy as earlier generations often judged
it to be; but while we cannot hope to learn everything we
would like to know about the Church's early worship, it is not
wholly impossible to say, even if only in a provisional way, a
certain amount about how that worship began and developed
in the first few centuries of the Christian tradition. When the
dots are carefully joined together, a faint picture can indeed
emerge.

NOTES

1. I am grateful to John Baldovin and the other members of the
Early Liturgy group of the North American Academy of Liturgy for

their many helpful comments and suggestions on an early draft of this paper.

2. Paul F. Bradshaw, "The Search for the Origins of Christian Liturgy: Some Methodological Reflections," *SL* 17 (1987): 26–34.

3. This is, for example, the judgment made by Anton Baumstark, *Comparative Liturgy* (London/Westminster, MD, 1958), pp. 31–32, in spite of his earlier affirmation (pp. 16ff.) that liturgical evolution proceeded from variety to uniformity.

4. Robert F. Taft, "How Liturgies Grow: The Evolution of the Byzantine Divine Liturgy," *Orientalia Christiana Periodica* 43 (1977): 355 = idem, *Beyond East and West* (Washington, DC, 1984), p. 167.

5. See further Paul F. Bradshaw, *Daily Prayer in the Early Church* (London, 1981/New York, 1982).

6. See further Robert F. Taft, "Historicism Revisited," *SL* 14 (1982): 97–109 = idem, *Beyond East and West*, pp. 15–30.

7. See further Paul F. Bradshaw, *Liturgical Presidency in the Early Church*, GLS 36 (Bramcote, Notts., 1983), pp. 11–14.

8. Caesarius of Arles, for example, makes this claim with regard to the use of Ps. 104 at the daily evening service (*Serm.* 136.1). He maintains that as a result it "is so well known to everybody that the greatest part of the human race has memorized it"; whereas in reality its use at this service seems to have been restricted to parts of the West, and in the East Ps. 141 was instead the standard evening psalm.

9. For example, Demetrius, patriarch of Alexandria in the third century, made such a claim with regard to the practice of preaching by those who were not ordained ministers, though the custom was defended by the bishops of Caesarea and Jerusalem and seems to have other traces of its former existence (see Bradshaw, *Liturgical Presidency*, pp. 18–20).

10. See further Bradshaw, *Daily Prayer*, p. 115.

11. John Chrysostom, *De Baptismo Christi* 4 (PG 49.370).

12. See Louis Villecourt, "Le Livre du chrême," *Muséon* 41 (1928): 58–59.

13. For further details see Bradshaw, *Daily Prayer*, pp. 48–62; and idem, *Ordination Rites of the Ancient Churches of East and West* (New York, 1990), pp. 39–44.

14. The most recent critique of the reliability of this document

is by Marcel Metzger, "Nouvelles perspectives pour la prétendue *Tradition apostolique*," *Ecclesia Orans* 5 (1988): 241–59.

15. See further Paul F. Bradshaw, "The Liturgical Use and Abuse of Patristics," in Kenneth Stevenson, ed., *Liturgy Reshaped* (London, 1982), pp. 134–45.

16. F. L. Cross, "Early Western Liturgical Manuscripts," *Journal of Theological Studies* 16 (1965): 63–64.

17. With regard to this particular example, see further David A. Fiensy, *Prayers Alleged to Be Jewish: An Examination of the "Constitutiones Apostolorum,"* Brown Judaic Studies (Decatur, GA, 1985).

18. Joachim Jeremias, *The Prayers of Jesus* (London, 1967), p. 26.

19. See Paul F. Bradshaw, "Baptismal Practice in the Alexandrian Tradition, Eastern or Western?" in Paul F. Bradshaw, ed., *Essays in Early Eastern Initiation*, JLS 8 (Bramcote, Notts., 1988), pp. 5–17.

20. Robert F. Taft has already done much to explore for a slightly later period how liturgical units grow and change. See especially "The Structural Analysis of Liturgical Units: An Essay in Methodology," *Worship* 52 (1978): 314–29; and "How Liturgies Grow: The Evolution of the Byzantine Divine Liturgy," *Orientalia Christiana Periodica* 43 (1977): 355–78. Both of these are reproduced in his book, *Beyond East and West*, pp. 151–92.

Reconstructing Ritual
as Identity and Culture

LAWRENCE A. HOFFMAN

[Editors' note: Lawrence Hoffman, Professor of Liturgy at the Hebrew
Union College–Jewish Institute of Religion, New York, looks to the human
sciences for guidance in interpreting the context behind the text. He challenges liturgists to go beyond the reconstruction of liturgical practice in
antiquity by seeing that practice as a ritualized celebration of Christian or
Jewish identity and as a window on to underlying cultural motifs that made
Judaism or Christianity the unique religious civilizations that they were.
Working from the perspective of paradigm theory in the sciences, he sum-
marizes how liturgy has been studied in the past and works out some of the
methodological principles necessitated by the paradigm he advocates: the
application of the human sciences, particularly anthropology, to the interpretation of inherited texts, in order to reconstruct Jewish and Christian identity
and culture.]

Paradigms, Programs, and Problems: The Structure
of Scientific Revolutions

This volume reexamines what we really know about the
development of Jewish and Christian liturgy. "What we know"
about anything, of course, is determined by two factors: the
raw data we are fortunate to have, on one hand, and the
method by which we process that data on the other. It is worth
looking at both of these variables briefly, as we consider ex-
actly what we can say with surety, and why we can be so sure
in the first place.

The first variable, our data—that is, the sources at our
disposal—is largely a matter of happenstance. Our knowledge
of late antiquity was revolutionized simply because an Arab

shepherd happened to be wandering in the vicinity of some caves back in 1947; similarly, our information about Jewish life under later Islamic conditions took a quantum leap forward only because some authorities more or less fell upon the Ben Ezra Synagogue in old Cairo. To be sure, we owe a tremendous debt of gratitude to the people who recognized the significance of what they found—Who knows how many treasure troves potentially as significant as the Dead Sea Scrolls or the Cairo Genizah have been thrown back into natural vaults and caves by naive hikers (or even scholars?) who did not have the foresight to know just what they had in their hands? But by and large, we depend on archeological ruins and manuscript remains that other people dig up; and we can hardly be self-congratulatory about the good fortune that finds us living later than the long line of scholars who preceded us and who would probably have seen what we see, if only they had had the same data that we do.

The long line of theories about the origin of the *Tefillah* is a good example of our dependence on the latest data available. Over a century ago, the venerable Leopold Zunz theorized that this series of benedictions began to take shape at some ancient point beyond which our meager evidence takes us, but some time after the return from Babylonian exile; the prayer then grew steadily, he thought, as blessing after blessing was added to the original core, until finally, during the patriarchate of Gamaliel II, at the end of the second century, it reached its final form. Recognizing that another term for this prayer is the *shemoneh esrei*, the Eighteen Benedictions, even though it contains not eighteen but nineteen blessings, he set himself the task of finding what that "extra blessing" was and why it had been appended. Since Gamaliel was the end of the line, it had to have been added by him, and indeed, the Babylonian Talmud itself held that his selection of the benediction—really a malediction—against the heretics (*Birkat minim*) was the culprit. Zunz quickly concurred.

But Zunz formulated his theory before the Genizah cache was uncovered. He couldn't have known what Ismar Elbo-

gen—in many ways, the dean of historical liturgical study to
this very day—was able to know, simply by looking at the
new evidence from Cairo. One of the scholars who had stum-
bled upon the fragments, Solomon Schechter, had published
an alternative version of the *Tefillah* that he found buried
there, a version that had the requisite eighteen, not nineteen,
benedictions. As other eighteen-benediction versions were
pieced together from the fragments, it became evident that
what we had was not some deviation from the nineteen-bene-
diction norm but a genuine tradition in its own right, a tradition
that seemed to be the one from which the normative label, the
Eighteen Benedictions (*shemoneh esrei*), derived.

Elbogen had only to compare the standard form of nineteen
benedictions that we use to this day—it is inherited from the
Babylonian tradition by way of the Babylonian Talmud—with
the Cairo tradition in order to see that Gamaliel's benediction
against the heretics was not the one missing from the latter.
On the other hand, he readily observed that the normative
fourteenth and fifteenth blessings (14, for Jerusalem; 15, for
the arrival of a Davidic messiah) appeared together as a single
petition in the shorter Cairo version, whence he theorized: (1)
the original eighteen-blessing version had been expanded to
nineteen blessings, but only in Babylonia; (2) the original
name, Eighteen Benedictions, accurately portrayed what the
original Palestinian practice contained; (3) the Cairo fragment
was the old Palestinian form, still used by some Jews in the
tenth and eleventh centuries; (4) the Babylonians had divided
one blessing into two, thus arriving at an extra blessing in their
Tefillah, so that it was natural for a later editor of the Babylonian Talmud to reflect upon the quandary of a prayer containing more blessings than its name implied that it should.

I mention this lengthy example only as an instance in which
new knowledge comes about by virtue of new evidence for
which we may properly be grateful, but for which we can take
no credit. To be sure, it takes some foresight to decide in the
first place that a newly uncovered text is worth studying, and

insight too, to determine how the new text has an impact on older texts and theories. Manuscripts rarely have tables of contents alerting us to their time, place, or authorship, and even if they are signed, they are not apt to carry an appendix telling us where they should be filed in the scheme of things we call wisdom. I have no intention, therefore, of depriving the people who unearth, publish, and decode new findings of their very real and deserved place of honor in the scholarly community. But I do want to say that there is another variable determining what we believe to be true, and it has less to do with the data before us than with the approach that we bring to the data in the first place.

More than anyone, Thomas Kuhn drew our attention to this matter of approach. He demonstrated that scientists do more than go drone-like through their data, drawing empirically and objectively on whatever their data tell them. He differentiated between "normal science" and "paradigm" formation. By "normal science," he meant "research firmly based upon one or more past scientific achievements, achievements that some particular scientific community acknowledges for a time as supplying the foundation for its further practice."[1] Elbogen was practicing "normal science" when he "based his research findings on the past scientific achievements" of Zunz (particularly); and he did so because he was already part of a "particular scientific community" that had already implicitly decided that Zunz's philological premises might profitably "supply the foundation" for liturgical study's "further practice." On the other hand, Zunz had established the criteria that Elbogen and others who constituted the "particular scientific community" took for granted. Zunz had established the paradigm. "Paradigms," says Kuhn, include "law, theory, application and instrumentation" that "provide models from which spring particular coherent traditions of scientific research."[2]

Another theorist of the scientific process (this time, of the social sciences), Robert Nisbet, sums things up nicely by comparing Durkheim and Darwin.

How did Durkheim get his controlling idea? We may be sure of one thing: he did not get it, as the stork story of science might have it, from a preliminary examination of the vital registers of Europe, any more than Darwin got the idea of natural selection from his observations during the voyage of the *Beagle*. The idea, the plot and the conclusion of *Suicide* were well in his mind before he examined the registers. . . . The creative blend of ideas behind *Suicide* . . . was reached in ways more akin to those of the artist than to those of the data processor, the logician or the technologist.[3]

Werner Heisenberg similarly recalls his once-naive conception that "science is empirical, and that we draw our concepts and our mathematical constructs from our empirical data." He had hoped "to introduce only such quantities as can be directly observed, and formulate natural laws only by means of this quantity." When he suggested this approach to Einstein, thinking that the latter, as a true scientist, must surely have discovered the theory of relativity by precisely this method, Einstein responded, "This may have been my philosophy, but all the same it is nonsense. It is never possible to introduce only observable quantities into a theory. It is the theory that decides what can be observed."[4]

To be sure, knowledge is not *independent* of observable reality. There is a world of some sort out there. But there is also our mind, which sees that world with predetermined approaches and guides what we observe. I said earlier that knowledge varies with data and with method, that is to say, with the world as presented to us and with the observations with which we greet that world. If the world more or less controls the data at our disposal, it is our mind that governs what we choose to observe and how we take our measurements—which is to say, the method we adopt. As Hilary Putnam puts it, "The mind and the world jointly make up the mind and the world."[5] Considerations of the method we employ are therefore vital if we are to continue in our task of reconstructing the world we call liturgy.

Let us return to Kuhn for a moment. Science is made of

paradigms that enjoy prominence for a period of time, as the people doing normal science push the paradigm they share as far as it will go in explaining the phenomena that they jointly consider important. They go merrily about solving one problem after another that had eluded previous generations who had worked under a different paradigm and thus had attended to different observations and problems. But eventually they find that one of two things occurs. First, certain problems that the new paradigm ought to resolve prove stubbornly resistant to solution. Nonetheless, they never run out of problems that are solvable, so even as the list of anomalies piles up, the list of successes and potential successes grows as well. If it were simply a matter of running out of things to do, old paradigms would never need overhauling. For some people, however, solving similar problems ad infinitum eventually becomes boring. It becomes harder and harder to go to work each day and write yet another article on yet one more finding regarding a subject about which we already suffer from information overload. At that point it is not so much the failure of the paradigm that matters as it is its redundancy. We adopt another paradigm now, not because the old one is exhausted but because our curiosity has taken us to a whole new enterprise for which the old paradigm was never intended, but which beckons us now precisely because no one has yet studied it.

Imre Lakatos, a prominent critic of Kuhn, prefers to speak of "scientific research programs" rather than of "paradigms," but he means roughly the same thing, and we can use the two terms interchangeably. Lakatos takes issue with Kuhn's presumed linear progression from one successful paradigm to another. Observing that several research programs (or paradigms) can and should coexist, he is forced to redefine "normal science." For Kuhn, who held that one and only one paradigm reigns supreme at any one time, "normal science" is simply what that paradigm's followers do while following the paradigm to its logical conclusion. But with several research programs or paradigms in place simultaneously, there must be several scientific communities doing the same thing at the same time, each working with a different, competing model of what should get done. Favoring such pluralism, Lakatos concludes, "The history of science has been and should be a history of competing research programs (or, if you wish, 'paradigms'). The sooner competition starts, the better for progress." Taking a closer look at Kuhn's alternative—a single paradigm claiming to be the sole model from which to work, and a hypothetical consensus among all scientists that "normal science" must proceed from that starting point— Lakatos warns us, "What [Kuhn] calls 'normal science' is nothing but a research program that has achieved a monopoly," a distinctly dismal situation, in his view.[6] Scientists should remain free to select any workable research program. Only thereby is progress assured.

Lakatos emphasizes the first of my two reasons for abandoning an old paradigm, namely, "A rival research program [or paradigm] explains the previous success of its rival, and supersedes it by a further display of heuristic success."[7] Kuhn admits also the "personal and inarticulate subjective, aesthetic considerations,"[8] among which is my second motivation for change: the fact that old problems start looking less interesting after a while, and simultaneously new challenges that old paradigms never even remotely considered worthy of investigation look better and better.

Paradigm Shifts and Normal Liturgy: The Structure of Liturgical Revolutions

What Kuhn and Lakatos say of science is true of the science of liturgical study no less than of the science of physics or of chemistry. Liturgical study too has seen its share of paradigms come and go, and it too is currently caught up in the very pluralism of research programs that Lakatos applauds.

The premodern world too offered an abundance of paradigms by which liturgy might be explored. Christians favored theological programs of research, while Jews preferred halakhic investigations. In either case, however, the data being investigated were treated as a synchronic whole, that is, even though the fact of the liturgy's changing over time was admitted, the liturgy was nevertheless studied as a timeless system laid out seamlessly for believers to ponder. Traditional Christian research programs are summarized and continued in works such as Edward J. Kilmartin's *Christian Liturgy*.[9] Kilmartin knows better than most how historically variable the liturgy has been, but his concerns are ahistorical: witness items like "the role of Christ in the institution and liturgical forms of the sacraments," about which he cites Hugh of St. Victor as an early example of the scholastic systematicians whose comprehensive exposition offered a paradigm advance over prescholastic piecemeal exegesis.[10] He is quite clear himself about the difference between historical analysis, which aims at uncovering the diachronic, or historical, development of the liturgy, and the synchronic approach that he, no less than Hugh, wishes to advance. Quite properly, he omits historical considerations entirely from a work that self-consciously defines "the specific character of liturgy" as "situating the liturgy within the framework of the totality of human existence, sanctified by the redeeming work of Christ."[11]

For a Jewish equivalent, albeit with less sophistication, consider Rabbi Nosson Scherman's commentary to the *ArtScroll Siddur*[12] published in Brooklyn in 1984 and currently in use as far away as England, where it threatens to replace the venerable *Singer Authorized Prayer Book* (the Orthodox Jewish world of Great Britain's equivalent to the *Book of Common Prayer*).[13] Kilmartin cites Hugh of St. Victor, and Scherman quotes "the sages." There is no history here either, but we do learn, for instance, that there are 248 important organs in the human body, corresponding to the number of positive commandments in the Torah, while there are 365 sinews in the human body, precisely the number of negative commandments. Meanwhile, the numerical equivalents of the Hebrew letters that make up the word *tsitsit*—the fringes on the prayer shawl (the *tallit*) that Jews wear—plus the 5 knots and 8 threads of each fringe make up a total of 613, which is precisely the number of positive and negative commandments taken together (248 + 365), thus indicating that when we wrap ourselves in the *tallit*, "we dedicate ourselves totally to the task of serving God."[14]

From the viewpoint of the university academy, systematics has survived as a respectable research program in the modern world better than Scherman's medieval Jewish exegesis. But even systematic theology has to reckon with the reality that its metier is no longer the dominant interpretive model in western intellectual thought. Joseph Jungmann's classic work on the Roman mass is entitled not just *The Mass of the Roman Rite,* but *The Mass of the Roman Rite: Its Origins and Development,*[15] just as the parallel Jewish classic by Elbogen is called *Jewish Worship in Its Historical Development.*[16] Clearly, the nineteenth century's historicism brought in its train a new paradigm: liturgy as a text that has a history. The medievals had known this to be the case but were uninterested in it. Nineteenth- and twentieth-century liturgists, on the other hand, found it fascinating. Neither Jungmann nor Elbogen was unconcerned with the traditional Christian or Jewish agenda: Jungmann was a Jesuit who turned regularly to theology,[17] and Elbogen wrote the introduction to the German *Einheitsgebetbuch* that was eventually to serve as the primary liberal book of worship for Europe's Jews.[18] But Jungmann's theology is informed by history—his book is subtitled, "an historical, theological, and pastoral survey"—and Elbogen's introduction to worship is intended to demonstrate how history can foster piety. He identifies the era in which each of the prayer book's various rubrics came into being, since from the very fact that liturgy has a history, we can learn that "the genius of the Synagogue has never rested. . . . Every generation [including Elbogen's own] has revived the ancient heritage through the expressions of its own time."[19]

In other words, if the ultimate religious goal of furthering spiritual worship remained the same, the academic paradigm out of which either Jungmann or Elbogen worked, as pastors rather than as academicians, had changed radically. They saw historical development as a scientific truth for liturgy no less than for Darwin's famous evolution of the species. The older agendas—systematic theology (for Christians) and exegetical theology (if we can call it that, for Jews)—never ran out of problems they could solve, but the problems they encountered no longer seemed appropriately scientific to a generation overwhelmed by scientific triumphalism. A new age called for a new research program: liturgy as a field of scientific study, by which was meant liturgy as evolved text.

Trace the evolution, and you have a scientific "truth." Know the relevant dates when this or that element entered the liturgical canon, and you have that canon's history. Compile its history, and.... Well, it wasn't clear what you had. But that problem was not to be raised until our time, when, in fact, it occasioned the next great paradigm change. In the meantime, "liturgy as text" generated "normal science" for more than a century, as one after another solution to its perceived problems found its way into print. Its rules of method were sharpened along the way. Form criticism altered the focus somewhat. But the goal remained the reconstruction of the diachronic process by which the text that we now have was born, shaped, and altered in time.

As the premodern paradigms never ran out of things to do, so too the historical paradigm is theoretically endless. The good thing about intractable problems, after all, is precisely their intractability: they remain eternally open for ever more alternative solutions. A Dura-Europos synagogue is unearthed only once in a lifetime, but we can probably count on digging up one synagogue or another with enough regularity to keep historians busy for the foreseeable future. Another Genizah may not be readily at hand, but the old one offers enough liturgical documentation to last several lifetimes. The *Didache* became easily available with its publication in 1883; an old manuscript of the Anaphora of Addai and Mari was published in 1966. Who knows what 2016 will bring? The detective-like search for novel clues to the chronicle of antiquity goes on and on, and even in the absence of striking new information, we

have the normal science on which progress within a paradigm
depends: sharpened vision as to what is possible to say about
a text and what is not; proper debate about which of several
reconstructions is most apt to be correct; spillovers from other
historical fields, including the study of history itself, telling
us more about the context in which textual formation occurred;
and reevaluations of virtual dogmas regarding the historical
study of liturgy, sometimes necessitating fresh looks at old
texts and revisionist theories that once were unthinkable and
now seem undeniable.

But side by side with developments within the historical
paradigm, we have seen a new research program arising: the
use of the human sciences in interpreting antiquity. As much
as any other, my own book, *Beyond the Text*,[20] has become
the manifesto of this new approach.[21] But almost simultaneously with that book, Jacob Neusner tried to get beyond the
text of life-cycle ritual to explore, among other things, the
"worlds of meaning" that marked "two Judaisms": premodern
Jewry on one hand, and post–World War II Jewry on the
other.[22] Four years before that, Wayne Meeks had applied
Levi-Straussian binary oppositions to first-century Christian
ritual, declaring expressly, "We are trying to see what baptism
did for ordinary Christians, *disregarding the question of where
its elements may have come from.*"[23] Back in 1980, I had tried
to get at the role of liturgical language—not in general, but
in tannaitic culture in particular,[24] and by 1989 the debate had
been joined by Naomi Janowitz, whose very title offered
"theories of language in a rabbinic ascent text."[25] This new
research program had grown significantly enough by 1988
that Kilmartin, who ignored the historical paradigm entirely,
felt the need to devote an entire chapter to the human sciences;
conceding on one hand that in a pastoral theology of liturgy,
"the human sciences should be continually reckoned with, . . .
ultimately, the life of faith is a life in Christ . . . only understandable from the background of the whole of the divine plan
of salvation for the world"[26]—which is to say, beyond the

meager insights that Kilmartin thinks the human sciences are in the end capable of producing.

The important point to be made here is that to construct the meaning of a ritual the human sciences had for years been used by anthropologists who lived and worked among observable subjects in the here and now. But the new paradigm of which I speak attempts to wed insights from those sciences to people and communities of the past, and thereby to ask new questions of the texts that those societies left us.

The impetus for this development has been a return to the nagging question left dangling several paragraphs back: What do you have, after all, once you compile the history of a text? In the nineteenth century, when history and text were the twin bases on which scientific knowledge rested, it was clear that you had a science, which was by nature a good thing, especially for religionists whom Enlightenment science branded prescientific, which is to say, premodern, which in turn is to say, irrelevant. Establishing the scientific credentials of those who study liturgy was equivalent to saying that liturgy was an appropriate topic of scientific study, which meant that it ranked right up there with all the other good things that constitute cultures: things like poetry, philosophy, great literature, law, and so forth. Nineteenth-century men and women reasoned that these are things that you have a right, if not an obligation, to take seriously—unlike folklore, witchcraft, and alchemy (for instance), which they relegated to the slag heap of yesterday's superstitions. August Comte had ushered in the new age of science, which would replace the old one of religion—that was the claim against which the scientific study of liturgy contended. What could be more religious than liturgy, and if liturgy too were to be displayed as a science, religion itself would be saved. The Christian mass and Jewish *siddur* could be shown to have a history; they were cultural artifacts worth serious attention no less than Homer's *Iliad*. That is why if you lived in the nineteenth century you had to compile the text's history. But why should we continue to do so today?

I don't really think scholars need justify what they do in their search for knowledge. We climb mountains because they are there and provide texts with histories because they have them. The landscape in either case—natural or historical—is interesting, even beautiful. Hike past the last ridge and get to the mountain stream that no one has seen before; see a prayer's origin in some ancient letter that no one has seen before—it's the same thing, a glimpse of the unknown, and a little more of nature's or humanity's incredible pattern swirling into recognizable shape before our very eyes. Some of us like that, myself included; that's why we do what we do.

But on the other hand the new paradigm promises an end beyond the text's reconstruction. A properly reconstructed text allows us to inquire about the people who used it. If it is a liturgical text, we can ask the same questions of those who used it as their ritual script as anthropologists do of people they encounter doing the actual ritualizing. What those questions ought to be and how we can phrase them with the hope of some scientific rigor are matters of discussion. Anthropologists themselves speak in a variety of different voices, after all. But it is the very nature of a paradigm in its early stages to develop slowly and uncertainly, not "by a single group conversion [but] in an increasing shift in the distribution of professional allegiances. A decision of that kind can only be made on faith."[27]

The Paradigm and Its Promise: From Text to Culture

Above all, we should be clear about what we are doing when we insist on expanding the traditional questions to go beyond textual and ritual reconstruction and encompass also questions of public meaning and personal identity. At the very outset, we need to determine the proper field of study, which is one thing for written text, but another for cultural context. What is the proper unit of study if you want to get behind the text to a reconstruction of the cultural ethos that the texts presuppose and the ritual encodes?

Systems theory faced a similar problem in its early years, when it wanted to avoid reductionism on one hand and expansionism on the other. Reductionism was the error of taking apart complex systems into their atomistic bits, but in so doing, destroying the system, such that one learns a lot about the bits but nothing about the system. Expansionism is the opposite error of maintaining the interconnectedness of the bits within the system, and then of that system with other systems, and so forth endlessly, until one is faced with studying either the universe in its totality or nothing at all. The solution was to recognize that the researcher has no option but to select an arbitrary subsystem somewhere in between the two extremes.[28]

But what is the liturgist's appropriate subsystem? In anthropological field work, the subsystem is given by the social system under investigation. One studies not *all* human societies—that would be expansionism, wonderful if we could do it, but beyond our grasp; nor just a single example of a ritual's performance with a view toward parsing the verbs used by the shaman—that would be reductionism, certainly achievable, but utterly useless, if your goal is getting at culture. The fieldworker establishes a relevant subsystem by choosing a society to observe in the here and now. Having decided in advance that he was going to study the African Ndembu, for example, Turner collected testimony from them, but not from the native American Crow. Unlike field-workers, however, liturgists' data precede the determination of the relevant field, since liturgists begin with textual data that have come to hand independently of their cultural aims. A Jewish liturgist, for instance, already has on hand the recorded voices, so to speak, of rabbis from Palestine both immediately before and immediately after 200. The former are recorded in the Mishnah; the latter only in later compendia called the Talmuds. On literary grounds— the old paradigm of reconstructing a liturgical text—one carefully avoids mixing the two sources, so as to recreate the state of a rite in the earlier Mishnaic era first, and then again, several centuries later, when the Talmuds were compiled. For the textual historian, therefore, there are two subfields to be investigated: literature prior to 200 and literature after 200. But literature is not culture. Jewish culture did not radically change the day the Mishnah came into being. Jews observed the Passover seder both before and after 200, for example, and there is reason to believe that a continuum of interpretation connects the two eras. At some point prior to 200 what we can call classical Palestinian rabbinic culture began, and at some point after 200 it started to become something else. The liturgist's relevant subsystem, then, is the cultural system of rabbinic Jews between these two hypothetical dates. But liturgists cannot just "move there." They have no option but to read through the texts listening carefully to what rabbis both before and after 200 say about the seder, until one gets a sense of a coherent cultural meaning that they saw in it. When the ritual begins to change sufficiently that we suspect we have a new set of public meanings, we assume we have reached a new subsystem, related to the first one, but also distinct enough to offer its own cultural patterns for deciphering.

Necessary ground work clearly includes dating our texts and attending to Paul Bradshaw's caveats (above) — which apply to Jewish texts no less than to Christian ones. When he says, for example, "Authoritative-sounding statements are not always genuinely authoritative" (principle 3), the Jewish liturgist thinks immediately of the author of the eighth-century *Letter of Ben Baboi,* an admirer of Yehudai Gaon, who echoed his master's ringing condemnation of Palestinian Jewry's stubborn retention of their own liturgical customs. Nothing sounds as authoritative as Yehudai's and Ben Baboi's denunciation of the Palestinians—except, perhaps, the vituperative charges against them by Amram, one of Yehudai's eminent successors. Palestinian Jews are "inveterate sinners," says Amram, "fools and ignoramuses." Taken at face value, his invective might lead us to suspect some kind of liturgical heresy in Palestine, whereas if there was any liturgical unorthodoxy here, it was the Babylonians' attempt to canonize what hitherto had been relatively free and decentralized. Eventually, the

Babylonians won the day, but at the time, a popular referendum would have judged as utter nonsense their authoritative claim that they alone held the key to proper Jewish tradition.[29] The same set of geonic pronouncements buttresses Bradshaw's fourth principle: "Legislation is better evidence for what it proposes to prohibit than for what it seeks to promote." Regularly, the Babylonian authorities promote their own liturgical preferences, as if they are already worldwide phenomena, when in fact, their boasts should be taken as evidence—generally in Palestine—of the healthy existence of precisely the practices that they seek to prohibit. When the Babylonian authorities say "everyone" does something, the only thing we should grant is that "they" do it—no one else.

The seventh principle too ("Liturgical manuscripts are more prone to emendation than literary manuscripts") is confirmed by geonic material. From that era comes *Seder Rav Amram,* our earliest instance of an authoritative comprehensive Jewish prayer book, which juxtaposes prayer wording with legal discussions of how, when, where, and by whom the prayer is supposed to be said. It has been recognized for a long time now that whereas the legal material has been retained with care in all the manuscripts, scribes through the ages played fast and free with the actual prayer texts[30]—precisely what Bradshaw's seventh law would predict.

This new paradigm, no less than the others, thus demands that we carefully sift through sources, sorting out the prayers and practices that were around at a given time from those that were not. The next step differs, however, for the authoritatively reconstituted textual history is only the beginning. We now read the text as if we were anthropologists personally observing the ritual's enactment. We take into consideration also nonliterary evidence: the class structure evident in the layout of ritual space, the ritual actions that people would have experienced (standing for emphasis, bowing in subservience, and the like); the hierarchical arrangement of leaders; the experience of music; and so on—some of which we deduce from the textual descriptions, and some of which we get from allied fields like archeology. We also test our theoretical observations against the actual witness of people who really did live then and who wrote about what they thought the rite in question meant. We analyze what we see and what they say, in categories taken from the human sciences: a people's sense of sacred space or sacred time; its sacred myths; its symbol system; its favored metaphors; and the like. We reconceptualize our account with ideas that social scientists have found useful in plotting their studies—performative language (from J. L. Austin), *communitas* (from Victor Turner), virtual experience (from Susanne Langer), and so forth;[31] we also do what they do, make up new conceptualizations of what we see, judging them to be true insofar as they work. Finally, we reconstruct a slice of culture, a bit of the social life and world view that characterized our chosen field: Palestine in the late Roman empire, say; or post-Crusade northern European pietism.

What we are after is the slippery notion that we call identity. In that regard, Gerald Lardner discerns my own decalogue in his reading of *Beyond the Text.*[32] It is not my intention here to tease out all the methodological regulations to which he alludes, but I emphasize again: the ultimate goal is cultural, not textual. We want to unpack the way a group's religious ritual encodes their universe.

Insofar as we begin by having to know the realities of when a text was written and how it changed through time, we remain true to the diachronical perception of the nineteenth century. Our ultimate goal, however, is a return to the synchronic point of view that preceded it. In the end, we want to posit discrete cultural systems that remain relatively impervious to change through a particular block of time. We want to know how Jews ordered sacred space, for example, or how symbol systems among Christians and Jews entailed common yet different trajectories for each faith in late antiquity. We can get at the former by investigating the Blessing of the Land in the Jewish grace after meals,[33] and the latter by attending to what Christians say about salvation through the blood of Christ and to what Jews say and do about the blood of circumcision and the blood of the paschal lamb. There is no single method here. There are many: Mary Douglas's grid and group analysis;[34] Clifford Geertz's intuitive "reading" of a ritual script (like his classic "Notes on a Balinese Cockfight");[35] Levi-Straussian binary oppositions;[36] and exceptional fieldwork reports of Jewish or Christian ritual today, such as Riv-Ellen Prell's analysis of aesthetics as a category for studying ritual among countercultural Jews in the 1970s,[37] and applicable also, I expect, though in different ways, to nascent Christianity as counterculture vis-à-vis rabbinic Judaism.

The list is endless, as well it should be, if this new research program is to have any future. The program is still in its infancy, requiring interdisciplinary cooperation by many scholars. Above all, it is promising and exciting, offering us a means to go beyond the text and find the people without whom there could be no liturgy at all.

NOTES

1. Thomas S. Kuhn, *The Structure of Scientific Revolutions* (Chicago, 1962), p. 10.

2. Ibid.

3. Robert A. Nisbet, *The Sociological Tradition* (New York, 1966), p. 19.

4. Werner Heisenberg, *Tradition in Science* (New York, 1983), p. 10.

5. Hilary Putnam, *The Many Faces of Realism* (LaSalle, IL, 1987), p. 1.

6. John Worrall and Gregory Currie, *The Methodology of Scientific Research Programmes: Philosophical Papers, vol. 1, Imre Lakatos* (Cambridge, 1978).

7. Ibid.

8. Kuhn, *Scientific Revolutions,* p. 157.

9. Edward J. Kilmartin, *Christian Liturgy I: Systematic Theology of Liturgy* (Kansas City, 1988).

10. Ibid., p. 262.

11. Ibid., p. 50.

40   LAWRENCE A. HOFFMAN

12. Rabbi Nosson Scherman, ed., *The Complete ArtScroll Siddur*, Art Scroll Mesorah (Brooklyn, 1984).

13. See Chaim Bernant, "On the Other Hand," *Jewish Chronicle* (November 24, 1989): 28.

14. Ibid., p. 5.

15. Joseph A. Jungmann, S.J., *The Mass of the Roman Rite: Its Origins and Development*, 2 vols. (1948), trans. Francis A. Brunner (New York, 1955).

16. Ismar Elbogen, *Der Jüdische Gottesdienst in seiner geschichtlichen Entwicklung* (1913), reprint ed. (Hildesheim, 1962).

17. See Joseph A. Jungmann, S.J., *The Mass: An Historical, Theological, and Pastoral Survey* (Collegeville, MN, 1976).

18. *Gebetbuch für das ganze Jahr bearbeitet im Auftrag des Liberalen Kultus-Ausschusses des Preussischen Landesverbandes jüdischer Gemeinden* (Frankfort, 1929).

19. Translation from Jakob J. Petuchowski, *Prayerbook Reform in Europe* (New York, 1969), p. 213.

20. Lawrence A. Hoffman, *Beyond the Text: A Holistic Approach to Liturgy*, Jewish Literature and Culture (Bloomington, IN, 1987).

21. See the review by Mark Searle in *Worship* 62 (1988): 472–75.

22. Jacob Neusner, *The Enchantments of Judaism: Rites of Transformation from Birth through Death* (New York, 1987), pp. 8–9.

23. Wayne A. Meeks, *The First Urban Christians: The Social World of the Apostle Paul* (New Haven, 1984), p. 154.

24. Lawrence A. Hoffman, "Censoring in and Censoring out: A Function of Liturgical Language," in Joseph Gutmann, ed., *Ancient Synagogues: The State of Research*, Brown Judaic Studies (Decatur, GA, 1981), pp. 19–37.

25. Naomi Janowitz, *The Poetics of Ascent: Theories of Language in a Rabbinic Ascent Text* (Albany, 1989).

26. Kilmartin, *Christian Liturgy*, p. 50.

27. Kuhn, *Scientific Revolutions*, p. 157.

28. See Arthur Koestler, *The Ghost in the Machine* (Chicago, 1967), pp. 45–58.

29. For details, see Lawrence A. Hoffman, *Canonization of the Synagogue Service* (Notre Dame, IN, 1979).

30. "A critical examination of the *Seder* shows that it was abused

to an extreme degree, and the portion that suffered most is the Order of Prayers specifically, rather than the Halakic explanations" (Louis Ginzberg, *Geonica*, vol. 1 [1909], reprint ed. [New York, 1968], pp. 125–26).

31. J. L. Austin, *How to Do Things with Words*, 2d ed., J. O. Urmsson and M. Sbisa, eds. (Cambridge, MA, 1975); Victor Turner, *The Ritual Process* (Chicago, 1969); Susanne K. Langer, *Feeling and Form* (New York, 1953).

32. Gerald V. Lardner, "'Hoffman's Laws': A Proposal," *Proceedings of the Annual Meeting of the North American Academy of Liturgy* (1989), pp. 142–46.

33. See Lawrence A. Hoffman, ed., *The Land of Israel: Jewish Perspectives* (Notre Dame, IN, 1986), editor's introduction.

34. Mary Douglas returns to grid and group analysis in many works, but see the original statement in her *Natural Symbols* (London, 1970).

35. Clifford Geertz, *The Interpretation of Cultures* (New York, 1973), pp. 412–53.

36. For Levi-Straussian binary oppositions, see Meeks, *First Urban Christians*, or Hoffman, *Beyond the Text*, pp. 20–45.

37. Riv-Ellen Prell, *Prayer and Community* (Detroit, 1989).

The Politics of Piety:
Social Conflict and
the Emergence of Rabbinic Liturgy

TZVEE ZAHAVY

[Editors' note: Tzvee Zahavy, Professor of Classical and Near Eastern Studies and Director of the Center for Jewish Studies at the University of Minnesota, criticizes the tendency of many recent liturgical scholars to disregard
what he calls the politics of piety as the primary force in the shaping of early
Jewish prayer patterns. He urges us to give credence to reports of political
strife around liturgical issues, holding that for religious leaders in antiquity,
prayer mattered sufficiently for offical parties to congeal around alternative
traditions. Though critical of early reductionist attempts to see liturgies as
simply political polemics against rival traditions, he holds that a nuanced
reconstruction of the parties of antiquity is still possible, and that we can
trace the origins of this or that prayer tradition to these parties, who contended with each other in the shaping of communal piety. His case in point
is the twofold central rubric of Jewish synagogue prayer: the *Shema* and its
blessings, on the one hand, and the *Tefillah*, on the other, each of which he
assigns to competing rabbinic factions as he posits a novel reconstruction of
the way rabbinic liturgy began.]

FROM HISTORY TO FORM CRITICISM AND BACK:
THE STUDY OF JEWISH PRAYER

In the past decade there has been renewed scholarly interest
in the development of Jewish prayer in its most formative
period, from 200 B.C.E. to 200 C.E. Current researchers are
now applying diverse social scientific and historical methods
to the study of the ancient world in general, and specifically
to the development of Judaic culture, enabling us to engage

in a more complex and fruitful historical mode of reconstructing the emergence of Judaic liturgy and ritual in late antiquity.
The most original of the contemporary investigators have
emphasized the need for interdisciplinary perspectives in this
area and have developed new modes of social scientific and
aesthetic criticism of Jewish liturgy.[1] This represents a third
stage in the critical analysis of Jewish liturgical development.
Nineteenth- and early twentieth-century scholarship (the first
phase) took a mainly reductionistic historical approach to Jewish prayer. That work is now outdated. The more recent form-
critical method dominated the second phase of research. That
mode of scholarship has proven unproductive.[2] In this essay I
summarize some of the shortcomings of these two previous
stages and then propose a fresh analysis of classical rabbinic
liturgy that does not abandon entirely the concern for historical
context that characterized the first stage but that obviates the
reductionism of that approach by using advanced methods of
analysis.

Critique of Earlier Research and Its
Methodological Premises

1. Early reconstructions of liturgical development were
often theological or apologetic.[3] No doubt the ideology of
Jewish ritual was significant in its time of origin and continued
to have theological impact afterward. Research in this area
must nevertheless avoid theological-apologetic explanations
of Judaic institutions and take care not to impute any unique
or timeless value to the philosophical content of Judaic ritual.

2. Rabbinism was a new Judaic system that took shape after
the destruction of the Temple in the first century. Its
worldviews and ways of life represent distinct configurations
in the history of Judaism, discontinuous in many ways with
prior Israelite systems in Hellenistic Israel and the Diaspora.
Most scholarly work of stages 1 and 2 reconstructed liturgical
development without differentiating rabbinic Judaism as a new
system of the postdestruction era. Research that sees Judaism

as a single linear progression from Moses or Ezra through the classical age of rabbinism rests on a subtle form of historicistic apologetics. Scholars with theological intent incline, for instance, to posit the early origin of the synagogue or the antiquity of certain prayers in the absence of evidence or in spite of abundant proof to the contrary.[4]

3. The Jews of first- to third-century Israel, the most formative interval of liturgical growth, lived under imperial Roman rule and within social configurations dominated by local leaders, often rabbis or other holy men. Their circumstances made them repress realistic aspirations of national political sovereignty. Their cultural output, including the formation of liturgical rituals, must be understood as a facet of this context. Many early reconstructions of liturgical development were based on deficient models of the social and political realities of the times.[5]

4. The main creative forces of rabbinic religious development derived from internal conflict and competition among the leaders of factions within Judaism. Among those who called themselves "rabbis" we assume were scribes, priests, members of the patriarchal house, and others seeking "leadership," that is to say, dominance and control, over local communal life. S. Talmon has developed a more advanced social scientific approach to liturgical development for Qumran. Some of his basic premises are informative, as the following summary statement illustrates:

> In order to compensate the loss of the sacrificial cult, and by reason of the group-centered ideology, the Covenanters especially promoted deindividualized, stereotyped forms of prayer that could be adapted without further qualification to communal devotion. Their egalitarian principles, the right of each member to scrutinize the deeds of his fellow, the hierarchical structure of the community, and the resulting system of close supervision of the lower-ranking by their superiors were conducive to the development of worship patterns fixed in time, openly observable, and removed from the sphere of subjective *ad hoc* decisions with their concomitant individualized forms of expression.[6]

We rarely find succinct, neutral assessments like this one in early reconstructions of liturgical development since they mainly misunderstood the internal dynamics, and especially the role, of prayer within Jewish culture and society in the first three centuries C.E.[7]

5. The artificial church-sect distinction of religious organizational life must be rejected as an inappropriate model for the description of the setting of late antique Judaism. That is to say, dynamics of ritual development cannot simply be attributed to reactions to heresies. Many early reconstructions of liturgical development, however, clung to the notion that prayers often developed within a normative Judaism specifically to oppose sectarian heresies. This supposition misled historians of Jewish liturgy to differentiate an urtext for prayers, which they associated with the imagined normative tradition, and variant versions of that urtext, which they declared deviant.[8]

6. We ought to assume that the primary targets of negative speech and action in ritual were those leaders closest in competition for allegiance of the populace at large. It is wrong to postulate readily that external challenges to the faith led to the formation of major components of Judaic rituals. Only where we find no likely candidate internal to the religion should we consider external competing systems of religion as targets of ritual polemic. Some early reconstructions of liturgical development placed too much emphasis on liturgy as a rebuttal to external forces such as early Christianity and Persian dualism.[9] Hoffman succinctly describes the assumptions of the historicist approach:

> The "original" prayer and subsequent additions to it all were explained as arising in response to various events and periods, as if prayer must always be a rational response to political persecution, a reaction to a foreign ideology, a blow against heresy, or an organism's response to the thousand and one other data that constitute a nation-folk's history.[10]

7. Both Hoffman and Sarason characterize how the philo-

logical approach dominated Jewish liturgical research and stood behind the work of the earlier historians and the form critics. Philologists did not claim to do Jewish history but did make many historical claims. Proponents of this text-based approach did not articulate a coherent model of social or historical circumstances for prayer and drew hasty and at times incomprehensible conclusions based mainly on unfounded assumptions.

8. Form criticism, based on a model for relating religious ritual to social institutions, replaced philology as a dominant paradigm for research. A shortcoming of the form-critical approach was that it postulated these institutions without appropriate evidence of their existence and without defining precisely what they were in comprehensible categories generalizable to the history of religion. Joseph Heinemann, for example, linked diverse liturgical forms to distinctive social settings,[11] but with questionable assumptions. He associated prayers with one or another *Sitz im Leben* in early rabbinism: the Bet Midrash or study hall, the Synagogue, the Law Court, and the Temple. Each of these was a complex and controversial institutional construct in its own right, a point to which Heinemann did not pay sufficient attention. He errs in his basic assumptions that these were uniform and mature institutions in the first and second centuries. His theory accordingly is built upon precarious foundations.

Hoffman's critique on this issue is milder: "Heinemann may at times have insufficient evidence to postulate details about the functioning of a given social institution, the workings of which he takes for granted in his etiology of a given prayer."[12] The speculative and arbitrary bases of liturgical form criticism rendered it a somewhat sterile method, unable to lead others to additional insights based on its assertions and conclusions.

9. Other facets of Heinemann's basic theory are counterintuitive, as for example: "At first many different forms of the same basic prayer grew up in a somewhat haphazard fashion, and . . . only afterwards, gradually in the course of time, did the rabbis impose their legal norms on this vast body of material."[13] Heinemann does not provide firm enough evidence to

establish an historical basis for a loose populist process of development of prayer. Furthermore, he neglected the essential role of the leadership of the elite in propagating liturgy to serve their political and social interests. He too often employed the unspecified passive voice to describe the growth of liturgical ritual. Other scholars both early and recent have lapsed often into the habit of describing liturgical growth as a kind of spontaneous generation. "Liturgy developed . . . ," said Stefan Reif in an article. Sarason declared, "The eighteen benedictions did not all come into being. . . ." At greater length Hoffman posits, "Worship is a category of human experience with rules of its own, and . . . these rules function in their own way to result in the formation of a liturgy."[14]

Considering these nine areas of weakness in the study of Jewish prayer we must take a fresh look at some basic issues. We ought not reject form criticism and return to the simple empirico-positivism of the past. We need to carry forward its basic idea that liturgy grows out of social and political institutional life. Fortunately, in the past few years Lee Levine has published an interdisciplinary study that represents one solid and sustained exercise in delineating the social ramifications of institutional structures in rabbinic culture.[15] Together with Saldarini's recent inquiry and the extensive critical studies of Jacob Neusner that relate the major corpora of rabbinic literature to the social world of late antique Judaism, we now have firmer underpinnings for a revisit to the complex formative world of classic Judaic liturgy.[16] The time has come to renegotiate aspects of the historical analysis of the growth of Jewish prayer based on current deeper and more complex understandings of the political and social circumstances of Judaism in Israel in late antiquity.

New analysis must be devoid of theological-apologetic intent. It must recognize the systemic discontinuities of rabbinism in Judaic history. It must take account of the relative influence of local and national forces over internal Jewish life and the role of religious ritual in those relationships. It must take seriously the effects of conflict on religious institutional change. It must broaden its view of religion and social life beyond the paradigm of norm against heresy. It must resist the temptation to posit changes in Judaism based on reactions to conditions outside the defined boundaries of the group's identity. These stated desiderata serve as crucial, though often implicit, grounding for the discussion that now follows.

THE FORMATION OF THE SHEMA AND TEFILLAH AS THE CORE OF RABBINIC LITURGY

Prayer services do not emerge spontaneously or arbitrarily in a vacuum. They are the public pronouncements of the central values and concepts of the religious leaders who initially propounded them and are social rituals that often emerge out of intense conflict and hard-fought compromise. Specific historical, social, and political conditions contributed to the distinct origin of two major rabbinic services. In the crucial transitional period after the destruction of the Temple in 70 C.E., the *Shema* emerged as the primary ritual of the scribal profession and its proponents. The *Tefillah* at this formative time was a ritual sponsored mainly by the patriarchal families and their priestly adherents. Compromises between the factions of post-70 Judaism later led to the adoption of the two liturgies in tandem, as the core of public Jewish prayer. But this came about only after intense struggles among competing groups for social and political dominance over the Jewish community at large, and concomitantly for the primacy of their respective liturgies. The political, social, and even economic dimensions of the religious life of the synagogues were crucial to the formation of nascent rabbinic Judaism.

Growth of Religious Ritual through Conflict

We are now more aware of the influence of conflict and differentiation internal to rabbinism in its historical development. Rabbinic traditions tersely report aspects of what must have been bitter and prolonged political battles over liturgical compromise. Talmudic sources recount that Gamaliel II of Yavneh was deposed from the patriarchate at the turn of the second century on account of a dispute over the regulation of prayers.[17] Other incidents, too, suggest that prayer had much more than merely spiritual and theological ramifications for late antique rabbinism and that diversity and conflict characterize the formulation of its liturgy.[18]

New Testament pericopes agree, depicting confrontations between Jesus and Paul and the Jews of various synagogues.[19] Richard Horsely's recent research into early Christianity explains that "in traditional historical societies there was no separation of life into different areas such as 'religion' and 'politics' and 'economics.'"[20] He remarks regarding the Gospels that "the intensity and variety of conflict that runs through the gospel tradition is still overwhelming. The situation in which Jesus heals and preaches is pervaded by conflict, some of it explicit, much of it implicit in stories and sayings."[21] Rabbinism in this era must be viewed in the same manner.

Once established as standard within a given community, prayers are not easily changed because their rituals must be accountable on a regular basis to a community of pious devotees. As Heiler says of institutionalized prayer in general, "The prayer formula is stereotyped and strictly obligatory; the wording is inviolable, sacrosanct; no worshipper may dare to alter the words in the slightest degree, any more than he would think of making a change in ritual acts of sacrifice, expiation, or consecration."[22] While we know that changes occur and variations exist, liturgy is basically one of the most conservative of all cultural commodities. Precisely because they resisted change, therefore, rabbinic prayers provide a window through which we may observe the development of formative Judaism in the first centuries of the common era.

Given these suppositions let us turn to the contents, motifs, and forms of the standard formulation that we possess of the two main liturgies, the *Shema* and the *Tefillah*. We shall see a progression in liturgical formulation summarized in three phases:

1. The *Shema* became the primary rite of the scribal brother-hoods, propounding the essential scribal themes. In this perspective the Exodus motif in the *Shema* functioned as a polemic of scribal triumphalism.
2. The *Tefillah,* by contrast, originated as the main liturgy of the deposed priestly aristocracy and was adopted by the patriarchate as a central ritual. Priestly and aristo-cratic themes were central to the *Tefillah.* In this per-spective the kingship motif served as a justification of priestly and patriarchal authority as postdestruction cli-ent rulers of the community, implicitly for Rome and explicitly for God.
3. Later, in the postdeposition era and in the wake of the defeats of the apocalyptic aristocracy in the Bar Kokhba revolt, rabbinic leadership amalgamated its social forces and merged the formerly distinct liturgical rituals into a single service.

The Scribes and Their Shema

Before we deal with the first phase, the institutionalization of the *Shema* in Israel in the first and early second centuries, a few words are in order regarding the social definition of the scribes in Israel. Matthew Black says the scribes "represented a distinctive class in the community. They practiced their legal profession throughout Palestine (and as certainly in the disper-sion)."[23] Saldarini's fresh and more complex definition pro-poses that "scribes do not seem to be a coherent social group with a set membership, but rather a class of literate individuals drawn from many parts of society who filled many social roles and were attached to all parts of society from the village to the palace and Temple."[24] We take note primarily of the struggle of the scribal faction within rabbinism for recognition in the composite social world of Hellenistic Israel.

This social group promulgated its liturgy to advance its ideas and influence. The *Shema* expressly emphasizes several dominant theological themes (e.g., love of God; unity of God; centrality of Torah) and gives priority to these ideas out of a rich repertoire of possible alternative biblical motifs.

The scribes' support of this prayer derives from their social realities. Saldarini discusses the overlapping roles of scribes who served in the Temple and were involved in the wisdom and apocalyptic movements of the time. Scribes, he says, served both in the village as copyists, teachers, and low-level functionaries, and in the government structures in Jerusalem and Galilee in middle-level bureaucratic official capacities.[25] It is likely that the scribal faction most active in rabbinic society derived its livelihood as teachers of the law and from the accompanying need for copies of the Torah, as well as the widespread use of phylacteries, *mezuzot,* and other required religious articles. The verses of the *Shema* stated plainly that Torah study and the observance of selected commandments were among the highest values in Israelite life.

The period of origin of the *Shema* as a popular scribal rite may be traced to the time of the Houses of Hillel and Shammai, wisdom fellowships of the first century. A number of rabbinic traditions associate rules and practices for reciting the *Shema* with the Houses.[26] Early Christian evidence in Mark 12:29–30 depicts Jesus reciting the first two verses of the *Shema* in the context of a debate with a group of scribes and as an opponent of the Temple hierarchy.[27] The scriptural verses of the *Shema* appear in the earliest phylacteries found at Qumran.[28] Of course, some of the values promoted by the *Shema* may be located even further back in Israelite history in the wisdom movements of the Hellenistic age.[29] Israelite sages and scribes commonly emphasized Torah and commandments as primary motifs of religious life.[30]

In formative rabbinic Judaism the liturgy figured prominently in daily ritual life. Both the inclusions and exclusions of the contents of the standard rabbinic text of this liturgy clearly define its focus and original intent. The primary motifs of the national cult in Jerusalem are noticeably missing from both the *Shema* and from the frame of blessings that surround it.[31] Such ideas and institutions as the Temple, the priesthood, Jerusalem, and Davidic lineage—all prominent motifs in the *Tefillah*—are not primary concerns of the framers of the *Shema*.

Conspicuous evidence of revision in the *Shema* shows that some disagreement arose over time among various subsequent sponsors of the liturgy. Mention of the patriarchal motif of kingship was added, intruding after the first biblical verse[32] and in the framing blessings. Mishnah Ber. 1:5 cites a dispute over the legitimacy of mentioning the Exodus in the evening *Shema*. Rabbinic pericopes indicate that there was significant disagreement over some main themes of the *Shema* liturgy.[33] It is fair to conclude that such materials probably reflect divisions between the local scribal brotherhoods, who sought independent authority over their adherents, and the national priestly aristocratic leadership, who likely served as part of the client governance of Israel on behalf of imperial Rome and accordingly advocated alternative values.[34]

Admittedly the case for the origination of the *Shema* in a scribal social context appears to be contravened by an oft-cited Mishnah pericope (Tamid 5:1) that projects the recitation of the *Shema* back to the priests in the Temple in Jerusalem. One might argue, however, that this evidence is secondary at best and may be suspected as a means to link artificially the *Shema* with ancient priestly authority. Priests in the Temple could hardly have been expected to sponsor and perpetuate a liturgy with the limited range of content and themes of the *Shema*.[35] It would be natural for a group sponsoring its own liturgical rite to seek legitimacy by establishing *post factum* a fictitious account of the antiquity and broad authority of the ritual. This pericope may just be a simple projection of a later ritual back to an earlier context. At best, it describes a variant precursor to the ritual "recitation of the *Shema*" that later historical and social forces adapted and adopted as a primary liturgical institution.[36]

A more subtle and possibly contrived association with the Temple is present in the first pericope of Mishnah. Berakhot 1:1 goes out of its way to link the *Shema* with the Temple and with the sons of Rabban Gamaliel the patriarch.[37] Other rabbinic evidence more firmly attests to the scribal provenance of the *Shema,* outside of the control of the Temple hierarchy. So, for instance, a Tosefta passage in Berakhot rules that scribes interrupt their professional duties when the time comes for the recitation of their main liturgy, the *Shema,* but not stop to recite the prayer of the patriarchal aristocracy, the *Tefillah.*[38]

Scribal values are conspicuous in the content of the *Shema's* texts. As I suggested, the blessings that became standard in later rabbinism for framing the *Shema* may have been established as late as the second century.[39] Still, they continue to focus on the scribal agendum and omit direct mention of such major themes as the Temple, the Priests, Jerusalem, and David—all crucial to the fostering of priestly and aristocratic ideals. The framing blessings refer prominently to cosmic motifs, suggesting the mystical dimensions of religious discourse; the Exodus and the promise of future redemption; the Torah and the commandments; and the value of the study of Torah— all essential thematic concerns of the scribal factions in post-70 Israel.

The standard blessings before the morning *Shema* make reference to cosmic-mystical dimensions of the world, mention the love of God, and refer to the return to the Land of Israel, but interestingly, not to Jerusalem.[40] The blessing recited in the morning after the scriptural passages of the *Shema* mentions the cosmic dimension and refers to the Exodus and the ultimate messianic redemption. The mention of the kingship of God appears only as a theme subsidiary to the Exodus. The blessings before the scriptural passages in the evening reiterate the cosmic references and rehearse the value of Torah study. After the passages the blessing in the evening returns to the theme of the Exodus, to a generalized statement of redemption, and to references to God as protector of Israel, apropos of the dangers of the night. This scribal liturgy builds its dramatic tension towards a promise of messianic redemption in alternation with reiteration of the miracles of the Exodus from Egypt.

The Scribes and the Seder

The invocation of the Exodus may have conjured a broader ritual complex, namely, the seder, through which participants reenacted the Exodus in the long-standing Israelite springtime ritual. Scribal political interests had much to gain by persistently recalling this theme. The rabbinic Passover, observed with a seder, was essentially a banquet for Torah study. Previously the most popular of Israelite festivals, it was celebrated through the cultic offering and feast of the paschal lamb. As the festival evolved, it became a primary means of annually reinforcing scribal social solidarity. The scribes promoted the seder as a ritual occasion to substitute for the sacrifice and as a vital way to promote their political and social aims.

Beginning even prior to the emergence of rabbinic Judaism but continuing later within rabbinism, these scribal factions renovated the festival and transformed the feast into an occasion for Torah study, as a deft means of usurping the authority for controlling ritual formerly claimed to be exclusively in the domain of the priesthood.[41] The fact that people participated in the seder, thus recognizing it as the authentic means to celebrate Passover, must have been a humiliation for the priests and their allies, as well as for their avowed successors, the patriarchal houses. These constituencies felt the loss of the Temple and its sacrificial cult most acutely at the time of the Passover festival.

The rabbinic-scribal seder was blatantly anticultic. Instead of describing the paschal sacrifice and its rite, the crux of the ritual was a recitation of questions and answers and rabbinic *midrashim* on the ten plagues and on various historical scriptural verses.[42] The seder mentions the paschal offering only reluctantly in the context of a statement ascribed to the patriarch Rabban Gamaliel. The passage arbitrarily insists that the offering be mentioned along with unleavened bread and bitter herbs. "Rabban Gamaliel said, 'Anyone who has not said these three things on Passover has not fulfilled his obligation: paschal offering, matzah, and bitter herbs.'" Note well that the unit concludes, "The paschal offering—on account of God having passed over the houses of our ancestors in Egypt . . . ," and not on account of the paschal offering brought to the Temple by generations of Israelite families from all corners of the land.[43] This attitude resonates as an undertone throughout the fellowship ritual.[44]

Another suggestive component of early traditions associated with the seder suggests close linkage among scribes, seder, and *Shema*. We hear of students who arrive in the morning after the seder to find that the rabbis have been discussing the Exodus all through the night; they declare, "Masters, the time has come for the morning recitation of the *Shema*." They make no mention of the *Tefillah*. This omission may be simply dismissed by assuming that the rabbis first would have recited the *Shema* and thereafter the *Tefillah*. But if we take the anecdote at its simple face value, the students remind their masters of the *Shema*, the rite of the scribes, not the *Tefillah*, the rite of the priests.[45]

Priests, Patriarchs, and the Tefillah of Eighteen Blessings

In striking literary and thematic contrast with the *Shema*, the *Tefillah* represents those themes most apt for reinforcing the primacy of the priestly aristocracy, including the priestly blessing itself. Elias Bickermann in fact labeled the *Tefillah*, the "Civic Prayer for Jerusalem."[46] His position is attractive because it appeals to the content and themes of the liturgy and because it posits a simpler genesis for the prayer. Let me therefore begin with that hypothesis and further scrutinize the evidence in light of the social and political ramifications of the promulgation of the liturgy in the first century after the destruction of the Temple.

Out of the nineteen blessings of the *Tefillah* (which follow), seven contain national or political themes that may be associated with priestly or patriarchal interests, i.e., blessings 5, 10, 11, 14, 15, 17, and 19.

1. Shield of Abraham, patriarchs
2. God's powers,[47] resurrection of the dead
3. Holiness of God, God's name
4. Knowledge [no explicit mention here of Torah]
5. Repentance [a cultic theme; mention of Torah with service]
6. Forgiveness
7. Redemption
8. Healing
9. Yearly sustenance
10. Liberation and ingathering of exiles [national motif]
11. Restoration of judges [political motif][48]
12. Slanderers, enemies, apostates
13. Righteous [reference to the "remnant of the scribes"]
14. Jerusalem [priestly theme]
15. Davidic salvation [priestly and patriarchal theme][49]
16. Hear prayer [followed immediately by prayer for restoration of cult]
17. Restore the cult, return presence to Zion
18. Thanksgiving
19. Peace, priestly blessing

Bickermann suggested that the last three blessings (17–19) were parts of the "High Priest's prayer," recited in the Temple, and were added as a unit to an earlier prayer that concluded with the present fifteenth blessing. Blessings 4–7 "form a group centered on the idea of sin. They enlarge upon the appeal to God's forgiveness made by the High Priest on the Atonement Day. The Sixth Benediction more or less repeats this pontifical prayer."[50] He further speculates that the first, eighth, ninth, fourteenth, and our sixteenth blessings form a single prayer invoking the patriarchs and concerning health, prosperity, Jerusalem, and an appeal for the acceptance of prayer. Bickermann argues that this group parallels similar Greek Hellenistic prayers recited for the well-being, health, peace, and prosperity of the polis. On this basis he concludes that

> the original Tefillah was the Civic Prayer for Jerusalem. Both, the Greeks and the Jews, asked for health and food. But while the Greek also prayed for peace or salvation of the city, the covenanted Jew expressed the same idea by supplicating the Deity to have mercy on Jerusalem.[51]

This prayer was recited, says Bickermann, in the Temple "by the people after the libation rite of the continuous sacrifice (Tamid). The prayer was post-exilic, and is first attested ca. 200 B.C. It was first said on the festival days only, but became a part of the daily sacrificial service after 145 B.C."[52]

Bickermann errs, I believe, in locating the initial official adoption of the full-blown liturgy in the second century B.C.E. This is too early, for we have ample data that factions among the rabbis in the first and early second centuries C.E. contended over its legitimacy. But as our evidence shows—based in part on Bickermann's analysis—this prayer formed the core of the priestly liturgy sponsored by the patriarchate after the destruction of the Temple. In the aftermath of the internal political crisis that led to the deposition of Gamaliel, the *Tefillah* was accepted by the scribal factions too, and, in return, the patriarch agreed to foster the *Shema*, with minor modifications. Together these prayers made up the composite liturgy that reflected a qualified compromise between priests, patriarchal aristocrats, and scribes/rabbis.

This line of argument is supported by several added points of importance regarding the *Tefillah*. First, in the *Tefillah* the thirteenth blessing refers to the "remnant of the scribes." Bickermann calls the allusion obscure and cites Liebermann, who

adds that it must be "very old." But it could in fact depict a
facet of the conflict between the two mainly distinct social
divisions that sponsored competing prayers as they strove for
dominance over the populace in the postdestruction era. This
terminology may be a negative reference to the adherents of
the scribal brotherhoods and a prayer for "mercy" for those
who adhere to that "decadent scribal group."[53]

Bickermann focused our attention on the agendum of the
liturgy. Prominently absent from the blessings of the *Tefillah*
are references to creation, to other aspects of the cosmic/mysti-
cal dimension of the world, and to the Exodus. Torah is mentioned, but only in the fifth blessing, in conjunction with
avodah, the sacrificial Temple cult. We may safely say that this
liturgy does not propound vital elements of a scribal agendum.

This understanding of the dynamic of the definitive first-
century stage of liturgical institutionalization helps us put prior
phases into perspective. So, for example, in T. Ber. 3:13 the
Houses of Hillel and Shammai dispute the number of blessings
to be recited in the case of a New Year or festival that coin-
cides with the Sabbath. The numbers alone are given, and they
descend from ten to seven, leaving us to decide to what blessings the Houses refer. One might argue that this passage is an
imagined projection of later practice to an earlier age. If so,
we might object that the dispute does not reflect an expected
simple picture of later practice by earlier masters. Hence the
disputes likely are not artificial. Even so, little can be deduced
from the tradition regarding the Houses' relationship to the
early use of the *Tefillah* on the Sabbath and festivals.[54] As
Petuchowski sums up, the most we can say is this: "Public
worship on Sabbaths and festivals antedated public worship
on weekdays, and an Order of Seven Benedictions for Sabbaths and festivals was in existence before the Order of Eighteen Benedictions for weekdays was devised at Yavneh."[55]

In further support of Bickermann's assertions, internal rabbinic evidence suggests that the *Tefillah* was a priestly rite,
later taken over by the patriarchate as its own ritual. The
relevant talmudic source provides two traditions regarding the

origin of the *Tefillah*. One source attributes the authorship to the Men of the Great Assembly, an institution about which we have little definite evidence. We can presume that this tradition seeks to associate the *Tefillah* with a public body attached to the Temple in Jerusalem. Another text links the *Tefillah* to the later Simeon Hapakoli under the supervision of Gamaliel the patriarch at Yavneh.[56] This unit leaves little doubt that patriarchal sympathizers sought to subsume the *Tefillah* as their own authorized liturgy. No comparable patriarchal-oriented tradition exists regarding the origin of the *Shema*.[57]

Based on our evidence we can go further than to say that the *Tefillah* and *Shema* were prototypical liturgies of competing social factions. We also can trace to a particular period the joint institutionalization of these prayers as permanent fixtures of rabbinic worship. Rabbinic texts preserve evidence of the main conflict and compromise that led to the "canonization" of the core of rabbinic liturgy. The deposition narrative that I alluded to earlier in this article centers on the struggle between first-century factions over the imposition of a liturgical ritual as obligatory. According to this narrative, Gamaliel was deposed from the patriarchate because he insisted that the rabbis recite the *Tefillah* at night. We have two versions of this deposition narrative that vary on some substantive details.

In the version of the narrative in the Palestinian Talmud (Ber. 4:1), the action begins in the Beit Va'ad (Gathering Hall) and continues in the Yeshivah. In the main action of the story, Eleazar b. Azariah, a priest descended from a scribe and himself an aristocrat, takes the place of Gamaliel after he is overthrown. Eleazar served as the interim patriarch as the scribes usurped control from the patriarchal aristocracy. He was described as a priest who supported the ideals of the scribes, a pragmatic political figure. Akiba, who was rejected as the compromise candidate for the patriarchate, is portrayed as lacking the practical ability to mediate between factions as an active politician. Tradition tells us that this political extremist supported the messianic rebellion of Bar Kokhba and suffered martyrdom at the hands of the Romans.[58]

The Babylonian version of the deposition narrative (Ber. 27b–28a) contains several additions. First, it locates all the action in the rabbinized study hall. It depicts a guard of shield-bearers supporting the patriarch. Here, the reform of the patriarchal court is effectuated by packing the membership of the house of study, by "adding benches." The deposition is followed by a reconciliation wherein Gamaliel reclaims the patriarchate, bowing to the new realities and the change in the balance of power in rabbinic leadership. As part of this process the patriarch visits the scribe's house and suffers debasing humiliation, counterbalancing Gamaliel's earlier humiliation of Joshua.[59] Once the deal is cut to restore Gamaliel, Eleazar is informed in priestly metaphor to yield his position back to the legitimate heir.

The deposition narrative compresses into stylized rabbinic form an account of events that probably stretched over a sustained period of social unrest and instability within rabbinic society itself.[60] Naturally, the struggle for dominance in the rabbinic community ought to be interpreted ultimately in light of all pertinent political, social, and economic factors. Nevertheless, we must not ignore the fact that the extant traditions link the struggle to liturgy. Other sources, too, indicate historical tension in the development of the *Shema* and *Tefillah*.[61] Prayer had a powerful and real impact within the community of the faithful.

Accordingly, we ought not assume that the liturgical account was just a peripheral means of reporting a broader conflict. Goldenberg dismisses the ostensible issue of liturgical reform as a mere excuse, referring to the "striking triviality of the dispute over the evening prayer."[62] However, there is reason enough to believe that the pivotal issue over which the patriarch was deposed is just as stated: the question of whether the recitation of the evening Prayer of Eighteen Blessings was optional or compulsory. Institutionalization of the *Tefillah* at night must have been seen as a move to displace the *Shema* from its place of liturgical primacy. It was in short a direct challenge to the authority of the scribal factions within rabbinism. Goldenberg alludes to political struggle:

> The Patriarchal regime was just beginning to consolidate its power. The rabbinic conclave in general must have resented this. At least two rival groups, the priests and Yohanan's circle, are likely to have had aspirations of their own. The stakes in the struggle—control over the remnant of Jewish autonomy in Palestine—were large.[63]

But he fails to take one more step: to acknowledge that promulgation of public prayers, the stated issue of the conflict that he discusses, was one of the primary means of exercising influence, dominance, and control over a community of the faithful.

THE POLITICS OF PIETY

To summarize, I have posited that liturgies within rabbinic Judaism arose out of competing social circumstances. I have argued that the scribes promoted the *Shema* together with particular motifs, such as the Exodus,[64] to foster their authority over Israelite society. Others seeking dominance employed their own competitive legitimizing liturgies. What Stefan C. Reif has written regarding the general characteristics of Jewish liturgy applies here: "The essence of Jewish liturgy is that it carries within it all these competing tendencies and successfully absorbs them all."[65]

Our reconstruction examined the development of two major liturgical rituals of early rabbinism as they progressed through several probable stages. During the initial transition after the destruction of the Temple, from about 70 to 90 C.E., the priests promulgated the *Tefillah* and the scribes promoted the *Shema*. At this time it would have been natural for the scribes to associate the *Shema* with the Temple Service. In the second phase of development, from about 90 to 155 C.E., the patriarchate sponsored the *Tefillah* to counter a growing scribal faction within the rabbinic movement. Scribes countered by rallying popular support, deposing Gamaliel, and effectuating a lasting compromise. Both liturgies were adopted in tandem and were made obligatory rabbinic rituals.

In the era from about 155 to 220 C.E., the rabbis amalgamated the *Shema* and the *Tefillah* in a compromise that led to the present shape of the composite rabbinic service. A probable result is that the *Shema* was revised to include the theme of kingship. In this era the priests were relegated to figurehead status in rabbinic communities. The patriarch continued to observe the conventional boundaries of his authority that were established after the deposition, and he was excluded from most internal rabbinic affairs. In effect the scribal faction triumphed in the internal rabbinic power struggle, severing rabbinic ritual from meaningful national political structures.

NOTES

1. See Lawrence A. Hoffman, *Beyond the Text: A Holistic Approach to Liturgy,* Jewish Literature and Culture (Bloomington, IN, 1987), and especially his introductory discussion of the history of the Jewish liturgy; Tzvee Zahavy, "A New Approach to Early Jewish Prayer," in Baruch M. Bokser, ed., *History of Judaism: The Next Ten Years,* Brown Judaic Studies (Decatur, GA, 1980), pp. 45–60; Stefan C. Reif, "Jewish Liturgical Research: Past, Present, and Future," *JJS* 34 (1983): 161–70.

2. See Hoffman, *Beyond the Text;* R. S. Sarason, "On the Use of Method in the Modern Study of Jewish Liturgy," in William S. Green, ed., *Approaches to Ancient Judaism: Theory and Practice* (Decatur, GA, 1978), pp. 97–172.

3. Examples of apologetics abound. See, e. g., Sarason's discussion of the work of Zwi Karl, "On the Use of Method," pp. 122–24. Popular works on Jewish liturgy have obvious apologetic purposes: cf. D. Holisher, *The Synagogue and Its People* (New York, 1955); Evelyn Garfiel, *Service of the Heart* (New Jersey, 1958); Abraham E. Millgram, *Jewish Worship* (Philadelphia, 1971).

These represent works of great devotion and erudition but avowedly with no critical agenda.

4. Nearly all major works in the discipline lack a consciousness of systemic shifts in Judaism. Abraham Z. Idelsohn, *Jewish Liturgy and Its Development* (New York, 1932); Ismar Elbogen, *Prayer in Israel in Its Historical Development* (Hebrew; Tel Aviv, 1972); and the work of Karl are but a few examples.

5. Examples of inadequate models of social and political life (Pharisee, Sadducee, Essene; plebeians, patricians) are common in the work of writers like Louis Finkelstein. See Sarason, "On the Use of Method"; Hoffman, *Beyond the Text,* pp. 8, 184, n. 16.

6. Shemaryahu Talmon, *The World of Qumran from Within* (Jerusalem, 1989), p. 239.

7. Examples of misunderstood internal dynamics include those who did not see Roman imperial domination as crucial; those who did not consider the distinction among priestly, scribal, and patriarchal interests; and those who did not recognize conflict as central to Judaism.

8. Hoffman, *Beyond the Text,* p. 4. See, e.g., G. Alon, E. E. Urbach, and S. Zeitlin, who frequently employ the model of "normative versus heretical."

9. Kaufmann Kohler, *The Origins of the Synagogue and Church* (New York, 1929), believed that liturgy reacted to Persian dualism; Elbogen thought that the *Tefillah* prayer for the restoration of the Davidic line was a polemic of the exilarch in Babylonia: see Sarason, "On the Use of Method," pp. 108, 110.

10. Hoffman, *Beyond the Text,* p. 5.

11. See Joseph Heinemann, *Prayer in the Talmud* (Berlin and New York, 1977). Heinemann also misinterprets some prayers, missing the main distinction between national and political ideology on the one hand, and the enunciation of scribal ideals on the other. For a view favoring political causality in the formation of the liturgy, see C. Roth, *"Melekh HaOlam:* Zealot influence in the Liturgy," *JJS* 11 (1960): 173–75; and cf. Louis Finkelstein, "The Development of the Amidah," *JQR* 16 (1925–1926): 142–69, regarding Zealot influence on the *Tefillah.*

12. Hoffman, *Beyond the Text,* p. 8.

13. Heinemann, *Prayer in the Talmud,* p. 7.

14. Reif, "Jewish Liturgical Research," p. 162; Sarason, "On the Use of Method," p. 101; Hoffman, *Beyond the Text,* p. 8.

15. Lee I. Levine, *The Rabbinic Class in Palestine during the Talmudic Period* (Hebrew; Jerusalem, 1985). This study deals mainly with the third and fourth centuries, but its method is applicable to earlier and later periods as well.

16. Regarding Saldarini's study, see below. Jacob Neusner's representative synthetic work for this period is *Judaism: The Evidence of the Mishnah* (Chicago, 1981).

17. B. Ber. 27b–28a; Y. Ber. 4:1; and see my *The Traditions of Eleazar ben Azariah* (Missoula, MT, 1977), pp. 146–59.

18. Confrontations involving prayer include those instances related in the Mishnah, such as the castigation of Tarfon (Ber. 1:3) for not reciting the *Shema* in the proper posture (bowing may have been suggestive of the priestly rite of the Temple on the Day of Atonement); the suspicion that Akiba and Eleazar b. Azariah were not reciting the morning *Shema* (T. Ber. 1:2); Roman concern over the recitation of the *Shema* in Akiba's house of study (T. Ber. 2:13), and the tradition that Akiba, a martyr of the Bar Kokhba war, recited the *Shema* at the time of his death (B. Ber. 61b).

19. See, for instance, Luke 4:16; Acts 9:2, 20; 13:5, 14; 14:1; 16:13; 17:1, 10–11, 17; 18:4, 19; 19:8.

20. R. Horsely, *Jesus and the Spiral of Violence* (San Francisco, 1987), p. 152. See also Anthony J. Saldarini, *Pharisees, Scribes, and Sadducees* (Wilmington, 1988), pp. 163–73.

21. Horsely, *Jesus and the Spiral of Violence*, p. 156.

22. F. Heiler, *Prayer* (New York, 1958), p. 58.

23. S.v. "Scribe," *The Interpreter's Dictionary of the Bible* IV (Nashville, 1962), pp. 246–48.

24. Saldarini, *Pharisees, Scribes, and Sadducees*, p. 275.

25. See Saldarini, *Pharisees, Scribes, and Sadducees*, pp. 241–97, for a full discussion of the social roles of scribes in Jewish society.

26. See, e.g., M. Ber. 1:3.

27. Regarding the role of scribes in the gospel traditions, see Saldarini, *Pharisees, Scribes, and Sadducees*, pp. 159–66.

28. See Y. Yadin, *Tefillin from Qumran* (Jerusalem, 1969).

29. The Nash Papyrus, c. 150 B.C.E., from Fayyum, contains the decalogue and the first two verses of the *Shema*.

30. See James Crenshaw, *Old Testament Wisdom* (Atlanta, 1981), pp. 27ff., regarding the sage as a member of a professional class. Crenshaw reflects on the Exodus motif in the Wisdom of

Solomon. Also see his prolegomenon to *Studies in Old Testament Wisdom* (New York, 1977) for the importance of the theme of creation in wisdom circles. Ismar Elbogen posits the *Shema* and its benedictions as the earliest form of the "synagogue service"; see *Studien zur Geschichte des jüdischen Gottesdienstes* (Berlin, 1907), pp. 38–44.

31. Even if we place the formalization of these blessings late in the second century, these expressions undoubtedly evoke the main themes of the earliest formulations of the *Shema*.

32. "Blessed be the name of his glorious kingdom for ever and ever"; and cf. T. Ber. 1:10.

33. See the discussion in T. Ber. 1:10 of whether reference to sovereignty (a patriarchal theme) must be removed when reference to the Exodus (a scribal motif) is inserted in the *Shema*. The pericope may be a political dispute rather than strictly a theological debate.

34. See Martin Goodman, *The Ruling Class of Judea* (Cambridge, 1987); idem, *State and Society in Roman Galilee, A.D. 132–212* (Oxford, 1983).

35. Josephus provides a more obvious exaggeration by associating the *Shema* with Moses in *Antiquities,* IV, vii, 13, and he avers it was part of the daily morning service in the Jerusalem Temple.

36. My thanks to Professor Israel Knoll, Hebrew University, for helping me clarify this point.

37. In M. Ber. 1:1. Gamaliel's children defy him by making reference to the *Shema*. By proposing to regulate their liturgy, Gamaliel asserts his authority over his rebellious sons: "Once [Gamaliel's] sons came from the banquet hall. And they said to him, 'We have not [yet] recited the *Shema*.' He said to them, 'If the day has not yet broken, you are obligated to recite [the *Shema*].'" Political conflict and social circumstances help explain the artificiality and awkwardness of this anecdote as part of this initial pericope of the Mishnah.

38. T. Ber. 2:6.

39. See my *Mishnaic Law of Blessings and Prayers: Tractate Berakhot,* Brown Judaic Studies (Decatur, GA, 1987), pp. 20–28.

40. This distinction may be too subtle. But consider that some modern anti-Zionists insistently employ the phrase "Land of Israel" rather than "State of Israel" in referring to modern Israel.

41. See Baruch M. Bokser, *The Origins of the Seder* (Berkeley, 1984). In parallel developments, the early Christians appropriated the seder in their own way.

42. For a discussion see Hoffman, *Beyond the Text*, pp. 86–102.

43. E. D. Goldschmidt, in *The Passover Haggadah* (Jerusalem, 1977), p. 51, n. 1, cites Alon's view that this passage be attributed to Gamaliel II at Yavneh, and refers to alternative opinions on its interpretation.

44. The folk song, the *Chad Gadya*, appended to conclude the seder, though it may be a later addition, may be viewed as a cynical reference to the paschal offering, mocking the two *zuzim*, the monetary interest, that the priests had in the sacrifice, and reinforcing their indignity in the wake of the destruction of the Temple.

45. A version in T. Pes. 10:12 has Rabban Gamaliel and the sages dealing with the laws of Passover all through the night. See Goldschmidt, *Passover Haggadah*, pp. 19–21.

46. Elias Bickermann, "The Civic Prayer of Jerusalem," *HTR* 55 (1962): 163–85. My purpose here is not to review all the theories of the origin of the *Tefillah*. The better-known views include that of Leopold Zunz who employed a problematic monolinear sequential historical model of its development, somewhat arbitrarily tracing its composite development to several distinct eras. For a critical assessment of Zunz's position see Sarason, "On the Use of Method," pp. 101ff. Kaufmann Kohler attributed its origin to other forces; see "The Origin and Composition of the Eighteen Benedictions with a Translation of the Corresponding Essene Prayers in the *Apostolic Constitutions*," *HUCA* 1 (1924): 387–425. Louis Finkelstein hypothesized yet another trajectory of development in "The Development of the *Amidah*," pp. 142–69. As we discussed above, Joseph Heinemann maintained an alternative position; see "Prayers of the Beth Midrash Origin," *JJS* 5 (1960): 264–80, and *Prayer in the Talmud*, passim.

47. Frederic Manns, *La Prière d'Israël à l'heure de Jésus* (Jerusalem, 1986), p. 146, n. 6, citing Urbach, sees in this expression (*gibbor*—"hero") an anti-Roman sentiment, implicitly demeaning the cult of the emperor.

48. Manns (ibid., p. 149) suggests that this blessing responds to the actual loss of juridical power prior to the destruction of the Temple.

49. The Genizah version conflates this blessing with the pre-

ceding. See Solomon Schechter, "Genizah Specimens," *JQR* 10 (1898): 656–57; J. Mann, "Genizah Fragments of the Palestinian Order of the Service," *HUCA* 2 (1925): 306–8.

50. Bickermann, "Civic Prayer," pp. 167–68, 172.

51. Ibid., p. 176.

52. Ibid., p. 185.

53. This is reminiscent of the polemics of our own day. Some Orthodox refer, for example, to Conservative Jews as "dead bark" or "at best, idolaters."

54. See my *Mishnaic Law,* pp. 70–72.

55. See Jakob J. Petuchowski, "The Liturgy of the Synagogue: History, Structure and Contents," in William S. Green, ed., *Approaches to Ancient Judaism* IV, Brown Judaic Studies (Decatur, GA, 1983), p. 16.

56. B. Meg. 17b–18a; see my *Mishnaic Law,* pp. 57–58. See also I. Schiffer, "The Men of the Great Assembly," in *Persons and Institutions in Early Rabbinic Judaism* (Missoula, MT, 1977), pp. 237–76. Also consider M. Ber. 4:3, the dispute between Gamaliel and Joshua over the formalization of the prayer, and T. Ber. 3:12, which draws specific parallels between the times for the prayer and the sacrifices of the Temple.

57. To make the picture even more complex, evidence also exists that the text of the Prayer of Eighteen Blessings may draw upon earlier formulas, e.g., from Ben Sirah, who appears to have been sympathetic to both scribal and priestly interests. See Petuchowski, "Liturgy of the Synagogue," pp. 7–11. Talmon (*World of Qumran,* pp. 200–243) has convincingly argued that the Covenanters at Qumran recited daily prayers with some parallels to the rabbinic *Tefillah.*

58. Elsewhere in rabbinic traditions, despite his aristocratic pedigree, Eleazar upholds a value of the scribal agendum, avowing that he understands why the Exodus must be mentioned at night. He thereby accepted and promoted practices of the scribes (M. Ber. 1:5). The rabbis applied his statement to the mention of the Exodus in the evening *Shema* and inserted it in the seder to warrant the retelling of the Exodus in the evening, the seder ritual itself.

59. As I explained above, in a touch of irony, M. Ber. 1:1 starts the primary rabbinic legal compendium by linking the *Shema* with the Temple and continues with Gamaliel's sons mocking him by telling him, as an excuse for their late return home from the "ban-

quet hall," that they did not recite the *Shema*. Instead of chastising them, Gamaliel is portrayed as reciting a ruling to them permitting them to recite the liturgy. Echoes of division and transition reverberate in this and other compressed narrative references to the liturgy.

60. In the B.T. version of the deposition narrative, the anonymous student responsible for the destabilization of the status quo is Simeon b. Yohai, the mystic apocalyptic—a force of provocation and instability in that era.

61. M. Ber. 4:3, for example, gives us a dispute between Gamaliel and Joshua over the formalization of the *Tefillah*.

62. Robert Goldenberg, "The Deposition of Rabban Gamaliel II," in *Persons and Institutions in Early Rabbinic Judaism*, p. 37.

63. Ibid., p. 38.

64. Regarding a dispute over the dominance of the theme of sovereignty over the Exodus as a liturgical subject, see T. Ber. 1:10.

65. Stefan C. Reif, "The Early Liturgy of the Synagogue," in *The Cambridge History of Judaism* III (forthcoming). See also his articles, "Some Liturgical Issues in the Talmudic Sources," *SL* 15 (1982–1983): 188–206; "Jewish Liturgical Research: Past, Present, Future," *JJS* 34 (1983): 161–70.

Using Archeological Sources

MARILYN J. S. CHIAT AND MARCHITA B. MAUCK

[Editors' note: In the first part, Marilyn J. S. Chiat, Adjunct Faculty Member of the Department of Classical and Near Eastern Studies and Fellow of the Center for Jewish Studies at the University of Minnesota, investigates what can be learned about early Jewish worship from the archeological study of synagogues. She questions the traditional assumption of the gradual evolution from a single type of building and suggests instead a much more pluriform development, in which the mutual influence of church and synagogue played a part. In the second part, Marchita B. Mauck, Associate Professor in the School of Art at Louisiana State University, undertakes a similar study of early Christian architecture, tracing the evolution from the house-church to the fourth-century basilica. Both authors stress the functional study of places of worship. Our knowledge of worship thus allows us to decipher the meaning of the spaces that we find; and the sacred sites inform us of the sacred rites they held.]

EARLY SYNAGOGUE ARCHITECTURE

Although the existence of early synagogues has been known since the nineteenth century, their study can still be considered in its infancy. This state of affairs is particularly evident when one examines current literature on the subject: even today, despite dramatic discoveries in Israel and the Diaspora, there are still scholars who continue to subscribe to an outmoded theory of the synagogue's evolutionary development first advanced over a half century ago.[1] In order to understand why the evolutionary model has retained its attraction and why it no longer can be considered valid, it is necessary to review, albeit briefly, the history of synagogue studies.

69

The Evolutionary Theory

In the latter half of the nineteenth century, American, English, and European explorers in Palestine began to publish the results of their surveys, including descriptions of the remains of buildings conjectured to be early synagogues.[2] In 1905 and again in 1907 expeditions from the Deutsche Orient-Gesellschaft, led by E. Hiller, Heinrich Kohl, and Carl Watzinger, and financed by the German-Jewish philanthropist James Simon, surveyed nine synagogues in Galilee and two in the neighboring Golan; their findings were published in 1916.[3]

Based on what they observed, Kohl and Watzinger proposed a synagogue type whose identity and date could be determined by the presence of certain specific characteristics: the use of basalt or limestone ashlars (square blocks of masonry laid, often without mortar, in horizontal courses with vertical joints); a richly carved ornamented facade facing toward Jerusalem (south); limestone slab pavements; an interior space divided by colonnades into a central nave with aisles on the east and west and occasionally on the north; and no evidence of a permanent repository for the Torah scrolls (*aron hakodesh*). Buildings with these characteristics became known by their locale as "Galilean." Kohl and Watzinger dated them to the reign of the Severans (c. 200 C.E.) and claimed that they had been destroyed by the mid-fourth century.[4]

This theory of a single type of early synagogue was widely accepted; it dovetailed nicely with contemporary scientific studies on rabbinic Judaism of the first centuries of the common era.[5] These theories were given their *summa* by G. F. Moore, who posited the existence of "normative Judaism," which was said to have its foundation in the Mishnah and Talmud and to have been followed by all Jews, except heretics, who, by definition, belonged to "fringe sects."[6]

Kohl and Watzinger's theory regarding the Galilean-type synagogue, and Moore's regarding normative Judaism, remained unchallenged for several decades. However, when new discoveries were made in Palestine in the 1920s and

1930s, it became apparent that the data required reevaluation. Synagogues excavated at Na'aram, Beth Alpha, Hammat Gadara, and Gerasa did not conform to Kohl and Watzinger's Galilean type. Setting these buildings apart were several important characteristics, including the addition of an apse (or niche) on the wall facing Jerusalem (supposedly to provide a permanent installation for the *aron hakodesh*—the ark for the Torah scrolls) and elaborately decorated mosaic pavements.

To explain the existence of these building without challenging the concept of normative Judaism, the eminent scholar and archeologist E. L. Sukenik proposed that "in the development of synagogue architecture in Palestine, two stages can be distinguished. In the earlier type of synagogue, the Ark of the Law was not permanently stationed in the main hall. . . . In the new type of synagogue we . . . find an apse for the Ark in the wall facing Jerusalem, and the doors in the opposite wall."[7] Another feature of the "new type" was the use of mosaics instead of flagstones for the floor.

By proposing that a "new" type of synagogue flourished in the Byzantine period, Sukenik was able to skirt the issue of diversity among Jews during the so-called Talmudic Era.[8] The "new" buildings represent nothing more than an evolutionary development in synagogue architecture: an improvement upon an old style. To suggest otherwise would have been to question the validity of the concept of normative Judaism.

In the conclusion of his book, Sukenik acknowledged that new discoveries "are being made in Palestine and the Diaspora which will undoubtedly add new details to our conceptions of early synagogues." But, he continued confidently, "we may safely predict that these details will not change the conception as a whole."[9]

But change it they did. It soon became evident that two synagogue categories were not sufficient. Yet another reevaluation of all synogogue data was called for by the unearthing of additional new evidence: the surprising discovery of a change in orientation in a so-called Galilean-type synagogue at Beth She'arim that transferred its focal point from a *bimah* (platform) built against the northwest wall to a niche created by the closing of the central door on the southwest wall facing Jerusalem; and the excavation of a broadhouse synagogue at Khirbet Shema in Galilee that was contemporary with its Galilean-type neighbor at Meron. The broadhouse-type synagogue, also found at Khirbet Susiya and Eshtemoa (as well as the synagogue at Dura-Europos, see below) has one of its broad walls, often with one or more niches or *bimot,* facing toward Jerusalem.

Michael Avi-Yonah, professor of classical archeology and history of art at the Hebrew University, proposed a theory that would account for the new evidence and yet not threaten the still-entrenched belief in the existence of normative Judaism.[10] According to him, there were three (not one or two) types of ancient synagogue, which were to be identified with three related chronological periods: (1) early (Galilean), as described by Kohl and Watzinger, dated to the second–third centuries; (2) transitional, a catch-all category for those buildings (including the broadhouse), that did not fit into either of the other types, dated from the late third to fifth centuries; (3) late, or Byzantine, characterized by an apse or niche facing toward Jerusalem and by mosaic pavements, dated to the fifth– sixth centuries. E. R. Goodenough, a student of Moore, adopted a similar division but used the terms Galilean, broadhouse, and synagogues with mosaic pavements.[11]

Although Avi-Yonah's theory received wide acceptance, particularly from classically trained Israeli archeologists and art historians, Avi-Yonah himself eventually became aware of its shortcomings. In one of his last articles on the subject he cautions against the use of "types" as a basis for determining chronology.[12] Eric Meyers, a Duke University archeologist who has excavated several synagogue sites in Israel, regularly urges scholars to move beyond Avi-Yonah's "old consensus" by accepting the theory that archeological evidence supports: not evolution from one type to another, but the coexistence until the early medieval period of several types.[13] While acknowledging that recent publications give the impression that synagogue studies are in many ways alive and well, Meyers laments the fact that on many key issues, particularly chronology and typology, a lack of scholarly consensus leaves the field betwixt and between in Israel and uninteresting to many American and European scholars. A further tragedy is that most sites in Galilee and the Golan still await excavation and restoration.[14]

Thus far, we have looked only at synagogues in Roman and Byzantine Palestine (see below, map of selected synagogue sites in Israel). A. Thomas Kraabel, an archeologist and religious historian, has written extensively on synagogues in the Diaspora, and his thoughtful observations offer additional insight into the issues confronting synagogue studies. The evidence from the Diaspora consists of six buildings: Dura-Europos, Sardis, Priene, Delos, Ostia, and Stobi. These differ in plan and decoration: according to Kraabel, the variety is due to the adoption by local Jewish communities of the iconography, architecture, and organizational form of their host culture.[15] Whereas Kraabel has used archeological evidence to reconstruct synagogues and their communities, Shaye Cohen has explored examples of diversity in Diaspora synagogues based on pagan and Christian literary evidence.[16] The diversity documented by Cohen and Kraabel is an important feature of Judaism in late antiquity.[17] As we examine synagogue architecture in the Diaspora, and more so in Palestine, clearly the "normative" theory regarding rabbinic Judaism and the three evolutionary stages for synagogue architecture that the theory supports can no longer be considered tenable.

Dura-Europos

It was in the Diaspora that one of the most dramatic finds was discovered, the synagogue at Dura-Europos. A study of this structure and its nearby neighbor, a small house-church (see below, p. 82, The Earliest House-churches), illustrates the need to study religious architecture not only within its larger cultural and historical contexts in general, but more specifically in its relationship to buildings belonging to different groups coexisting in the same environment. During the first centuries of the common era, Jews, Christians, and pagans did not live in isolation from each other. Dura-Europos, a trading outpost on the Euphrates river in modern Syria was subject to many cultural influences—Seleucid, Parthian, and Roman—before being destroyed by the Sassanians in 256.[18] The synagogue and the church were discovered in 1932 during excavations of an embankment that encircled the town. Built as a last-ditch fortification to thwart the Sassanian invasion, the embankment consisted of buildings located next to the city wall and filled in with dirt; one was a church, another a synagogue.

The synagogue complex occupied almost an entire city block in an area described as "one of the less desirable streets in the city."[19] The exterior of the complex did not differ in appearance from neighboring dwellings. It consisted of nine rooms and a colonnaded forecourt that preceded the sanctuary and was open to the sky. Destroyed by the Sassanians in 256, the synagogue can be dated by an inscription to 245; it was built on the site of an earlier building, a house, that by the late second century had been converted into a modest synagogue.

The synagogue is a broadhouse in plan, 14 meters × 8 meters; it is entered by two doorways in its long east wall, a large one in the center and a second one at the south end (see fig. 1, p. 94). Opposite the center doorway, on the west wall (the wall facing Jerusalem), is an elaborate niche, an *aron hakodesh*. Benches are attached to all the walls. Broadhouse-type synagogues have since been uncovered in Israel, but only one—at Khirbet Shema—is close in date to this.[20] Although both are broadhouses, they differ in several significant ways. For example, the synagogue at Khirbet Shema has a colonnaded interior; but a more significant difference is to be found in their decoration. The surviving decoration at Khirbet Shema consists of an eagle within a garland incised on a doorpost and a *menorah* (a candelabra) crudely carved on a lintel; a side room has frescoes with red and white geometric designs. At

Dura-Europos the sanctuary is elaborately decorated with spectacular wall-paintings that have been the source of discussion and controversy since their discovery nearly sixty years ago.[21] No similar cycle of synagogue paintings has yet been discovered, but the cycle's existence here in a remote caravan town would suggest that its source may be yet-unknown synagogues built in larger urban areas of the Diaspora; one possibility recently suggested is Palmyra.[22]

The Dura synagogue's plan and decoration suggest the development of certain cultic practices. For example, Joseph Gutmann has proposed that the prominence given to the yellow, rounded Torah ark-chest in the second band of paintings "suggests the possibility that it was related to a liturgical hymn sung by the congregation when the Torah ark was brought from outside the synagogue, where it was kept at that time, and then led in procession around the synagogue."[23] Regardless of what the wall-paintings may have meant to their congregants, when the synagogue is compared to the modest house-church located just down the block (see below, p. 83), it would appear that while both groups had places of worship suitable for their needs, the Jews of Dura were able to afford a larger and more elaborate complex and had available to them an established visual vocabulary, an iconography, capable of transmitting religious belief and practice.

The Interrelation of Church and Synagogue

Recent scholarship suggests that, like the wall-paintings at Dura, the elaborate decoration found in the mosaic pavements of some fourth- to sixth-century Palestinian synagogues may have been inspired by contemporary liturgical practices.[24] Whether this is indeed the case has yet to be established, but what can be proved by the archeological evidence is that synagogues constructed in Roman and Byzantine Palestine, even when contemporary in date, display a diversity of architectural styles. Moreover, during their centuries of use, many were extensively remodeled, or rebuilt, or both, resulting in dramatic changes in their original form. While a thorough examination of this phenomenon is impossible here, we can at least document several examples and suggest what may have precipitated the changes and what they indicate about the synagogue's use.

One point must be made clear at the outset: the concept of "art for art's sake" is modern. Changes were not made to a synagogue's plan or decoration as an exercise in "keeping up with the Joneses," who in Roman or Byzantine Palestine were increasingly Christian. The changes were certainly influenced by Christianity via its numerous churches that were beginning to cover the countryside—a dramatic reversal of the situation at Dura; but the alterations still had to serve the synagogue's function, namely, to provide a place of Jewish assembly and prayer.

One of the most famous synagogues excavated by Kohl and Watzinger is at Capernaum, the home of Peter the Fisherman, on the north shore of the Sea of Galilee.[25] Recent excavations by the Franciscans at this site have established the synagogue's date as being later than initially believed: it was probably not built until after 350, but its plan and decoration are similar to those of several nearby synagogues, such as Kefar Bar'am and Chorozin, which are dated earlier.[26] This similarity is what led Kohl and Watzinger to postulate the existence of a Galilean-type synagogue for all of Galilee and the neighboring Golan Heights.

The synagogue is an adaptation of a basilica, a building type developed by the Greeks but used by the Romans for a number of secular purposes ranging from warehouses to courts of law. The Capernaum synagogue is divided into a nave and three aisles by three rows of columns, two longitudinal and one transverse (see fig. 2). The main hall is entered through three doors that open off a narrow narthex located on the south; a large court adjoins the main hall to its east. Kohl and Watzinger conjectured the existence of an elaborate Torah ark *blocking* the main central entry. The Franciscans, however, recently uncovered what they believe to be foundations for a *bimah* and a Torah ark, *flanking* the central door. In either case, however, worshipers would have had to have made a 180-degree turn to pray towards Jerusalem. The awkwardness of this arrangement suggests that the building may have served the community in a variety of ways, of which prayer was only one.

Located practically across the street and south of the synagogue at Capernaum are the ruins of an octagonal church dedicated to Saint Peter. Built on the supposed site of Peter's house, the church is contemporary with the synagogue. Both are built of the same material, imported white limestone. Their plans, however, are quite different (see fig. 3).[27] The church was a pilgrimage site without a permanent congregation, and its octagonal plan was intended to remind the pilgrim of the central plan of the Holy Sepulchre in Jerusalem built over the tomb of Jesus. Like the Holy Sepulchre, Peter's church was intended to be a *martyrium,* although it lacked a tomb chamber since Peter had been martyred and buried at Rome. By way of contrast, the synagogue did not commemorate a particular event or individual but was designed to serve the needs, sacred and secular, of Jews living in the community.

One further observation can be made about these two buildings. In a small Galilean community in about the year 400, a beautiful synagogue and equally beautiful church stood practically side by side, indicating a level of religious pluralism not evident in either the writings of the church fathers or the talmudic rabbis. In this particular community, the two religious buildings are quite different in design and decoration, but, as will be shown, this is not always the case.

The majority of Palestinian churches are basilicas built along a longitudinal axis, usually terminating in one or more semicircular internal or external apses; at times, a single apse is flanked by rooms. The chancel area of the church is usually two steps higher than the nave and is enclosed on three sides by a low solid screen. The screen is built of stone panels set into small posts (90 cm. high) that enabled the congregation to see the service but kept them separate from the clergy.

The church at Beth Yerah, dated to the first half of the fifth century and located on the south shore of the Sea of Galilee, is typical of many Palestinian churches (see fig. 4).[28] Worshipers entered the church through three doors opening off a narthex and proceeded down the nave and aisles to the most sacred part of the building—the chancel that housed the clergy and altar. Thus, one sees here a longitudinal progression from the temporal (or secular) world to the most sacred, a progression similar to that of the Jewish Temple in Jerusalem, but remarkably different from that of the synagogue at Capernaum (see figs. 2 and 5). Christians may have borrowed from the Jewish people the concept of interior congregational worship and the use of the basilica plan to accommodate the ritual, but it could be argued that they added to it elements borrowed from the Jewish Temple cult, in particular the separation of the priestly class from the congregation and, perhaps more significantly, the separation of the sacred from the profane. The *devir* (Holy of Holies) of the Temple becomes the chancel of the church.

The synagogues constructed in the city-territory of the Scythopolis, known in Jewish sources as Beth She'an, do not resemble the synagogue at Capernaum.[29] Rather, they are similar to nearby churches, such as the one at Beth Yerah. The synagogue at Ma'oz Hayyim is one such example.[30] The original building was contemporary to the synagogue at Capernaum. In plan it was an almost square hall, 14 × 12.5 meters, divided into a central nave and flanking aisles by two rows of rectangular pillars; a single door may have opened on the east. Remains of what appears to have been a platform of unhewn stones in the middle of the south wall may have supported a *bimah* or Torah ark (see fig. 6).

Sometime after the middle of the fourth century the building underwent extensive remodeling. The hall, enlarged to 16.4 × 14 meters, was divided into a central nave and flanking aisles by two rows of five columns. An external raised semicircular apse was added to the south, the direction of Jerusalem. The apse appears not to have had a *bimah* in front of it, but it may have been enclosed by a marble chancel screen. Two entrances added on the east opened on to a courtyard that may have been extended to the north of the building (see fig. 7). An elaborate mosaic pavement replaced the hall's original pavement of limestone slabs.

About a century later, other changes were made (see fig. 8). The exterior of the building remained essentially the same, but a *bimah* was added in front of the apse; it appears to have projected into the nave up to the first pair of columns. Evidence further suggests that a screen separated this area of the hall from the nave.

What we see here is a synagogue that over the years came increasingly to resemble nearby contemporary churches.[31] Initially a building with undifferentiated space, the remodeled synagogue at Ma'oz Hayyim adopted some of the same characteristics of the Jerusalem Temple as did the churches.[32] In its last stage, the synagogue's chancel area is separated from its nave much as the *devir,* the Holy of Holies, of the Temple was separated from the rest of the Temple space. The substantive changes made in the appearance of the synagogue suggest that the building had acquired a sacral quality lacking in its earlier stages, perhaps because of a shift in emphasis regarding its use: prayer may have become the synagogue's primary function.

The archeological evidence raises other issues as well. For instance, what was happening to the Jewish people in Palestine in the middle of the fourth century that brought about the extensive remodeling of synagogues such as the one at Ma'oz Hayyim? Jacob Neusner has described the fourth century as "marking the point of intersection between the histories of the two religions, Judaism and Christianity."[33] One could consider the synagogue remains uncovered in Israel as visible evidence of the Jewish people's response to these historical events, including the legalization of Christianity, Julian's death and the debacle of the Temple rebuilding, Jews becoming a minority in their own country, and the subsequent blanketing of their land with churches, large and small.

The Jewish people of Capernaum who lived alongside

Christians chose to construct a synagogue quite different in design from that of their neighbors' church. By contrast, the Jews in Ma'oz Hayyim had no compunction about remodeling their synagogue to resemble nearby churches. In order to understand fully the implications of this evidence, it is necessary to follow the suggestions of scholars such as Lawrence Hoffman, Jacob Neusner, Tzvee Zahavy, A. Thomas Kraabel, and Eric Meyers who have pointed out that, in order for synagogue studies to advance, scholars must make use of all available evidence.[34] Since many of the literary sources are ignored by archeologists and the archeological material is ignored by those studying literary evidence, it is time for a cross-fertilization of disciplines to begin. The same is true with regard to scholars working on Christian material—literary and archeological. Synagogues and churches, Jews and Christians, coexisted in Palestine and the Diaspora during the Roman and Byzantine periods: it is time we began to understand more accurately the nature of their relationship.

EARLY CHRISTIAN ARCHITECTURE

The Shift from a Theological to a Liturgical Approach

The history of early Christian architecture has seldom been looked at as a source for the reconstruction of liturgical history. Since the nineteenth century, scholars have preferred to concern themselves with the technical development of architectural forms and their theological/polemical presumptions.[35] A great surge of archeological research in the second half of the twentieth century has radically changed the map of early Christian architecture. Recent discoveries have invalidated many earlier conclusions, including the dating of specific monuments, chronologies, styles of architecture, and liturgical functions. Revisionist historians whose research relies on modern sociological, anthropological, and cultural insights are calling into question earlier presumptions about the low economic and social status of early Christian communities, thus altering our perceptions of the context of the worshiping assembly and the nature of its patronage of places of worship.[36]

The preeminent modern scholar of early Christian architecture is Richard Krautheimer. His book, *Early Christian and Byzantine Architecture*, first appeared in 1965; in addition, a four-volume work on early Christian churches in Rome, *Corpus basilicarum christianarum Romae,* by Krautheimer, Frankl, and Corbett, was published from 1937–1970. Along with Krautheimer's numerous articles, these works provide the bedrock of contemporary insight about early Christian architecture. Revised editions of *Early Christian and Byzantine Architecture* (1975, 1979, 1981, and 1986) illustrate both the rapid pace of research discoveries and the breadth of Krautheimer's lively intellect, ever willing to assess the consequences of new information and to revise his opinions in response. Unlike some other historians, he sees early Christian architecture as a last phase of late antiquity and not as a preamble to medieval architecture, which really has an entirely different character. In the "theoretical" realm he has shifted the academic discourse to follow the ground-breaking path of inquiry of Thomas Mathews, who provided a method for understanding liturgy as a determining factor in church architecture.[37]

Inquiry based on liturgical sources differs markedly from the prevalent alternative, which orients research around the theological aspect of early Christian architecture. That position, represented primarily by Friedrich Wilhelm Deichmann and his disciples, distinguishes a secular understanding of places of Christian worship prior to 313 C.E. from sacral notions of place instituted during the fourth century.[38] In this view, Jesus himself is both focus and locus of the holy, requiring neither temple nor sacred space. As in the early synagogue of Second Temple Judaism, the *ecclesia* thus meets in places of a neutral nature. The conclusion is that the emperor Constantine paganized Christianity, and fourth-century developments of distinctively religious church architecture subverted the normative postures of the apostolic period. This point of view, by which a meetinghouse is the only authentic norm for Christian worship, says more about post-Reformation polemic than about the actual relationship of liturgical practice to architectural form.

The new liturgical path of inquiry, however, has thrown architectural studies wide open. Intriguing at present, for example, are questions concerning the origin and function of duplicate apses, choirs, and altars in North Africa.[39] Was one set for liturgy and the other for sheltering important graves or relics? Or was there some duplication of liturgy? What do these North African instances have to do with similar later expressions in northern Europe? What is the purpose of the fourth-century "double basilicas" (two churches, side by side, connected by a hall) along the Istrian coast of Italy and north of the Alps? How were they used? What is the relationship of monumental mosaic or painted images decorating early churches to the rituals celebrated in their midst? These are essentially unexplored questions, since art historians have concerned themselves with stylistic or iconographic analyses and have shied away from liturgical interpretations. The field is thus rich for study.

The Earliest House-churches

The New Testament does not tell us anything about the places where the earliest generations of Christians gathered for worship. The most important element was that they gathered. The Acts of the Apostles states that the first converts in Jerusalem broke bread in their homes (2:42). Thus our first intimation is of a domestic environment for the celebration of the eucharistic liturgy.

Archeological evidence confirms that in the early third century, Christians were still meeting in the homes of community members. Prior to Constantine's Edict of Toleration in 313, the members of any sect whose activities might appear to conflict with the cult of the emperor generally found it prudent to be as inconspicuous as possible. The best-known example of such a Christian meeting place is the ordinary domestic house which served as a church at Dura-Europos, mentioned earlier.[40] Along with the neighboring Jewish synagogue, this house-church was destroyed when the city walls were fortified in 256, since both buildings were incorporated into the earthworks supporting the wall on its inner side. Excavations of the building revealed the date 231 scratched into the wall, possibly indicating the time of an earlier renovation of the house occasioned by the growth in the size of the community. One wall on the west side of the house was removed so as to merge two small rooms into a single large one accommodating fifty or sixty people. This new assembly room included a platform for the bishop's chair along the east wall. A second room on the west side which opened into the large room, into the central courtyard, and into a room to its north, might have been used for the instruction of those preparing for baptism. The room on the right of it had been converted into a baptistery complete with a tub covered by a canopy (see fig. 9).

The *Didascalia,* a Syrian church order of the third century that offers guidelines for the arrangement of the assembly for liturgy, indicates that the bishop's chair and those of his presbyters are to be located on a platform on the east side of the building, precisely as at Dura-Europos.[41] The document also calls for a table for the eucharist and another for the offerings, both presumably movable. There might be a railing separating the laity from the clergy, or a railing enclosing the altar/ table.[42] By the middle of the third century an ordinary house alone would probably not have provided without some renovation the assembly place together with separate rooms for baptismal instruction, baptism, and storage for the community's charities.

That the arrangement of people within the liturgical assembly was a concern in the third century is understandable because of the growth in numbers in many places. By then the Christian population in Rome alone approached fifty thousand, while fully 60 percent of Asia Minor was Christian.[43] By 312, twenty-five Christian community centers in Rome were identified by name. These centers, each called *domus ecclesiae* (house of the church), presumably along with many others to accommodate the large numbers of Christians in the city, were the origins of the present-day *tituli* churches.

Constantinian Churches

The *domus ecclesiae* survived until Constantine's proclamation of the Edict of Milan in 313 C.E. At this point a public Christian ecclesiastical architecture emerged as a direct consequence of the emperor's patronage. Although he was baptized—if at all—only on his death bed in 337, Constantine encouraged Christianity from the very beginning of his reign. Both architecture and liturgy shifted into a new, public, imperial mode colored by lavish court ceremonial and shaped by the new and exhilarating elevation of the Church to the realm of power.

It is one of the old warhorses of art history that the Roman secular basilica is the prototypical plan for Christian churches in the west from Constantine's time almost to the present. But, as Krautheimer puts it, "the Christian basilica both in function and design was a new creation within an accustomed framework."[44] Actually, diversity prevails in Constantinian churches with at least four distinct designs responding to fourth-century liturgical interests: (1) cemetery churches, (2) *martyria*,[45] (3) shrine churches, and (4) episcopal and parish churches.

For each of these types it is possible to speak in a general way of a longitudinal basilican plan. The Roman basilica was an all-purpose structure meeting a variety of needs ranging from markets and assembly places to law courts and imperial reception halls complete with a throne. Generally speaking, they were rectangular with a wide central aisle flanked by one or more side aisles that might continue around all four sides of the building. The entrance could be on any side, but was often on one of the long sides opening into the forum. There would be one or more apses, that is, semicircular areas housing the chair of the magistrate or the throne of the emperor. The secular basilica's symbolic display of imperial power and splendor, coupled with its large unencumbered spaces, offered an appealing model for the new buildings of a sect whose founder was now represented as a king clad in gold, seated in the heavens and waiting for the second coming at the end of time. Christian basilicas shift the axis from a lateral one opening onto a busy forum to a longitudinal one whose forum "migrates" from the side to form an atrium courtyard in front of the new door placement.[46] Now the axis is from the entrance door to the apse at the opposite end where the Christian altar was located. Within this generic type numerous possibilities emerge for quite distinctive purposes (see fig. 10).

The covered cemeteries are perhaps the closest in form and function to their pagan prototypes.[47] It was an ancient custom to celebrate the anniversaries of deaths with banquets at the burial places. Christians continued the practice but included the celebration of the eucharist. That the covered cemeteries were equipped for this purpose is evident from entries in the *Liber Pontificalis* describing imperial gifts of altar vessels to these churches. Literally paved with tombs, these basilicas constituted roofed cemeteries for those wishing to be buried in the vicinity of a martyr's tomb. They were not open to the sky because the lavish anniversary banquets required a covered space. As the festivities surrounding the banquets grew more rowdy in the course of time and finally died out by the end of the fifth century, so too did these cemetery basilicas, which were either abandoned or rededicated.

The *martyrium* churches are closely related to the cemetery churches in that they too are funerary and are located outside the city walls. As was the case with the cemetery churches, no clergy were assigned to them. The difference is that they were built either above the tomb of a martyr buried in an underground catacomb or around the martyr's tomb in a cemetery, enclosing it within the structure. Since the focal point of these churches was the tomb, a new architectural response was needed to clarify the focus on the martyr.

Although not evident in today's Renaissance and Baroque church, the upper part of the tomb-shrine of St. Peter in Rome protruded above the nave floor in Constantine's church of the fourth century. To set apart this area of the building as the sacred shrine, a transept (a tall transverse hall at a right angle to the nave) was inserted between the nave and the apse, creating a cross shape (see fig. 11). Above the tomb stood a canopy resting on spiral columns, now incorporated into Bernini's seventeenth-century baldacchino. In the vast church of Old St. Peter's, some 390 feet long, the transept was the *martyrium,* a space with a special meaning distinct from both nave and apse.

The designation of a sacred site by means of a special architectural form was not limited to the graves of martyrs. It extended also to places especially significant in the life of Christ, such as the site of the nativity in Bethlehem, or the presumed site of the holy sepulchre in Jerusalem. These functioned as shrine churches, related to but distinct from the *martyria.* In each of these places a special structure is incorporated into the basilican plan to emphasize the historical site.

In Bethlehem at the Church of the Nativity the solution to the need for both assembly space and a separate zone to enshrine the cave of the nativity was the construction of an octagonal structure to terminate the nave and protect the cave underneath (see fig. 12). Pilgrims ascended several steps to an opening over the grotto into which they could peer. Above the grotto was a circular window in the roof of the octagon opening to the sky. Thus, the octagon became the *martyrium.*[48] The Jerusalem Church of the Holy Sepulchre included several focal points unified in an interconnected whole. A basilica with atrium led beyond itself across a courtyard, past the rock of Calvary, to the domed sepulchre (see fig. 13).[49]

The octagonal structure terminating the basilica at Bethlehem and the domed building over the holy sepulchre derived from a structure in antiquity known as the imperial mausoleum. These mausolea were all "central-plan." It is important to note that they were more than just elaborate burial places. They were also *heroa,* "tomb temples designed to commemorate the dead emperor, raised to the gods, and to pay him divine honors."[50] Interestingly, Constantine's architects appropriated the *heroon/martyrium* only for the sites associated with events in Jesus' life. Krautheimer notes, "the transept of St. Peter's appears as an emergency solution, newly invented because the imperial *heroon* type reserved for Christ was not considered appropriate for any martyr, not even St. Peter."[51]

Episcopal or congregational churches are typified by St. John of the Lateran in Rome, one of two churches built within the city walls by Constantine. Begun in 313, it was a longitudinal basilica with a central nave flanked by double side-aisles, terminating in an apse (see fig. 14). Unlike any of the plans considered so far, this building served a regular congregation and was presided over by the bishop of Rome. There were no burials within it, and it had no *martyrium;* nor was it associated with any site of historical significance for Christians. The building functioned primarily as a gathering place for the celebration of the eucharist and as an audience hall for the Lord.[52]

The outermost side-aisles terminated in small winglike rooms that projected outside the structure.[53] These did not form a transept (which we recall was the *martyrium* at St. Peter's). Instead, they may have been storage rooms for the community's collection of food, clothing, and other goods to be distributed to the poor. Seats for the bishop and clergy were located in the apse, across the front of which stood an elaborate silver screen called a *fastigium*. The *Liber Pontificalis* describes this *fastigium* as including silver sculptures, facing the clergy, of the resurrection of Christ, and, facing the people in the nave, of Christ as teacher flanked by the apostles.[54]

Behind the church stood Rome's only baptistery, because usually only the bishop baptized. This was a central-plan structure whose resemblance to the imperial mausolea appropriated for the *martyria* of Christ in the Holy Land is not coincidental. We have only to recall Paul's query to the Romans: "Are you not aware that we who were baptized into Christ Jesus were baptized into his death? Through baptism into his death we were buried with him, so that, just as Christ was raised from the dead by the glory of the Father, we too might live a new life" (Rom. 6:3–5). Here we glimpse how carefully the form of the structure has been chosen to create symbolic resonance. Baptism is an experience of death and it takes place in a mausoleum.

All of the structures considered, the domestic house-churches of pre-Constantinian times as well as the later splendid imperial churches, express practical as well as symbolic understandings of the community's life. In the house-churches the gathered assembly was the focus, and the presiding minister was among the people as they celebrated the eucharist at a simple table placed in position at the appropriate time. Suitable spaces were also arranged for instruction of converts and the baptism of new members.

As the context of the church shifted, so too did the scale and function of its places of worship. Cemetery and *martyrium* churches were funerary in nature and accommodated burials and anniversary funeral banquets at which the eucharist was also celebrated. In *martyrium* churches and shrine churches special canopylike shapes were chosen to cover the sacred sites. Congregational churches, devoid of tombs or *martyria,* accommodated the Christian community's ongoing life. They also reflected the new sacralization of the clergy, who were now separated from the assembly by elaborate chancel screens or colonnaded canopies around and over the altar, such as was seen at the Lateran. The distinction of the clergy from the laity was affirmed in 399 by the Council of Elvira's call for clerical celibacy, a step underlining a different lifestyle and underscoring an emerging sense of a cultic priesthood in the tradition of Old Testament priesthood. These shifts in ecclesiology find direct expression in the shape and arrangement of the worship spaces.

NOTES

1. See, for example, Yoran Tsafrir, "The Byzantine Setting and Its Influence on Ancient Synagogues," in Lee I. Levine, ed., *The*

Synagogue in Late Antiquity (Philadelphia, 1987), pp. 147–48.

2. See E. L. Sukenik, *Ancient Synagogues in Palestine and Greece* (London, 1934), pp. 3–5.

3. Heinrich Kohl and Carl Watzinger, *Antike Synagogen in Galilaea* (Leipzig, 1916).

4. For a complete description of these buildings and others in Roman and Byzantine Palestine see Marilyn J. S. Chiat, *Handbook of Synagogue Architecture,* Brown Judaic Studies (Decatur, GA, 1982).

5. See Jacob Neusner, "Judaism in Late Antiquity," *Judaism: A Quarterly Journal of Jewish Life and Thought* 15.2 (Spring, 1966): 230.

6. G. F. Moore, *Judaism in the First Centuries of the Christian Era* I (Cambridge, MA, 1927), p. 109. According to Moore, "normative Judaism" was a development of the Babylonian and Palestinian rabbinic academies and was to be distinguished from other so-called nonnormative or fringe sects of Judaism. For comments on Moore's theories, see Jacob Neusner, "'Judaism' after Moore: A Programmatic Statement," *JJS* 31 (1980): 141–56.

7. Sukenik, *Ancient Synagogues, p. 27.*

8. On the use of the term *talmudic archeology* to refer to the study of the artifactual heritage of Greco-Roman Palestine, see Eric M. Meyers and A. Thomas Kraabel, "Archeology, Iconography, and Nonliterary Written Remains," in Robert A. Kraft and George W. E. Nickelsburg, eds., *Early Judaism and Its Modern Interpreters* (Decatur, GA, 1986), p. 175.

9. Sukenik, *Ancient Synagogues,* p. 78.

10. Michael Avi-Jonah, "Synagogue Architecture in the Late Classical Period," in Cecil Roth and Bezalel Narkiss, eds., *Jewish Art: An Illustrated History,* 2d ed. (New York, 1971), pp. 65–82.

11. E. R. Goodenough, *Jewish Symbols in the Greco-Roman Period* I (New York, 1953), pp. 181–267.

12. Michael Avi-Jonah, "Ancient Synagogues," *Ariel* 32 (1973): 38–42.

13. Eric M. Meyers, "The Current State of Galilean Synagogue Studies," in *The Synagogue in Late Antiquity,* p. 128.

14. Ibid., p. 127.

15. A. Thomas Kraabel, "Unity and Diversity among Diaspora Synagogues," in *The Synagogue in Late Antiquity,* p. 58.

16. Shaye J. D. Cohen, "Pagan and Christian Evidence on the

Ancient Synagogue," in *The Synagogue in Late Antiquity,* p. 166.

17. See, for example, Meyers, "Galilean Synagogue Studies," p. 133.

18. There is an extensive bibliography on the excavations at Dura-Europos. For the synagogue, see C. H. Kraeling, *The Synagogue Excavations at Dura-Europos, Final Report VIII, 1* (New Haven, 1956); Joseph Gutmann, ed., *The Dura-Europos Synagogue: A Reevaluation* (Missoula, MT, 1973); idem, "The Dura-Europos Synagogue Paintings: The State of Research," in *The Synagogue in Late Antiquity,* pp. 61–72.

19. Kraeling, *The Synagogue,* p. 328.

20. See Chiat, *Handbook,* pp. 31–36, 224–28, 230–35.

21. For current bibliography on the paintings, see Gutmann, "Dura-Europos Synagogue Paintings."

22. Ibid., p. 65.

23. Ibid., p. 63.

24. Ibid.

25. Chiat, *Handbook,* pp. 89–97.

26. Ibid., pp. 27–31, 97–102.

27. See Stanislao Loffreda, *Recovering Capharnaum,* Studium Biblicum Franciscanum Guides 1 (Jerusalem, 1985).

28. See Asher Ovadiah, *Corpus of Byzantine Churches in the Holy Land* (Bonn, 1970), pp. 40–44.

29. Chiat, *Handbook,* pp. 121–46; idem, "Synagogue and Churches in Byzantine Beit She'an," *Journal of Jewish Art* 7 (1980): 5–24.

30. Chiat, *Handbook,* pp. 136–38; Vassilios Tzaferis, "The Ancient Synagogues at Ma'oz Hayyim," *Israel Publication Journal* 32.4 (1982): 215–44.

31. Tsafrir ("Byzantine Setting," p. 152) comments on the fact that the shape of the synagogue prayer hall approaches a square rather than the elongated rectangle characteristic of the church. He claims the church's "mystical rites" dictated the longitudinal arrangement, whereas the synagogue with its "direct, intellectual approach . . . omitted any ornamentation that might have augmented tendencies toward the mystical." Furthermore, the architect's intent "was to promote closeness and attentiveness between the individual worshiper and the public reader of the Torah, disdaining any hierarchy between reader and worshiper." He does not provide documentation to support these contentions.

32. See Marilyn J. S. Chiat, "Synagogue and Church Architecture: A Comparative Study," in *Proceedings of the Eighth World Congress of Jewish Studies* (Jerusalem, 1982), pp. 35–42. Other synagogues in the region, such as Beth Alpha, did have their entrances on the north, opposite the apse: see Chiat, *Handbook,* pp. 121–44.

33. Jacob Neusner, *Judaism and Christianity in the Age of Constantine* (Chicago, 1987), p. x.

34. Meyers and Kraabel, "Archeology, Iconography, and Nonliterary Written Remains," p. 176; Lawrence A. Hoffman, *Beyond the Text: A Holistic Approach to Liturgy,* Jewish Literature and Culture (Bloomington, IN, 1987), p. 17; Jacob Neusner, "The Symbolism of Ancient Judaism: The Evidence of the Synagogues," in Joseph Gutmann, ed., *Ancient Synagogues: The State of Research,* Brown Judaic Studies (Decatur, GA, 1981), pp. 12–13; Tzvee Zahavy, "A New Approach to Early Jewish Prayer," in Baruch M. Bokser, ed., *History of Judaism: The Next Ten Years,* Brown Judaic Studies (Decatur, GA, 1980), p. 17.

35. Cf. Paul Corby Finney ("Early Christian Architecture: The Beginnings," *HTR* 81.3 [1988]: 319–39), who divides post–World War II scholarship into either theoretical or practical concerns.

36. See Wayne A. Meeks, *The First Urban Christians* (New Haven, 1983); Daniel J. Harrington, S.J., "Sociological Concepts and the Early Church: A Decade of Research," *Theological Studies* 41 (1980): 181–90.

37. Thomas F. Mathews, *The Early Churches of Constantinople: Architecture and Liturgy* (University Park, PA, 1971).

38. See Finney, "Early Christian Architecture," for an outline of Deichmann's thesis as well as the extension of his ideas in the work of Sussenbach and Turner; Friedrich Wilhelm Deichmann, "Vom Tempel zur Kirche," in *Mullus: Festschrift Theodor Klauser* (Münster, 1964); idem, *Einführung in die christliche Archäologie* (Darmstadt, 1983); Uwe Sussenbach, *Christuskult und kaiserliche Baupolitik bei Konstantin* (Bonn, 1977); Harold W. Turner, *From Temple to Meeting House* (New York, 1977).

39. See N. Duval, *Sheitla et les églises africaines a deux absides,* 2 vols. (Paris, 1971; 1973); Richard Krautheimer, *Early Christian and Byzantine Architecture,* 4th ed. (Harmondsworth, 1986), pp. 187ff.

40. See above, p. 73. See also Richard Krautheimer, *Early*

Christian and Byzantine Architecture, p. 27; Meeks, *First Urban Christians,* p. 80; Clark Hopkins, *The Discovery of Dura-Europos* (New Haven, 1979), pp. 242–49.

41. *Didascalia* 12. See Willy Rordorf et al., *The Eucharist of the Early Christians* (New York, 1978), p. 201.

42. Krautheimer, *Early Christian and Byzantine Architecture,* p. 26.

43. Ibid., p. 24.

44. Ibid., p. 42.

45. The major study of martyrial churches is André Grabar, *Martyrium,* 2 vols. (Paris, 1943–1946).

46. See Richard Krautheimer, "The Beginnings of Early Christian Architecture," in *Studies in Early Christian, Medieval, and Renaissance Art* (New York, 1969), p. 15.

47. See Richard Krautheimer, "Mensa-Coemeterium-Martyrium," in *Studies,* pp. 35–58; G. T. Armstrong, "Constantine's Churches: Symbol and Structure," *Society of Architectural Historians' Journal* 33 (March, 1974): 5–16.

48. See Krautheimer, *Early Christian and Byzantine Architecture,* p. 60; Armstrong, "Constantine's Churches," p. 15.

49. Krautheimer (*Early Christian and Byzantine Architecture,* pp. 60–63) provides a new plan of the church, based on recently excavated remains of the fourth-century structure, which is significantly different from earlier speculations and eliminates a domed structure terminating the central nave of the basilica.

50. Ibid., p. 64. See also Armstrong, "Constantine's Churches," pp. 11–12.

51. Krautheimer, *Early Christian and Byzantine Architecture,* p. 42.

52. Armstrong, "Constantine's Churches," p. 7; Richard Krautheimer, *Rome, Profile of a City, 312–1308* (Princeton, 1980), pp. 21–24.

53. Richard Krautheimer, "The Constantinian Basilica of the Lateran," in *Studies,* p. 24.

54. Krautheimer, *Early Christian and Byzantine Architecture,* p. 48.

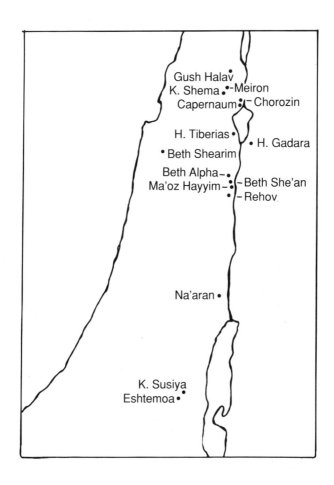

MAP OF SELECTED SYNAGOGUE SITES IN ISRAEL

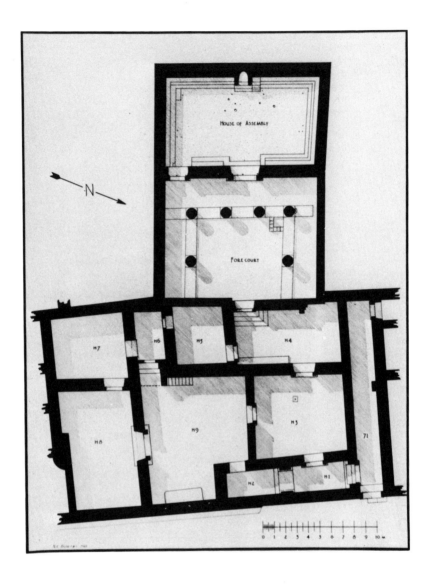

FIG. 1. DURA-EUROPOS SYNAGOGUE SITE, SYRIA
Courtesy Yale University Art Gallery, Dura-Europos Collection.

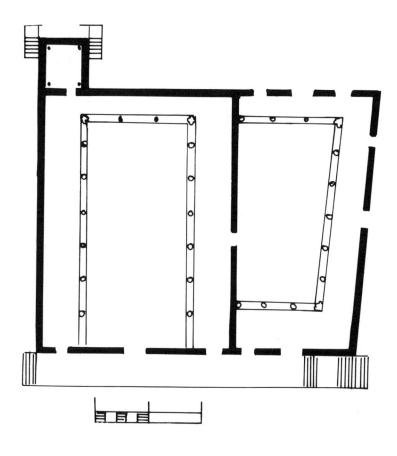

FIG. 2. CAPERNAUM SYNAGOGUE, ISRAEL
Illustration by H. J. Chiat, after Stanislao Loffreda, *Recovering Capharnaum,* Studium Biblicum Franciscanum Guides, 1 (Jerusalem: Edizioni Custodia Terra Santa, 1985).

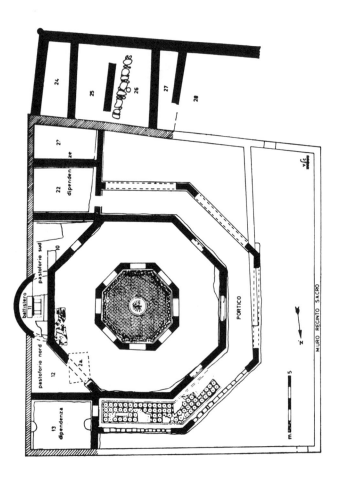

FIG. 3. St. Peter's Church, Capernaum, Israel
Courtesy Studium Biblicum Franciscanum.

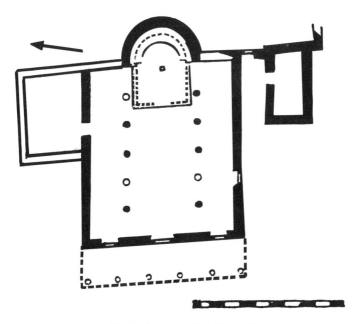

FIG. 4. CHURCH AT BETH YERAH, ISRAEL

Illustration by H. Chiat, after Asher Ovadiah, *Corpus of Byzantine Churches in the Holy Land*, trans. by Rose Kirson, Theophaneia: Beiträge zur Religions- und Kirchengeschichte des Altertums, 22 (Bonn: P. Hanstein, 1970).

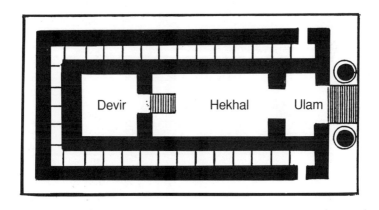

FIG. 5. JEWISH TEMPLE, JERUSALEM

Illustration by H. J. Chiat, after Carl Watzinger, *Denkmäler Palästinas: Eine Einführung in die Archäologie des Heiligen Landes*, 2 vols. (Leipzig: J. C. Hinrichs, 1933–1935).

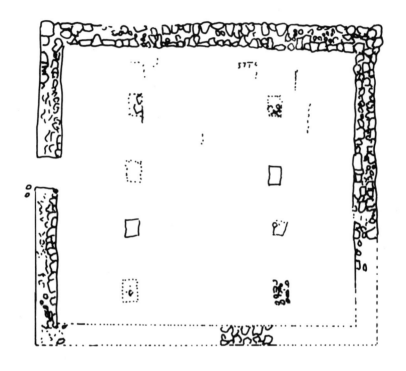

FIG. 6. MA'OZ HAYYIM I, ISRAEL
Courtesy *Israel Exploration Journal*, Israel Antiquities Authority.

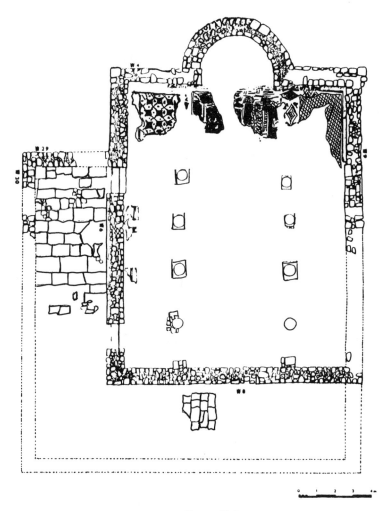

FIG. 7. MA'OZ HAYYIM II, ISRAEL
Courtesy *Israel Exploration Journal*, Israel Antiquities Authority.

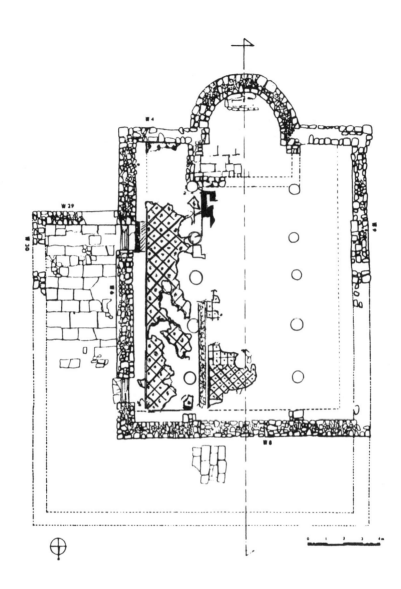

FIG. 8. MA'OZ HAYYIM III, ISRAEL
Courtesy *Israel Exploration Journal*, Israel Antiquities Authority.

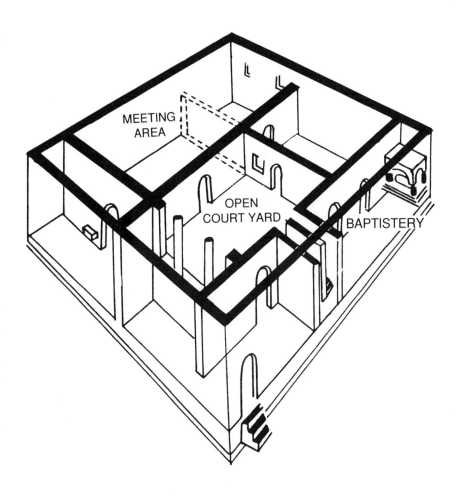

FIG. 9. HOUSE-CHURCH AT DURA-EUROPOS, SYRIA
Illustration by Armando Garzon-Blanco.

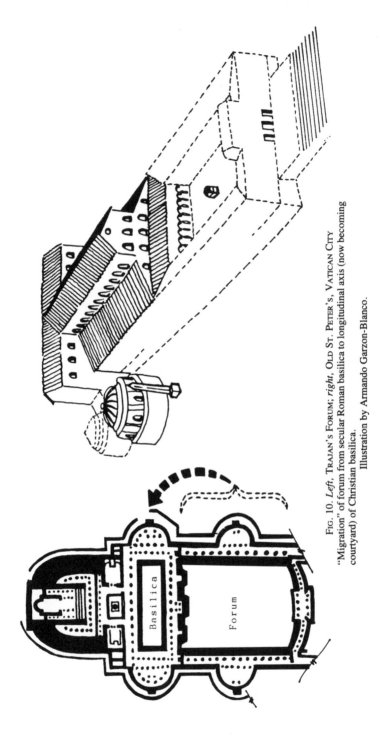

Fig. 10. *Left*, Trajan's Forum; *right*, Old St. Peter's, Vatican City "Migration" of forum from secular Roman basilica to longitudinal axis (now becoming courtyard) of Christian basilica.

Illustration by Armando Garzon-Blanco.

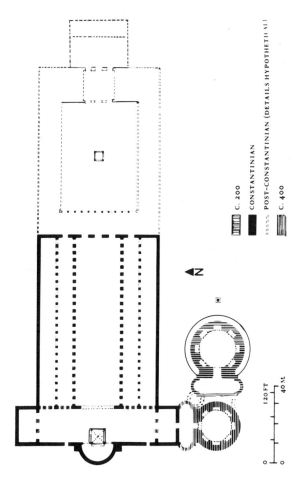

C. 200

CONSTANTINIAN

POST-CONSTANTINIAN (DETAILS HYPOTHETICAL)

C. 400

Fig. 11. Old St. Peter's, Vatican City

Reprinted from Richard Krautheimer, *Early Christian and Byzantine Architecture*, The Pelican History of Art, 4th ed. (Harmondsworth: Penguin, 1986), p. 55. Copyright © Richard Krautheimer, 1965, 1975, 1979, 1981, and (with Slobodan Ćurčić) 1986. Reproduced by permission of Penguin Books Ltd.

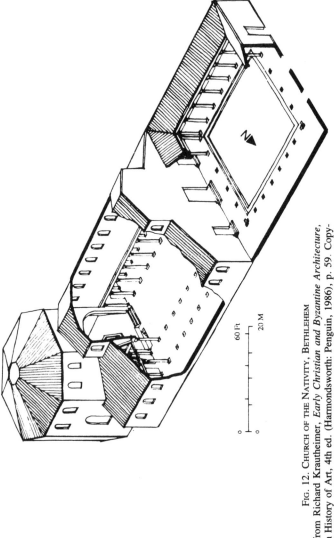

60 Ft

20 M

N

Fig. 12. Church of the Nativity, Bethlehem

Reprinted from Richard Krautheimer, *Early Christian and Byzantine Architecture,* The Pelican History of Art, 4th ed. (Harmondsworth: Penguin, 1986), p. 59. Copyright © Richard Krautheimer, 1965, 1975, 1979, 1981, and (with Slobodan Curcic) 1986. Reproduced by permission of Penguin Books Ltd.

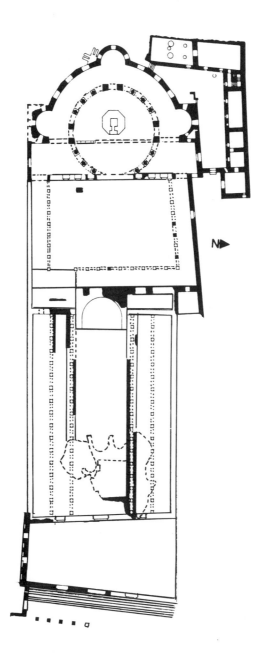

FIG. 13. CHURCH OF THE HOLY SEPULCHRE, JERUSALEM
Reproduced, with permission, from V. Corbo, *Il Santo Sepolcro di Jerusalemme*,
Studium Biblicum Franciscanum 29 (Jerusalem: Studium Biblicum Franciscanum,
1981), plate 1.

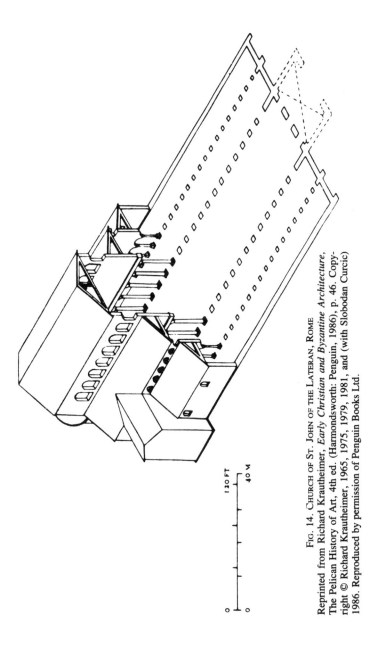

FIG. 14. CHURCH OF ST. JOHN OF THE LATERAN, ROME
Reprinted from Richard Krautheimer, *Early Christian and Byzantine Architecture,*
The Pelican History of Art, 4th ed. (Harmondsworth: Penguin, 1986), p. 46. Copyright © Richard Krautheimer, 1965, 1975, 1979, 1981, and (with Slobodan Curcic)
1986. Reproduced by permission of Penguin Books Ltd.

PART 2

Evolution and Change

The Early History of Jewish Worship

STEFAN C. REIF

[Editors' note: Stefan C. Reif, Director of the Genizah Research Unit of the University of Cambridge, England, compares what is known of the worship practices of early Judaism with the liturgical evidence of ninth/tenth-century geonic Babylonia, contrasting the fluidity of the early period with the liturgical fixity of the latter. The evidence suggests a radical reconsideration of early rabbinic liturgy, acccording to which we must imagine a great deal more flexibility and creativity than has traditionally been assumed. He sums up what we know of the many strands of Jewish liturgy from their inception in the first few centuries of rabbinic culture and takes us briefly to the period in which liturgical traditions were consolidated into prayer books and rites that have proved lasting ever since. Of particular significance, he shows how the discoveries from the Cairo Genizah can illuminate our understanding of the process by which prayer books and rites evolved out of liturgical traditions.]

The function of this contribution to our discussion of the liturgical traditions of Christianity and Judaism is to explain how a formal, authoritative liturgy emerged in the history of rabbinic Judaism; when and where this process took place; and what factors dictated the adoption of such an office among the religious commitments of the Jewish community at large. In order to achieve an adequate explanation of such developments it will obviously be necessary to take as our starting point that period of Jewish religious history when a recognizable form of rabbinic liturgy may be identified and to describe in general terms the various characteristics of that form as contemporary research has identified them. A leap of some centuries will then be made to bring us to a situation when a Jewish liturgical codex was given a position of some respect among the literary sources of the religious tradition and there-

fore to a time when it may no longer be doubted that there
existed a written guide for regular communal worship sanctioned by a leading figure, or a number of such guides emanat-
ing from various such authorities.

A comparison, or rather a contrast, will then be drawn
between the primitive form and the subtle shape that it later
acquired, and it will be possible to pinpoint the differences
that had emerged in the intervening centuries. Reference will
be made to the attempts of various generations of Jewish liturgical scholars to account for any differences that may be
detected between the earlier and later sources and to demonstrate, by and large, that these were differences of degree
rather than of essence. By way of contrast and as a result of
recent research in the fragmentary manuscripts from the Cairo
Genizah, it will be suggested that what may be traced here are
pivotal developments in the history of Jewish liturgy that have
only recently gained the attention of scholars and that indeed
characterize a period of Jewish history that has yet to give up
all its secrets to the researcher. It will then be possible to set
such developments in a larger context and thereby to achieve
the aims set for this essay.

Jewish Liturgy in the Fourth Century

By the fourth century of the common era it is fairly certain
that there existed (1) an authoritative body of tannaitic traditions relating to biblical interpretation and the application of
Jewish law, and (2) at least the early, dialectic responses, both
supportive and disputatious, of the *amoraim* to these traditions. The process of developing these responses, or *Talmud,*
as it came to be called, was under way in both Jewish Palestine
and the major Diaspora community of Babylon; and the Jewish
religious reaction to the loss of its temple, its holy city, and its
independent state had had time to mature over a period of three
centuries.[1]

What is more, whatever the length of the period during
which the Jews and the early Christians, or Jewish Christians,

enjoyed close religious and social contact, they had by that time gone their separate ways. The situation had been much more fluid in the first Christian century than is often claimed. At that early stage, neither the founders of Christianity nor the precursors of the talmudic tradition had a definitive theory or practice with regard to worship outside the Jerusalem Temple, and various competing forces had been seeking to dominate the liturgical scene. Whatever mutual influences were at work on the earliest, recognizable forms of rabbinic and Christian liturgy, these are more likely to date from the second and third centuries, when the two communities were still operating in the same, or closely connected contexts. Be that as it may, the schism was completed by the fourth century, and later effects, positive and negative, whether the result of emulation or reaction, were those of one religion on another and not of a single religion's internal affairs. For all these reasons, it may be assumed that by the fourth century the foundations had been laid of what ultimately became talmudic Judaism and that the liturgical customs in vogue by then may fairly be identified as the early form of what later evolved into the rabbinic prayer book.[2]

It is beyond dispute that the wide variety of prayers and blessings that are attested in the talmudic literature were normally recited from memory and transmitted orally, and that there was a distinct disapproval of committing them to an authoritative, written text. While there is no doubt in the talmudic sources about the existence of such pieces of liturgy, there are no unanimous views recorded there about its degree of importance in Jewish practice, its essential character, and its detailed application. Not without controversy was it sometimes given a theological centrality equal to that accorded to Torah study and charitable behavior and directly linked with the cultic obligations that had once been met in the Jerusalem Temple. Where, when, towards which site, how often, in which language, with whom, and for how long observant Jews—certainly men, but possibly women as well—should conduct their prayers, were questions that elicited a host of

responses from the Babylonian and Palestinian rabbis. By the
same token, the formalization of the reading and interpretation
of the Hebrew Bible was already a feature of synagogal activity, but the precise content and structure of the lectionary was
clearly open to debate and variant usage.[3]

As far as the synagogue itself was concerned, it was only
gradually being transformed from a center of social and intellectual activity, particularly in the Diaspora, to the successor
of the Temple as *a* central but not *the* central, focus of Jewish
liturgical activity. The synagogue was attracting to itself more
and more of the disparate elements of earlier Jewish expressions of worship and their symbols, but arguments could still
be made for alternative sites, such as the home and the academy, perhaps even for alternative cultic sites in the form of
Jewish temples, and a distinction could still be drawn between
prayer as the expression of individual piety and supplication
and liturgy as the religious commitment of the community,
whatever form that might have to take now that there was no
Jerusalem Temple. The architecture and function of the synagogue were by no means standard, but the trend was moving
away from the simple towards the complex and from the functional to the symbolic. Although there were honorific titles and
functions for leading members of the synagogue, the service
could be led by any male congregant, no special mediator,
professional or theological, being required.[4]

In the matter of prayer, as in so many other detailed elements of their daily religious activities, the rabbis of the Talmud, perhaps even more than those of the Mishnah, adopted
a fairly pluralistic approach. This, of course, assumes that
what they have to say is to be regarded as a reflection of reality
rather than a collection of theoretical reflections of relevance
only to their intellectual system of argumentation. Some
stressed the mystical and the poetic while others opted for a
more prosaic order and guidance. The student of liturgical
issues in the oldest talmudic sources soon becomes aware of
what I have, in a different context, called "the tensions, controversies, stresses and strains that accompanied early rabbinic

Judaism's attempt to define the place of prayer in the framework of its religious ideology." This is not to say that there were no halakhic requirements and that it was left entirely to individuals to treat prayer as they pleased. Some traditions had existed long enough among the ordinary folk to have acquired a popular status, others were clearly attached to special occasions of one sort or another, and there were, no doubt, those that were treated as authoritative because of their origin in the Jerusalem Temple. In the detailed recitation, however, as well as in the degree of standardization of all the customs and the theological assessment of their importance, there lay the substantial pluralism just noted. Although many specific items of prayer and prayer custom are referred to, they often appear only as a title or as a few initial words, disembodied liturgy as it were, or they are offered in a variety of different forms. Types of prayer are mentioned, and numbers of words are sometimes specified; but to the critical observer it is not obvious where the theory ends and the practice begins.[5]

Before an attempt is made to summarize what constituted the corpus of Jewish prayer in about the fourth century, two further points need to be stressed. It should not be taken for granted at any stage of Jewish religious history that what the rabbis said and legislated was already the communal norm. There were certainly periods and areas in which rabbinic authority and centralization were dominant, but these were at least as often the exception as they were the rule. Talmudic statements may consequently reflect a rabbinic struggle to impose certain ideas and practices and need not necessarily record the contemporary, communal reality. Conversely, it is possible that what the rabbis record as accepted custom may to an extensive degree include items that had their origin among the common folk rather than the intelligentsia. But until we have fuller liturgical texts dating from that period, if we ever do, we can only speculate on the relative proportions of liturgical theory and practical application.[6] The second point to be made is that two major Jewish communities existed during the talmudic period, one in the Holy Land and the other in Babylon. There was considerable intercourse between the two, and influence was exercised in both directions. Some evidence suggests that in Eretz Yisrael, to put it in Heinemann's words, "a certain amount of freedom and variety remained," and it may therefore be the case that the pluralism of the talmudic sources with regard to prayer will ultimately turn out to be a division between the popular, aesthetic, and liberal trends of one community against the elitist, standardized, and authoritative preferences of the other.[7] A further complication is the existence of Jewish communities in the Greek-speaking Diaspora who might have been more open to external influences than those in Babylon and Eretz Yisrael. Some inscriptions point in such a direction, but the major sources are still the Palestinian Talmud and *midrashim*. Again, the necessary analysis remains to be undertaken, and it is not certain that such research can successfully be completed on the basis of the literary sources alone, as these have obviously passed through the hands of various editors and redactors since they were first compiled.[8]

Which Jewish prayers, then, were already in existence and use by the middle of the talmudic period? It seems clear that at least two paragraphs of the *Shema* were recited, morning and evening, and that a formal invitation to communal prayer, as well as benedictions concerning the natural order of the day and the unique role of Israel, preceded it. The *Tefillah* (or *Amidah*) was also to be recited in the morning and afternoon, but some doubts were voiced about its obligatory nature in the evening. Efforts were being made to ensure a continuity between the *Shema* and the *Tefillah* by the adoption of passages, with suitable benedictions, expressing faith in God's special relationship with Israel, as demonstrated in the past, and confidence in God's response to its more immediate needs. The daily *Tefillah* recorded these needs, but it is doubtful whether each of its benedictions had yet obtained a definite structure. Perhaps the first three and last two or three were less fluid than the remainder. These were also recited on Sabbaths, festivals, and fasts together with one or more appropriate central benedictions relating in some way, also yet to be categorically defined, to the particular nature of the occasion. Elements of what had originally been individual prayer and benediction were gradually becoming absorbed into communal or synagogal worship, and remnants of the public ritual once carried out on Mount Zion were being adopted and adapted for more personal use. It was not, however, universally assumed that the formal patterns suitable for the liturgy of the community were necessarily applicable to private devotions. Such devotions, generally pietistic or penitential, were associated with the names of individual rabbis and couched in the first person, although there were also poetic supplications that may have originated in the Jerusalem Temple.[9]

The other function of the synagogue—perhaps indeed its major and earlier function—was as a center of Bible reading and instruction. Pentateuchal scrolls were publicly read and expounded on Sabbaths, festivals, fasts, and on the market days of Monday and Thursday, and, while it was becoming customary to associate particular passages with related occasions, it is still anachronistic to refer to a fixed lectionary at this time. There was controversy about the place of the Decalogue and a tendency to make a theological point by abandoning its daily recitation in spite of its long and respectable pedigree. Translations from the Hebrew into Aramaic and interpretations of the text were a central part of what amounted to this system of regular religious education for the community. Parts of the prophetic and hagiographical books also played a part in such public readings, but the process had yet to be liturgically formalized. The earliest manifestation of a custom to include a formal recitation of a set of psalms in the communal liturgy was the use of Psalms 113–118 as the *hallel,* but the wider liturgical use in a communal context of what has often been viewed as the hymn book of the second Jerusalem Temple was still a development of the future.[10]

As previously implied, liturgy for the talmudic Jew was not restricted to prayer but was expressed in the observance of *mitzvot,* the study of Torah, and in domestic customs. It therefore occasions no surprise to find the academy and the home as the normal settings for the remainder of talmudic prayer. Declarations of God's sanctity, with the use of the *trishagion,* and pious aspirations for the establishment of God's ultimate dominion were components of the praises that came to be associated with sessions of Torah study. At home, the commencement and conclusion of Sabbaths and festivals were marked by formulas that declared the sanctity of God and of the special day and that distinguished between various examples of the holy and the profane. Some prayers were couched in Aramaic, others in Hebrew, and there was even no objection in principle to the use of Greek in certain contexts. Among the oldest Jewish liturgical forms are the Passover Haggadah and the Grace after Meals, and it should not be forgotten that benedictions were used to acknowledge God's bounty in providing for human sustenance. Even the contract of marriage had, by talmudic times, developed its own set of benedictions on the themes of the creation of humankind, marital joy, and the return to Zion; the setting here, however, was not the synagogue but the independent entity of wedding ceremony and feast. The benediction, like the oath and the vow, had evolved from its popular origins into a more formal structure and, as has been argued by Heinemann, was gradually being applied as such to various liturgical contexts.[11]

Jewish Liturgy after the Ninth Century

Since the earliest forerunners of what became the standard rabbinic prayer book can be traced back to the period of the ninth to the twelfth centuries, it will now be necessary to move on to that era of Jewish history and describe the liturgical situation that then obtained. It is a useful point of reference for other reasons, too. During these years the once dominant Jewish community of Babylon began to see its power drift away to new centers, and the Palestinian Jewish community, which for all its vicissitudes and crises had always made its influence felt in the far-flung Diaspora, was virtually destroyed by the Crusaders. Furthermore, the primary sources available to the researcher multiply significantly, and the relative silence of a number of centuries is broken.[12] Also during these years the Jewish prayer book made its first appearance. Leading scholars, among them the Babylonian leaders from the eighth to the eleventh centuries, known as *geonim,* issued guidelines on what should constitute the regular blessings and prayers and answered questions about the validity of particular customs. They systematically applied the various principles that occur from time to time in the Talmud to various parts of the liturgy and offered definitions of what qualified to be included under the headings of each of the different, liturgical categories. They and their successors in a much wider geographical area, ultimately including countries as far apart as England in the west and Persia in the east, laid down detailed regulations for prayer and attempted to explain its theoretical basis and its historical evolution. Some types of accretion to the basic talmudic framework were firmly rejected while others were welcomed and sanctioned. In those cases where what they regarded as an unsatisfactory custom had established itself too stubbornly to be dislodged, a new interpretation was given to it that could justify its retention even in the light of the strictest categorizations.[13]

Two new types of liturgical composition had made their way into the regular practice and were now given specific places in the standard prayers. The *piyyutim,* or liturgical poems, the earliest forms of which had first made their appearance in the Holy Land towards the end of the talmudic age, were incorporated into those sections of the liturgy with which they could incontrovertibly be linked. Their structure, content, and language were, however, brought under control in the process and their degree of creativity thereby reduced, with the result that their composers had to find other outlets for their originality and aesthetic expression.[14] A similar limitation was imposed upon prayers of the more mystical bent. Certain compositions were allowed to enter, or remain, in such contexts as the recitation of the *trishagion,* but there was a clear policy of restricting any unfettered development and adoption in the synagogue.[15]

At this stage, too, individual communities, or sets of communities, merged what they had inherited as their established liturgical custom with what they were told by their authorities was acceptable and produced an identifiable *nusach* or rite of their own. These rites, generally referred to by the geographical areas where they were practiced (e.g., French, German, Italian, North African, Spanish, Yemenite, and Romanian), differed from each other in detail but were all substantially based on the format and content earlier dictated by the Babylonian authorities. Minor and vestigial elements of non-Babylonian provenance occasionally appeared, but a great deal more of the nonstandard was lost than was retained.[16]

As far as the text of the major prayers is concerned, there was a reluctance to approve any subtractions or additions. Clear rules were laid down for the benedictions that were to accompany particular prayers: how many they should be, of what form and content, and how much variation from the norm was to be permitted to take account of special occasions such as Sabbaths, festivals, and fasts, some allowances always being made for variety between rites.[17] Where a ceremony was regarded as important, such as the lighting of Sabbath lamps, a benediction was even introduced and justified.[18] A concern for precise language, grammar, vocalization, and punctuation soon began to be expressed and was a factor in the liturgical editions from then until the modern period. Liturgical Hebrew was the chosen medium of prayer and, at least in the major communities influenced by the authority of the Babylonian Talmud and the codification of its *halakhah,* Aramaic was used only when it had already been associated with a particular prayer for so long that it appeared to be an act of revolution to alter it. Once a *siddur* existed as a Jewish literary entity, commentaries on its contents soon became a feature of rabbinic scholarship.[19]

Even more interesting is the transfer of what had originally been domestic or academic liturgy into the synagogue and its incorporation into the standard prayer book. Benedictions relating to morning activities such as rising, washing, and dressing ultimately entered the communal liturgy, as did the recitation of psalms by way of preparation for prayer proper. The *Kaddish,* the *Alenu,* the praises associated with the academy, even the *Kiddush* and *Havdalah,* which were still recited at home, became integral parts of the synagogal liturgy, and reasons were advanced to justify their retention there, or sometimes, indeed, to challenge it. The synagogue itself became a more elaborate entity and a degree of ceremonial was introduced of which there is little mention in the talmudic sources. A regular cantor and choir, special seats for dignitaries, processions, use of the Torah scroll, *tallit* and *tefillin* as integral parts of the ritual, all now became familiar elements of communal worship in the synagogue.[20] Formal ceremonies associated with *rites de passage* were not yet working their way into the synagogue, but the process of evolution had begun that would in the long term lead to such a development.

In the matter of the reading of the Pentateuch and the Prophets, a more definite lectionary was now in existence, and the annual cycle of the Babylonian Jews had virtually replaced all the others, particularly the triennial cycle of Palestinian Jewry, which some refugees from the Crusades apparently brought with them to Cairo and succeeded in preserving for at least a few decades. During his visit to Cairo in about 1170 the famous Jewish traveller, Benjamin of Tudela, noted that the Palestinian emigrés had no completion of the annual cycle to celebrate at the end of Sukkot each year and therefore joined their Babylonian coreligionists for the occasion. When read, the scroll was taken from the ark and returned to it with some accompanying verses, and its presence among the worshipers was made the occasion for the recitation of special prayers. It may also have been at this time that the lectionary ceased to be distributed among various participants who read and expounded it, and that it came to be performed by a competent and knowledgeable individual while the required number of participants made formal benedictions to begin and end each section. A set of benedictions had also by this time been attached to the reading from the Prophets at the outset and the conclusion.[21]

A Comparison of the Two Periods

If stock is now taken of these developments, it will become apparent that significant changes have occurred during the centuries between the talmudic period and the Middle Ages, and that they concern the theory, practice, and location of Jewish prayer and prayer customs. To begin with the first of these, it is no longer a matter of debate whether prayer has a central role in the theological priorities of rabbinic Judaism, and the stress is rather on finding all manner of justifications—historical, philosophical, and halakhic—for the central role that it has come to occupy. The contradictions inherent in a pluralistic approach to liturgical expression have given way to the consistencies of a system in which clearcut definitions and applications iron such awkward creases out of the fabric of prayer. Instead of limited guidance and extensive creativity, the worshiper is faced with the prospect of extensive guidance and limited creativity. A standard, hitherto vague and adjustable, has taken on a stricter form and makes demands for adherence. In sum, a text has emerged to replace what had for centuries been an oral medium, and the authoritative, written version now has a major relevance to discussions in which the previous consideration had been one of options.

A close examination of the practice is also instructive. Differences between versions are no longer the major matter that they were for the talmudic Rabbis. Disputes now generally concern minor details, and, explode in number as these details might, they will not constitute significant variation until the modern period, when different considerations are destined to apply. While neither the need nor the method for distinguishing a prayer from a benediction or for institutionalizing popular forms of liturgical expression had been apparent to the *amoraim,* authorities are now laying down rules for the structure and content of prayer texts and applying these in an increasing number of contexts. To be sure, Aramaic still has a place in the newly produced texts of the *siddur* but not of the same nature as before: once, the language of a prayer first depended on its original context and was then subject to change and exchange; now, Hebrew is to be dominant and, as far as popular Aramaic prayers are concerned, matters are frozen as they stand and arguments are offered in favor of the status quo, not just as such but as a sanctified tradition with a profound significance. The evidence from around the ninth century provides the first hints of a move from a widespread pluralism towards an authoritative format; the sources from around the twelfth century indicate the existence of a pull, however limited by the clearly expressed regulations, away from centralization towards regional autonomy of a sort.

In matters of location, too, the theme is one of transformation. The variety of centers—domestic, academic, and cultic—has given way to the dominance of the synagogue, which has absorbed the forms originally associated with these alternative loci. Whatever has been seen to be of lasting significance among the prayers and supplications of the individual has been incorporated into the communal rites. While, at the earlier stage, part of the emerging liturgy modeled itself on the practices of various individuals or groups of individuals, the position is reversed at the later stage, individuals having to follow much of the communal pattern when they choose to recite their prayers outside the synagogue. Ceremonial has also become an integral rather than an occasional element of synagogal worship, with the attendant adjustments in the physical and organizational structure. What is even more interesting is that the educational and exegetical significance of the scriptural reading has, to a considerable extent, given way to its ritual and ceremonial function. It would appear that it has become more important to read precisely the relevant section of the Hebrew Bible, with or without its standard translation of one sort or another, than to engage in the public exposition of a suitable text. That latter exercise has acquired an existence

independent of the formal biblical reading, though not necessarily of its detailed content, and has taken to including as
much general, moral, and religious guidance as it does direct
interpretation of verse after verse.[22]

Before an explanation is offered of what occurred in Jewish
religious and literary history between the late talmudic and the
immediate postgeonic periods that brought about such developments in the liturgy, it may clarify matters if some reference
is made to the way in which previous generations, from as
early as medieval times until current works of scholarship,
have viewed the relationship between these two periods and
to the new evidence that calls into question many of their
presuppositions.

An earlier understanding of the situation—but an understanding still encountered today—has been that the text of the
two Talmuds accurately reflects talmudic rather than geonic
practice, and little attention is paid to the possibility that major
editorial revision was undertaken at a time when liturgical
customs had substantially been altered. Where technical terminology is employed, whether with regard to the prayers and
benedictions themselves or to the synagogue, its functionaries
and ceremonies, the natural tendency is to equate the sense
borne in one generation with that used in another, and if the
abbreviated title or introductory phrase of a prayer is encountered it is taken for granted that the full text, though not given,
is substantially the same as it later came to be known. Where
the view of a talmudic authority does not accord with later
custom, it is regarded as an individual quirk rather than the
reflection of an existing practice, or it is somehow explained
away. Sometimes it is forgotten that the talmudic system of
presentation is not geared towards codification but is rather a
dialectic method aimed at defining the issues and factors, and
that when a decision is clearly recorded it may well be that of
a posttalmudic redactor. Above all, it is commonly presup-
posed that Jewish liturgical development consistently moves
in one direction, either from the original, pristine form to

various corruptions of it, or, indeed, from a variety of possibilities towards an authoritative version.

It is acknowledged that the *siddur* did not exist before about the ninth or tenth century, but at the same time its contents are regarded as a written version of what had already existed for an extended period in oral form. The *geonim* are viewed as the continuators of the talmudic tradition and credited with no more than the finalization of a textual, exegetical, and codificatory process that was already well under way some centuries earlier. Wherever any suspicion of creativity on their part is encountered, it is explained as a response to a particular set of circumstances, be they catastrophic or restrictive. The emergence and/or development in talmudic and posttalmudic times of such genres as *midrash, targum,* and *piyyut* are seen as the gradual accretion of creative expansions that actually come into conflict with the basic form of liturgy or lectionary to which they are added. Differences in liturgical practice are attributed to geographical variation, such as the earliest one of Palestine and Babylon, and later rites are traced to one or other of these two original forms. As in the case of general historians who once interpreted the darkness of the "dark ages" as a reflection of the ignorance of those times rather than of their own lack of knowledge and understanding of that part of history, scholars of Judaic studies have supposed that the limited nature of their information about the geonic period may indicate that there was not much of significance to report and that the talmudic and medieval periods may conveniently be linked together without reference to any intermediate stage.[23]

Lest it be thought that the most novel of historical theories makes no assumptions based on its own attitudes rather than on the historical evidence, one may point out that we sometimes choose to forget or ignore the fact that the rabbis of all posttalmudic generations viewed everything in terms of *halakhah*. They were not biblical critics, midrashic analysts, or liturgical historians, but religious leaders anxious not only to interpret God's original word and current message but also to

follow procedures for communicating with God in a way that
could somehow be seen as authoritative and sanctioned by
tradition. With our modern scientific approaches, we tend to
overlook the fact that all Jewish religious developments had a
practical, halakhic aspect to them, even if we are entitled to
look beyond that and to theorize about their historical nature.[24]

The Illumination Offered by the Cairo Genizah

That all these presuppositions may now be exposed as faulty
and that some light may now be shed on the "dark" geonic
ages are due to the discoveries made in the remarkable collection of documents from the Cairo Genizah. As is well known,
some two hundred thousand fragmentary texts, many of them
at least a thousand years old, survived in the storeroom of the
Ben Ezra Synagogue in the old section of Cairo and are today
housed in famous libraries around the world, about three-
quarters of them at Cambridge University Library. It is beyond
dispute that these Genizah fragments represent the most important discovery of new source material for every aspect of
scientific Hebrew and Jewish studies ranging from the early
medieval period until the age of emancipation. As they have
been deciphered and identified, especially as a result of the
work of the Cambridge Genizah Unit, previous ignorance has
given way to detailed information and earlier theories have
been drastically modified. Among the fields of research that
are now benefiting most from these developments are the
analysis of talmudic study in the geonic period, the history of
Jewish Bible reading and exegesis at that time, and the emergence of posttalmudic Jewish liturgy. Although the majority
of Genizah texts are generally dated from the tenth to the
twelfth centuries, it is clear that there are a substantial number
of earlier date and that in the nature of things the adoption of
liturgical customs and rituals must anticipate their earliest recorded usage, even by some considerable time. What is more,
the authoritative sources cited from the eleventh and twelfth
centuries refer to what their authors were clearly interested in

establishing as the standard, while fragments from the Genizah provide evidence of practice at all levels, as much by the Jew in the pew as the rabbi in his code. The chronological range of material from the Cairo Genizah also makes it possible for the historian to obtain a more accurate overview of a great variety of activity rather than a narrow perspective based on the sight of a few specific landmarks.[25]

With regard to the Talmud, that overview is gradually indicating the major role played by the *geonim* in bringing all aspects of talmudic study, ideology, and practical guidance to the center of Jewish religious activity. It was they who transmitted, expounded, and perfected the traditions and ultimately made it possible for actual copies of texts to be circulated and for commentaries to be composed. In their heyday study circles became major academies; in these academies decisions were made for appending to long talmudic discussions, the first elementary codifications were drawn up, and responsa were dispatched to far-flung communities who sought advice on Jewish religious procedure. The *geonim* constituted the essential link between the mass of source material available in the talmudic texts and the exploitation of that material for the construction of a system of Jewish law that could be comprehensively codified by such later scholars as Maimonides.[26]

The Genizah evidence that relates to biblical matters is no less revealing, although it may often have more to do with the Palestinian scholars than their Babylonian counterparts. Whatever the precise origins of the developments, it was in the geonic period that various systems of Hebrew vocalization were attached to the biblical text and that schools of Masoretes laid the foundations for what was ultimately to become a standard text of the Hebrew Bible but was yet far from it. It was also at that time that regulations came to be written down, as in *Massekhet Soferim,* for the writing of a Torah scroll. Such a wealth of lectionary variation has been uncovered that it can no longer be suggested that the talmudic rabbis, let alone their predecessors in the time of Jesus, followed specific systems that can today be clearly identified. While it was once suggested that the bulk of known *midrashim* developed in the talmudic age and that an authoritative *targum* emerged at a similar time, the riches of the Genizah are now providing scholars with quite a different impression. All manner of midrashic and targumic creativity in the geonic centuries is now being recorded, and it is only towards the end of that period, and perhaps in the century or two following it, that authoritative and standard versions may justifiably be recognized.[27]

And so to the numerous aspects of the synagogal liturgy that are preserved for us in thousands of Genizah fragments. Although there are fairly full versions of the prayers that can be attributed to such leading *geonim* as Saadiah and identified with what later became the norm, there are also previously unknown benedictions and prayer texts, some of them in flagrant contradiction of instructions recorded in the talmudic texts. One little-known, but remarkable, example is the benediction for the public recitation of the second chapter of the tractate *Shabbat* on the subject of the Sabbath eve. Novel, messianic, and mystical "expansions" associated with the *trishagion,* the benedictions surrounding the *Shema,* and such domestic prayers as *Kiddush, Havdalah,* and the Passover Haggadah have come to light. If it was once possible to state categorically that a certain type of text form was of the standard Babylonian kind while another was of its Palestinian equivalent, such a confidence is becoming progressively more misplaced. Having recently discovered significant variation within the liturgical practice of each of these major Jewish communities, scholars must now proceed with greater caution and, instead of referring to two standard forms with hybrid adaptations, are obliged to acknowledge a plethora of trends and tendencies, perhaps leading later to an attempt at arriving at one standard in various centers.[28]

It is not only in the realm of the messianic and the mystical that Genizah texts provide us with greater variety and more extensive content than is available from the standard sources and the later rites. The same situation applies with regard to the choice of language for some prayers and to the incorporation of *piyyutim* in others. It is no longer surprising to encounter an Aramaic version of a well-known Hebrew prayer or vice versa, and for the last half century it has been almost commonplace to discover new poems, unknown poets, novel uses of poetry, and unfamiliar poetic versions of familiar prose texts within liturgical settings being revealed among these worn but distinguished fragments. Above all, the existence of so many texts convincingly demonstrates that any remaining apprehensions about the dangers of committing prayer texts to writing have either been allayed or have given way to greater fears of the consequences of not doing so.[29]

Conclusion

Having discussed the differences between Jewish liturgy as it was in the time of the talmudic rabbis and as it emerged in the postgeonic centuries, and having demonstrated the contrast between the assumptions made about the intervening, geonic period and the hard facts that have been revealed in the contents of the Cairo Genizah, it remains for this study to offer some explanation of what these facts indicate in terms of general liturgical development within the history of Jewish religious tradition.

The overall liturgical theme of the early geonic age was one of creativity and expansion. The basic foundations of rabbinic prayer, and Bible reading in its widest sense, having been laid down earlier, every opportunity was taken, perhaps especially in the tranquil periods of that age, to build all manner of structures. It is not clear whether at this stage *piyyutim, midrashim,* and *targumim* were, as has often been claimed, an intrinsic part of liturgy as such or were rather, as seems more likely, developments out of the original centrality of the biblical lesson. Either way, the tolerance and, indeed, encouragement of diversity applied among these genres no less than in the area of prayers and benedictions and the earliest Genizah texts are a reflection of the extent of that unregulated productivity.[30]

In liturgy, as in other manifestations of the Jewish religious tradition, there are of course crests and troughs of creativity, and periods of innovation are followed by years of conservative retrenchment in which yesterday's novelty is retained only because it has become today's established tradition. There are also inbuilt tensions within the liturgy between spontaneity and rigidity, synagogue and home, law and mysticism, Hebrew and vernacular, and brevity and protraction, to cite but a few, and at times laxity about the choice gives way to a strong stand about what represents the preferable alternative in each case. Such changes appear to have occurred in the latter part of the geonic period and to have reached their peak in the century or two immediately afterwards. The theme then became one of standardization and consistency, and all the authority of *halakhah* was employed to ensure that variation from the established norm was kept to a minimum.[31]

This was not, however, the whole story. A process of ritualization also took place in which those paraliturgical activities associated with the study and interpretation of the Hebrew Bible were virtually incorporated into the liturgy and given a ceremonial role. Particular parts of the poetic, exegetical, and mystical traditions were digested by the standard liturgy and other parts diverted to different functions. The centralization of Jewish worship according to the particular Babylonian rites acceptable to such figures as Saadiah was also undertaken, and what Hoffman has called the "canonization of the synagogue service" became a reality.[32]

The question yet to be answered is why this change took place. As with all historical developments, there were surely a number of factors. The new authority of the talmudic text and interpretation as laid down by the *geonim;* the success of the rabbinic leadership in spreading their religious ideas and practice to a wide body of the Jewish public; the need for a clearly defined response to the religious challenges of Christianity and Islam from without and Karaism from within; and the general intellectual atmosphere of the day which favored authority and centralization over variety and pluralism—there are strong grounds for regarding these influences as major.[33]

It is not, however, unlikely that the dominant theme is to be sought elsewhere. While the Jews had for many centuries attained high levels of literacy and had recorded various aspects of their religious teachings on papyrus and on leather scrolls, the rabbinic tradition had been a predominantly oral one, and there is a singular lack of manuscript evidence of any sort from the second to the ninth century. The versatile nature of the codex had already been recognized by the Christian community a few centuries earlier, but it would appear not to have been adopted by the Jews for their major corpora of talmudic and related traditions until some time between the seventh and ninth centuries. During that time, what had previously been restricted to oral circulation was committed to codices, and this produced precisely the effect that some rabbis feared and that others no doubt welcomed. The authority of the written word now spread from the biblical field to its rabbinic counterparts; the bound volume became the medium for the dissemination of authoritative texts. As a result, what had previously been the exclusive terrain of the scholar became familiar ground to the literate Jew, and, by the same token, the attempts of the leading schools and champions of rabbinic Judaism to establish authoritative guidance for the populace could achieve success by the circulation of volumes newly composed and sanctioned by them.[34]

In the field of liturgy too, then, the codex became the medium for the transmission of authorized sets of prayers, and a process was initiated that was ultimately to lead to the *siddur* acquiring what amounted to a form of popular canonization. The existence of thousands of Genizah texts representing almost every area of the Jewish religious tradition provides ample evidence of the growing tendency to commit the relevant teachings to authoritative, written form, and it is perhaps in the light of this development that the later literary history of *midrashim, piyyutim,* and *targumim* should be viewed.

Once the emerging prayer book had chosen what it wished to include from these and other such fields, the remaining material gradually, or perhaps contemporaneously, formed itself into written corpora suitable for the codex and thereby moved from a paraliturgical function to a purely literary one. This may be a more controversial point; what is, however, beyond dispute is that the written prayer book preserved much of the centralized liturgical tradition of the leading Babylonian *geonim* long after the authority of those leaders had waned and the centers of Jewish cultural activity had moved elsewhere.[35]

NOTES

1. Schmuel Safrai, ed., *The Literature of the Sages.* Part One: *Oral Tora, Halakha, Mishna, Tosefta, Talmud, External Tractates* (Assen/Maastricht and Philadelphia, 1987); D. Weiss-Halivni, *Midrash, Mishnah, and Gemara* (Cambridge, MA, 1986); Jacob Neusner, *A History of the Jews in Babylonia,* 5 vols. (Leiden, 1965–1970); G. Alon, *The Jews in Their Land in the Talmudic Age 70–650 C.E.* (Jerusalem, 1980–1984).

2. Stefan C. Reif, "The Early Liturgy of the Synagogue," in W. D. Davies and Louis Finkelstein, eds., *The Cambridge History of Judaism* III (forthcoming); M. Meyers and J. F. Strange, *Archaeology, the Rabbis, and Early Christianity* (London, 1981); Paul F. Bradshaw, *Daily Prayer in the Early Church* (London, 1981/New York, 1982).

3. B. Gerhardsson, *Memory and Manuscript* (Uppsala, 1961); Stefan C. Reif, "Some Liturgical Issues in the Talmudic Sources," *SL* 15 (1982–1983): 188–206; Joseph Heinemann and Jakob J. Petuchowski, *Literature of the Synagogue* (New York, 1975); Jakob J. Petuchowski, ed., *Contributions to the Scientific Study of Jewish Liturgy* (New York, 1970), pp. xvii–xxi.

4. Joseph Gutmann, ed., *Ancient Synagogues: The State of Research,* Brown Judaic Studies (Decatur, GA, 1981); Lee I. Levine, ed., *Ancient Synagogues Revealed* (Jerusalem, 1981); idem, ed., *The Synagogue in Late Antiquity* (Jerusalem, 1987); Baruch M. Bokser, *The Origins of the Seder* (Berkeley, 1984); J. Schwartz,

"Jubilees, Bethel, and the Temple of Jacob," *HUCA* 56 (1985): 63–85; Joseph Heinemann, *Prayer in the Talmud* (Berlin, 1976); Bernadette J. Brooten, *Women Leaders in the Ancient Synagogue: Inscriptional Evidence and Background Issues,* Brown Judaic Studies (Decatur, GA, 1982); B. Meg. 10a, A. Z. 52b, Men. 109b.

5. Reif, "Some Liturgical Issues," especially p. 191. Ezra Fleischer (*Eretz-Israel Prayer and Prayer Rituals as Portrayed in the Genizah Documents* [Hebrew; Jerusalem, 1988]) takes a less skeptical view than Heinemann (*Prayer in the Talmud*) about the degree of formality already in existence in talmudic prayer. See also Joseph Heinemann, *Studies in Jewish Liturgy,* ed. A. Shinan (Jerusalem, 1981); Ismar Elbogen, *Der jüdische Gottesdienst in seiner geschichtlichen Entwicklung* (Frankfort, 1931; updated Hebrew edition, Tel-Aviv, 1972).

6. Robert Goldenberg neatly sums up the problem of using talmudic sources for historical reconstruction in his essay in Barry W. Holtz, ed., *Back to the Sources: Reading the Classic Jewish Texts* (New York, 1984), pp. 129–75.

7. Salo W. Baron, *A Social and Religious History of the Jews* II (New York, 1952); Heinemann, *Prayer in the Talmud,* pp. 285–87.

8. Brooten, *Women Leaders*; L. Roth-Gerson, *The Greek Inscriptions from the Synagogues in Eretz-Israel* (Hebrew; Jerusalem, 1987).

9. E.g., M. Ber. 1–5, Taan. 2:2–3, Yoma 7.1, Tamid 5.1; T. Ber. 1–3; B. Ber. 4b, 27b–29b. See L. Ginzberg, *A Commentary on the Palestinian Talmud* (Hebrew; New York, 1941), I, pp. 215–16, III, p. 359. See also Stefan C. Reif, "Liturgical Difficulties and Geniza Manuscripts," in S. Morag, I. Ben-Ami, N. A. Stillman, eds., *Studies in Judaism and Islam Presented to S. D. Goitein* (Jerusalem, 1981), pp. 99–122; Heinemann, *Prayer in the Talmud,* pp. 137–92, 218–50, and the various relevant essays in the collection edited by Shinan, *Studies in Jewish Liturgy;* Tzvee Zahavy, *The Mishnaic Law of Blessings and Prayers: Tractate Berakhot,* Brown Judaic Studies (Decatur, GA, 1988).

10. Philo, II *Som.* XV 3.127 and *De Opificio Mundi* 43.128; Josephus, *Contra Apionem* 2.17.175; Luke 4:16–21, Acts 13:15, 15:21; M. Meg. 3–4; B. Meg. 21a–32a; Elbogen, *Der jüdische Gottesdienst,* pp. 155–84 (Hebrew edition, pp. 117–38); Petuchowski, *Jewish Liturgy;* Heinemann, *Studies in Jewish Liturgy;*

G. Vermes, "The Decalogue and the Minim," *Beiheft zur Zeitschrift für die Alttestamentliche Wissenschaft* 103 (1968): 232–40 = idem, *Post-Biblical Jewish Studies* (Leiden, 1975), pp. 169–77; Ernst Würthwein, *The Text of the Old Testament, An Introduction to the Biblia Hebraica*, 4th ed. (London, 1980), pp. 75–79; B. Pes. 117b, Arakhin 10b, Ber. 56a.

11. Heinemann, *Prayer in the Talmud*, pp. 27–29, 218, 256–75; M. Ber. 7, 8.1, 5, Pes. 10; B. Ber. 20b, Pes. 53a–54a, 106b, Keth. 7a–8b; R. Posner, U. Kaploun, and S. Cohen, *Jewish Liturgy: Prayer and Synagogue Service through the Ages* (Jerusalem, 1975), pp. 35–38; Reif, "Early Liturgy," paragraph on liturgical language.

12. Baron, *Social and Religious History*, VI (1958), pp. 152–313; M. Gil, *Palestine during the First Muslim Period* (Hebrew; Tel-Aviv, 1983); M. Ben-Sasson, *The Jewish Community of Medieval North Africa* (doctoral dissertation, in Hebrew, Hebrew University of Jerusalem, 1983); M. Beit-Arié, *Hebrew Codicology* (Jerusalem, 1981), pp. 9–11.

13. For the works of Natronai, Amram, Saadiah, Hai, Maimonides, Rashi, and Simchah of Vitry, see L. Ginzberg, *Geonica* II (New York, 1909), pp. 109–10, 114–17; E. D. Goldschmidt, *Seder Rav Amram Gaon* (Jerusalem, 1971); T. Kronholm, *Seder Rav Amram Gaon* (Lund, 1974); Israel Davidson, Simchah Assaf, and B. I. Joel, *Siddur Rav Saadja Gaon* (Jerusalem, 1963); Tsvi Groner, "A List of Rav Hai Gaon's Responsa," in *Alei Sefer* 13 (1986); E. D. Goldschmidt, *"Seder Hatefillah shel Harambam,"* *Studies of the Research Institute for Hebrew Poetry* 7 (1958): 183–213 = idem, *On Jewish Liturgy* (Jerusalem, 1978), pp. 187–216; Solomon Buber and J. Freimann, *Siddur Raschi* (Berlin, 1911); S. Hurwitz, ed., *Machzor Vitry* (Nuremburg, 1923); Baron, *Social and Religious History*, VII (1958), pp. 62–134. For the earliest known Persian and English rites, see S. Tal, *The Persian Jewish Prayer Book* (Jerusalem, 1980); I. Brodie, *The Etz Hayyim* (Jerusalem, 1962–1967).

14. E. Fleischer, *Hebrew Liturgical Poetry in the Middle Ages* (Hebrew; Jerusalem, 1975); T. Carmi, ed., *The Penguin Book of Hebrew Verse* (New York, 1981), pp. 13–31. In addition to the standard works of G. G. Scholem, J. Dan, and I. Gruenwald, reference may also be made to the recent survey of M. Bar-Ilan (n. 28 below).

15. Baron, *Social and Religious History* VII (1958), pp. 73–79.

16. Posner, Kaploun, and Cohen, *Jewish Liturgy*, pp. 249–53; Abraham Z. Idelsohn, *Jewish Liturgy and Its Development* (New York, 1960), pp. 56–63; Lawrence A. Hoffman, *Beyond the Text: A Holistic Approach to Liturgy*, Jewish Literature and Culture (Bloomington, IN, 1987), pp. 40–49.

17. The clearest and most concise and consistent example is the prayer book of Maimonides as cited in Goldschmidt, *"Seder Hatefillah shel Harambam."*

18. B. M. Lewin, *"Letoledot Ner Shel Shabbat,"* in I. Davison, ed., *Essays and Studies in Memory of Linda R. Miller* (New York, 1938), Hebrew part, pp. 55–68; J. Z. Lauterbach, "The Sabbath in Jewish Ritual and Folklore," *Rabbinic Essays* (Cincinnati, 1951), pp. 454–70; B. S. Jacobson, *Netiv Binah* II (Tel-Aviv, 1968), pp. 25–29; Lawrence A. Hoffman, *The Canonization of the Synagogue Service* (Notre Dame, 1979), pp. 86–89.

19. Stefan C. Reif, *Shabbethai Sofer and His Prayer-book* (Cambridge, 1979); Posner, Kaploun, and Cohen, *Jewish Liturgy;* C. Rabin, "The Linguistic Investigation of the Language of Jewish Prayer" (Hebrew) in Jakob J. Petuchowski and E. Fleischer, eds., *Studies in Aggadah, Targum, and Jewish Liturgy in Memory of Joseph Heinemann* (Jerusalem, 1981), pp. 163–71; Maimonides, *Mishneh Torah, Tefillah* 1.4; Idelsohn, *Jewish Liturgy*, pp. 56–70.

20. Posner, Kaploun, and Cohen, *Jewish Liturgy*, pp. 109–23, 224–26; Idelsohn, *Jewish Liturgy*, pp. 73–89, 148–49; Jacobson, *Netiv Binah* I, pp. 100–103, 127–28, 145–73, 190–92, 276–77, 313, 360–76; II, pp. 388–92; Elbogen, *Der jüdische Gottesdienst*, paragraph 53.6; A. Neubauer, *Mediaeval Jewish Chronicles and Chronological Notes* (Oxford, 1887), pp. 83–85; *Massekhet Soferim* 10–14, ed. M. Higger (New York, 1937), pp. 208–73.

21. Elbogen, *Der jüdische Gottesdienst;* Jacobson, *Netiv Binah*, II, pp. 207–20; M. N. Adler, *The Itinerary of Benjamin of Tudela* (London, 1907), Hebrew section, pp. 62–63, English section, pp. 69–70; *Massekhet Soferim*, ed. M. Higger.

22. All this becomes progressively clearer when one traces and compares the attitudes to prayer and communal worship as they evolve in the earliest liturgical guides cited in n. 13 above. The writer hopes to return to a more detailed analysis of the theories underlying such attitudes in a future study. In the meantime, see David R. Blumenthal, "Maimonides: Prayer, Worship, and Mysti-

134 STEFAN C. REIF

cism," in idem, ed., *Approaches to Judaism in Medieval Times* III,
Brown Judaic Studies (Decatur, GA, 1988), pp. 1–16.

23. The tendency to underestimate or virtually ignore the major
geonic influence on the talmudic material itself and on the development of rabbinic liturgy is apparent not only in the relevant medieval works but also in Baer's *Avodat Yisrael* and in many aspects
of the modern scientific treatments cited above. Although ques-
tioned in the Hebrew edition (p. 204), Elbogen's lead is followed
by many scholarly and semischolarly works, and the liturgical innovation and productivity of the talmudic and medieval periods are
viewed as vastly superior to what emerged in the geonic era. Interestingly, Baron makes a much more favorable assessment of liturgical creativity at that time (*Social and Religious History* VII [1958],
pp. 62–134).

24. If I have a criticism of Hoffman's *Beyond the Text,* it is
encapsulated in the fact that in a wideranging study of Jewish liturgy
covering history, theology, sociology, and linguistics, the word *halakhah* does not have to make a single appearance in the index.

25. *Encyclopaedia Judaica* (Jerusalem, 1972) XVI, 1333–42;
S. D. Goitein, *A Mediterranean Society* I (Berkeley and Los Ange-
les, 1967), pp. 1–28; idem, *Religion in a Religious Age* (Cambridge, MA, 1974), pp. 3–17, 139–51; Stefan C. Reif, *A Guide to
the Taylor-Schechter Genizah Collection* (Cambridge, 1973, 1979);
"Genizah Collections at Cambridge University Library" (Hebrew),
Te'udah I, ed. M. A. Friedman (Tel-Aviv, 1980), pp. 201–6; idem,
"The Taylor-Schechter Genizah Research Unit," in *Newsletter* no.
19 of the World Union of Jewish Studies (August, 1981): 17–21;
idem, "1898 Preserved in Letter and Spirit," *The Cambridge Review*
103, no. 2266 (29 January, 1982): 120–21; idem (with G. Khan),
"Genizah Material at Cambridge University Library," *Encyclopaedia Judaica Year Book 1983/85* (Jerusalem, 1985), pp. 170–71; and
idem, *Published Material from the Cambridge Genizah Collections:
A Bibliography 1896–1980* (Cambridge, 1988), introduction.

26. S. Abramson, *Bamerkazim Uvatefutsot Bitekufot Hage onim*
(Jerusalem, 1965) and *Inyanot Besifrut Hage onim* (Jerusalem,
1974); D. M. Goodblatt, *Rabbinic Instruction in Sasanian Babylonia* (Leiden, 1975); Tsvi Groner, *The Legal Methodology of Hai
Gaon,* Brown Judaic Studies (Decatur, GA, 1985); R. Brody, "The
Testimony of Geonic Literature to the Text of the Babylonian Talmud," a Hebrew paper delivered at the Ninth World Congress of

Jewish Studies in Jerusalem in 1985 and scheduled for publication in a collection of essays by the Talmud department of the Hebrew University of Jerusalem.

27. Israel Yeivin, *Introduction to the Tiberian Masorah* (Missoula, MT, 1980); idem, "Masorah" in *Encyclopaedia Judaica* XVI, 1401–82; J. Mann, I. Sonne, and B. Z. Wacholder, *The Bible as Read and Preached in the Old Synagogue* (Cincinnati, 1940, 1966, 1971); Z. M. Rabinovitz, *Ginzé Midrash* (Tel-Aviv, 1976); Stefan C. Reif, "A Midrashic Anthology from the Genizah," in J. A. Emerton and Stefan C. Reif, eds., *Interpreting the Hebrew Bible* (Cambridge, 1982), pp. 179–225; Michael L. Klein, *Genizah Manuscripts of Palestinian Targum to the Pentateuch* (Cincinnati, 1986).

28. N. Wieder, *"Berakhah Bilti Yeduah," Sinai* 82 (1978): 197–221. The many recent articles of N. Wieder and E. Fleischer in *Sinai* and *Tarbiz* have taken much further the earlier seminal work of Jacob Mann and the important contributions of Joseph Heinemann. See also M. Margaliot, *Hilkhot Eretz Yisrael min Hagenizah*, ed. I. Ta-Shema (Jerusalem, 1973), pp. 127–52. Among younger scholars, see Tsvi Groner, *"Haberakhah al Havidui Vegilguleha," Bar-Ilan Annual* 13 (1976): 158–68, and *Genizah Fragments*, no. 13 (1987): 2; Lawrence A. Hoffman, *Canonization of the Synagogue Service;* Stefan C. Reif, "Festive Titles in Liturgical Terminology" (Hebrew), *Proceedings of the Ninth World Congress of Jewish Studies* (Jerusalem, 1986), Division C, pp. 63–70; M. Bar-Ilan, *The Mysteries of Jewish Prayer and Hekhalot* (Hebrew; Ramat Gan, 1987).

29. The pioneering efforts of M. Zulay and J. Schirmann and individual publications by A. Habermann and A. Scheiber have now been substantially supplemented by E. Fleischer in such works as his *The Yozer: Its Emergence and Development* (Hebrew; Jerusalem, 1984). See also M. Sokoloff and J. Yahalom, "Aramaic Piyyutim from the Byzantine period," *JQR* 75 (1985): 309–21; W. J. van Bekkum, *The Qedushta'ot of Yehudah according to Genizah Manuscripts* (Groningen doctoral dissertation, 1988).

30. In addition to the work of the scholars cited in the previous note, and that of Petuchowski and Heinemann cited in notes 3–5 above, see the relevant essays by A. Shinan and J. Yahalom in *The Synagogue in Late Antiquity*, pp. 97–126; and by Barry W. Holtz in *Back to the Sources*, pp. 176–211; and Gary G. Porton, *Understanding Rabbinic Midrash* (Hoboken, NJ, 1985).

31. Jakob J. Petuchowski, *Understanding Jewish Prayer* (New York, 1972); Reif, "Early Liturgy of the Synagogue"; idem, "Some Liturgical Issues."

32. Hoffman's work, *Canonization of the Synagogue Service,* is an important contribution to our understanding of this process, although he has probably been too ambitious in attempting to identify precise and discrete trends within particular timespans and on the part of individual authorities.

33. For the general history of the period see Baron's *Social and Religious History,* III–VIII (New York, London and Philadelphia, 1957–1958); Haim H. Ben-Sasson, *A History of the Jewish People* (London, 1976); Cecil Roth, *The World History of the Jewish People* (London, 1966).

34. M. Haran on scrolls in *Eretz Yisrael* 16 (1982): 86–92; *JJS* 33 (1982): 161–73; 35 (1984): 84–85; *HUCA* 54 (1983): 111–22; 56 (1985): 21–62; M. Beit-Arié, *Hebrew Codicology;* C. H. Roberts and T. C. Skeat, *The Birth of the Codex* (London, 1983); Stefan C. Reif, "Aspects of Mediaeval Jewish Literacy" in Rosamond McKitterick, ed., *The Uses of Literacy in Early Mediaeval Europe* (Cambridge, 1990), pp. 134–55.

35. The writer gratefully acknowledges the assistance received from Dr. Robert Brody during his year as a Visiting Research Associate at the Genizah Research Unit (1987–1988) as well as the most efficient data-base management demonstrated by his wife in the preparation of this paper.

Jewish Worship
since the Period of Its Canonization

ERIC L. FRIEDLAND

[Editors' note: Eric L. Friedland, Sanders Professor of Judaic Studies at (jointly) the United Theological Seminary (Dayton, Ohio), the University of Dayton, and Wright State University, surveys Jewish liturgical development from the period when the first comprehensive prayer books were composed. His narrative thus takes him from ninth-century Babylonia to the high Middle Ages in western Europe, and then eastward to the Ottoman empire and Poland. Finally, he examines Reform liturgy, first in Germany, where the Reform movement was born in the nineteenth century, and then in America, where it was imported by German immigrants. He illustrates well the constant penchant of premodern Jewish liturgy to grow with ever more strata illustrative of novel theological developments: the penitential piety of German Hasidism in the twelfth and thirteenth centuries; the Lurianic Kabbalah in the sixteenth and seventeenth centuries; and Polish Hasidism in the eighteenth century. Only with later movements, of which Reform was a major expression, was the cumulative tendency reversed, as revisers not only added prayers representative of nineteenth-century thought, but also removed earlier strata that they deemed unacceptable to their post-Enlightenment conscience and aesthetics.]

Even as one observes the vicissitudes of the Jewish prayer book down through the centuries one cannot help continually being aware of its timeless qualities. Just the same, there was hardly ever a time when it was not somehow in a state of flux. The Jews' worldwide wanderings may explain some of this liturgical malleability. Despite their fidelity to, and pride in, a tradition that harks back to a past, immediate and remote, the Jewish people has tended generally to be hospitable to new ways of approaching that venerable tradition, notably in eras and societies not given to restrictive or discriminatory excesses. This pattern was to hold in the Middle Ages, given the qualifications mentioned, not much less than in our highly mobile, changeful age.

The High Middle Ages in France and Germany

Just as the liturgical compilations of Amram (ninth century),[1] Saadiah (882–942),[2] and Moses Maimonides (1135–1204)[3] in the East went a long way toward consolidating the labors of the past in the area of worship, so *Siddur Rashi*[4] (reflective of the school of thought developed by the doyen of medieval biblical and talmudic commentators, Rabbi Solomon ben Isaac of Troyes [1040–1105]) and *Machzor Vitry*[5] (by Simchah ben Samuel of Vitry [died before 1105], a leading disciple and possibly colleague of Rashi) were to pave the way for similar efforts in the West. While depending heavily upon earlier non-European efforts (*Seder Rav Amram* in particular), both *Siddur Rashi* and *Machzor Vitry* are indigenously Franco-German. *Siddur Rashi* provides the *halakhot* for prayers whereas *Machzor Vitry* stipulates these rules and regulations and furnishes the prayer texts as well.

The high Middle Ages thus gave rise to a series of such geographically specific volumes, representative of regional rites, each known as a *minhag: Minhag Rhinus* (the Rhineland rite), for instance, and *Minhag Österreich (Böhm)* (the Austrian or Bohemian, i.e., eastern European, rite). These rites are generally conceptualized as belonging to larger families of rites, particularly *Minhag Sefarad* (the rite of the Iberian Peninsula) and *Minhag Ashkenaz* (the rite of northern Europe). *Minhag Sefarad* eventually made its way throughout the Mediterranean, via Jewish emigrés from the Spanish Inquisition and expulsion of 1492, just as *Minhag Ashkenaz* was carried by successive waves of Jewish migrants from western and central Europe to eastern centers like Poland and Russia.

The medieval period witnessed not only a gradual crystallization of the prayer book but also the composition of many new poetic works (*piyyutim*) beyond those written by the perdurable Palestinian poets of the earlier Byzantine age, such as Yannai and Kallir. Two types of *piyyut* that dominated the Ashkenazic orbit were the *selichah* (forgiveness), for penitential services,[6] and the *kinah* (lament), for days commemorating national or communal tragedies. These received their impetus in Italy and were developed in Jewish communities along the Rhine by the Kalonymide family, among many others. Without doubt, the vulnerable position in which the Jews as a minority and as adherents of a despised faith found themselves and their all-too-frequent persecution and martyrdom were conducive to the mood and mindset responsible for the composition of such heartrending *selichot* and *kinot*.

Penitential piety reached its high point in eleventh- to thirteenth-century Germany in the movement known as German Hasidism (*Chasidei Ashkenaz*), which reinforced and deepened devotional life by intensifying and interiorizing Jewish moral teaching. Its founder, Judah ben Samuel Hechasid ("the Pious"; died 1217), and his key disciple, Eleazar ben Judah of Worms (1165–1238), taught meditation, mystical prayer, and asceticism. Theurgy and theosophical speculation formed important parts of the belief system upheld by these pietists.

The worship of German Hasidism could be simple and direct at one moment and theologically complex the next. On the one hand, the value of simple, sincere prayer was recognized, as is attested by this moving utterance of the cowherd "who knew not how to pray":

> Master of the universe,
> It is revealed and known to Thee,
> That if you had cattle and gave them to me to tend
> For everyone else I tend expecting pay
> But for Thee I would tend for free
> Because I love Thee.[7]

The pietists would have had no difficulty endorsing this mystical aphorism on the subject of prayer: *Tefillah beli kavvanah keguf beli neshamah* ("Prayer without sincere intention, or proper inwardness, is like a body without a soul").[8] On the

other hand, they created a textured hymnody that shows both
literary and theological sophistication, particularly in the
Hymns of Unity (*Shirei Hayichud*) to be recited on successive
days of the week. The best known of these is the Hymn of
Glory (*Shir Hakavod*), or *Anim Zemirot* ("Sweet Hymns and
Songs Will I Recite"),[9] which today is customarily sung in
Orthodox synagogues towards the end of services on Saturday
morning. The text of *Anim Zemirot* is found, interestingly
enough, *in toto* or *in parte*, in every American non-Orthodox
rite since the 1940s. Unlike any other contemporary rite, traditional or otherwise, the 1945 edition of the Reform *Union
Prayer Book* II reproduced, in English rendition, portions of
the Hymn of Unity appointed for Sunday:[10]

How shall I come before God, the Most High? And how shall I
bow before the God of old?

If the mountains were an altar, and all the wood of Lebanon laid
thereon;

If all the cattle and all the beasts were slain, and lain as a sacrifice
upon the wood;

All Lebanon would not suffice for fuel, nor all the beasts for
burnt-offering—

Lo! all these were not enough to serve, to come therewith before
the God of glory,

For Thou, our King, art exceedingly glorious; how then should
we bow before our Lord?

Verily none living can honor Thee—how can I, Thy servant?

For Thou hast multiplied good things for me—for Thou hast
magnified Thy mercy unto me.

Great are the debts I owe Thee for the good Thou hast wrought
for me.

I have not served Thee in accordance with Thy benefits: one in
ten thousand I have not repaid Thee.

If I say, I will declare their number, I know not how to count
them.

And what shall I return unto Thee, seeing that Thine are the
heavens, and the earth also is Thine?

It is written: I, the Lord, will not reprove thee for lack of sacrifices or thy burnt-offerings.

> Concerning your sacrifices and your burnt-offerings I com-
> manded not your fathers.
> What have I asked, and what have I sought of thee but to fear
> Me?
> To serve with joy and a good heart; behold to hearken is better
> than to sacrifice,
> And a broken heart than a whole offering. The sacrifices of God
> are a broken spirit.
>
> I will build an altar of the broken fragments of my heart, and
> will bow my spirit within me.
> My broken spirit—that is Thy sacrifice; let it be acceptable upon
> Thine altar.
> I will proclaim aloud Thy praise; I will declare all Thy wonders.

The Influence of Kabbalah

The Jewish mystical tradition reached its culmination in the publication of the *Zohar,* a virtual "Bible" for another stage in the mystical development known as Kabbalah. A major part of it was written in Spain pseudonymously by Moses de Leon (1250 – 1305). The influence of the *Zohar* on the theology of prayer has been incalculable. One's "state of contemplation" (*kavvanah*) during the recitation of prayer was held to impinge inescapably upon the Sephirotic realm of divine emanations, that is to say, upon the various manifestations of divinity itself.[11] For all that, this classic of the Kabbalah is not conspicuous for its immediate *literary* contributions to the liturgy. A solitary example of a prayer that found entry into the Sephardic and Ashkenazic rites is the Aramaic one invoked in front of the open ark before a Torah scroll is taken out for a public reading:[12]

> Blessed be the name of the Lord of the universe! Blessed be thy crown and thy dominion. May thy good will ever abide with thy people Israel. Reveal thy saving power to thy people in thy sanctuary; bestow on us the good gift of thy light, and accept our prayer in mercy. May it be thy will to prolong our life in happiness. Let me also be counted among the righteous, so that thou

mayest have compassion on me and shelter me and mine and all
that belong to thy people Israel. Thou art He who nourishes and
sustains all; thou art He who rules over all; thou art He who rules
over kings, for dominion is thine. I am the servant of the Holy
One, blessed be He, before whom and before whose glorious
Torah I bow at all times. Not in man do I put my trust, nor do I
rely on any angel [literally: 'son of God'], but only in the God
of heaven who is the God of truth, whose Torah is truth and
whose Prophets are truth, and who performs many deeds of good-
ness and truth. In Him I put my trust, and to His holy and
glorious name I utter praises. May it be thy will to open my heart
to thy Torah, and to fulfill the wishes of my heart and the heart
of all thy people Israel for happiness, life, and peace.[13]

The next stage in the development of the Kabbalah, however, was to have a pivotal impact on Jewish worship. This
stage came into being in Safed with the promulgation of the
teachings of Isaac Luria, also popularly known by an acronym
made up of his name and title, Ari (1534–1572). We witness
a breathtaking efflorescence not only of new mystical doc-
trines rooted in the *Zohar* and its antecedents but also of novel
approaches to the standard liturgy and the creation of extraliturgical practices and hymnody. Luria was behind the institution of (1) special preparatory meditations called *kavvanot*
(singular: *kavvanah*), intended to induce the proper inner state
in the worshiper so as to effectuate change on the cosmic level;
and (2) *yichudim* (singular: *yichud*), prayers designed to
achieve "unity" among the manifest aspects of the Godhead,
which Kabbalistic theology held to have been fragmented in
the process of God's creation of the cosmos. He set up noctur-
nal vigils (*tikkun chatsot*) as well, particularly on the night of
fateful occasions, one a semifestival and the other a major
festival, Hoshana Rabbah and Shavuot, respectively. In addition, both he and his many disciples produced a rich store of
hymns that in time were disseminated the world over. A surprising number of the Sabbath table songs that continue to
enchant emanated from the Lurianic circle.

To give a slight idea of the style and attitude found in this eruption of postbiblical devotional prosody in the Hebrew language, we reproduce in the fairly literal, if a little labored, translation of the *ArtScroll Siddur* a now-popular love song to God by a Safed Kabbalist in his own right and author of the important *Sefer Charedim,* Elazar ben Moses Azikri (1533–1600). Normally sung just prior to the commencement of the public worship on Shabbat eve, the amatory hymn of longing and healing is called *Yedid Nefesh* (Beloved of the Soul).[14] Its mystical significance lies in the fact that the four Hebrew letters beginning the four verses spell the sacrosanct four-letter name of God (YHVH). While reciting this love poem to God, the mystic concentrated on the four letters of the name, until the divine name was unified, as, it was hoped, fragmented divinity itself would again be.

> Beloved of the soul, Compassionate Father, draw Your servant to Your will. Then Your servant will hurry like a hart to bow before Your majesty. To him Your friendship will be sweeter than the drippings of the honeycomb and any taste.
>
> Majestic, Beautiful, Radiance of the universe —my soul pines for Your love. Please, O God, heal her now by showing her the pleasantness of Your radiance. Then she will be strengthened and healed, and gladness will be hers.
>
> All-worthy One—may Your mercy be aroused and please take pity on the son of Your beloved, because it is so long that I have yearned intensely to see the splendor of Your strength. Only these my heart desired, so please take pity and do not conceal Yourself.
>
> Please be revealed and spread upon me, my Beloved, the shelter of Your peace. Illuminate the world with Your glory that we may rejoice and be glad with You. Hasten, show love, for the time has come, and show us grace as in days of old.

Polish Hasidism

During the first half of the eighteenth century in Poland the Lurianic phase of the Kabbalah underwent a popularizing,

proletarianizing process. Kabbalah's elitism and esotericism
were blunted; its teaching, streamlined and transformed, was
brought to the masses. This new phase, Polish Hasidism—not
to be confused with the earlier German Hasidism—was
founded by Israel Ba'al Shem Tov (acronym: Besht; c. 1700–
1760), who preached simplicity, fervor, and hope in the aftermath of the Chmielnicki massacres and the Sabbatean fiasco.
In 1648 Chmielnicki had led a peasants' revolt which deci-
mated the Jewish population in Poland, and that same year the
most famous of the medieval false messiahs, Sabbatai Zevi,
had declared himself. In 1665 Sabbatai Zevi converted to Islam, crushing the hopes of Jews worldwide. In the wake of
these events, this new form of Hasidism invested prayer with
new dimensions.[15] It offset, as well, the academic formalism
of the Lithuanian *yeshivot* and the inaccessibly arcane quality
of Lurianic Kabbalah as it had evolved up to the start of the
eighteenth century. *Hitlahavut* (enthusiasm) became a primary
criterion for bona fide worship. One's heartfelt commitment
and total involvement might be disclosed in, say, somersaults
in worship, dance, zesty melodies, and the like. (Parallels in
revitalization drawn from the history of American religions
include such enthusiastic utopian-communitarian movements
of the nineteenth century as the Shakers.)

A crucial factor in the success and cohesiveness of the
Hasidic movement is the emergence of the charismatic figure
of the *tsaddik* (the righteous one) or *rebbe*. Dynasties—"gal-
axies" might not be an inappropriate term—of such spiritual
leaders appeared. Each *tsaddik* had his own particular style
and placed his unique stamp on his group or conventicle within
the larger movement. The generations of *rebbes* succeeding
the Besht diverged in specifics and style with respect to prayer,
all the while maintaining a recognizably common Hasidic
mode. In his exquisite, short manual of select Hasidic apho-
risms, *Ten Rungs,* Martin Buber includes a modest number of
penetrating statements on prayer (one of the "rungs"), two of
which merit repeating here:

This is how the words of prayer: "Hear us, when we call for help, hear our cries, Thou who knowest what is hidden," are expounded:

We do not even know how we are supposed to pray. All we do is call for help because of the need of the moment. But what the soul intends is spiritual need, only we are not able to express what the soul means. That is why we do not merely ask God to hear our call for help, but also beg Him, who knows what is hidden, to hear the silent cry of the soul.[16]

Or this poignant reworking of the ancient rabbinic version of the Parable of the Prodigal Son:[17]

A king's son rebelled against his father and was banished from the sight of his face. After a time, the king was moved to pity for his fate and bade his messengers go and search for him. It was long before one of the messengers found him—far from home. He was at a village inn, dancing barefoot and in a torn shirt in the midst of drunken peasants. The courtier bowed and said: "Your father has sent me to ask you what you desire. Whatever it may be, he is prepared to grant your wish." The prince began to weep. "Oh," said he, "if only I had warm clothing and a pair of stout shoes!"

See, that is how we whimper for the small needs of the hour and forget that the Glory of God is in exile!

Two of the premier *tsaddikim,* each the head of a prominent branch of the Hasidic movement, Shneur Zalman of Liadi (founder of the highly visible Lubavitcher group) and Nachman of Bratslav, developed well-defined approaches to Hasidism and hence towards prayer and the accompanying inner preparations. The Lubavitcher *rebbe* combined mainstream Kabbalistic thought, particularly its Lurianic phase, with the staunch philosophical endeavors of Moses Maimonides. This intellectualist brand of mysticism is very much in evidence in Shneur Zalman's treatment of prayer and *kavvanah* as found in his *Tanya.*[18] Nachman of Bratslav on the other hand, though certainly no antinomian or nonconformist when it came to statutory prayers and ritual observances, broke new ground, both in what he encouraged and in what he did himself. Solitude (*hitbodedut*) in prayer, especially in a rustic setting, receives a fresh emphasis; so does spontaneous prayer in the vernacular, in this case Yiddish, touching on matters of immediate, pressing concern to the individual.[19] Some of his deepfelt extraliturgical private meditations, as recorded by his key disciple and amanuensis, Nathan of Nemirov, have, not surprisingly, found their way into the most recent official prayer books of the Reform and Conservative movements in the United States[20] and their counterparts in Great Britain. In its "Passages for Silent Devotion," for example, the editors of the British Reform *Forms of Prayers for Jewish Worship* included this example of Nachman's outpourings of the soul:[21]

My Father in heaven,

Save and help me from this moment to be in the fields every
    night . . .
To cry to You from the depths of my heart . . .
To set forth all the burdens and negations that remove me from
    You, Light of Life,
And give strength to strengthen myself in spite of everything—
With happiness that has no end,
Until my heart lifts up my hands to clap, to clap, to clap, and
    my legs to dance until the soul swoons, swoons.
And help me ever make a new beginning and to be a flowering
    well of Torah and prayer,
To work always with quickened spirit,
And to stand with powerful strength against the scoffers and
    mockers,
Who go about in our days—days of double darkness . . .
But oh, against all the troubles and burdens,
Your joys and Your delights are strong and powerful . . .
O, our great Father, home of delights and wellspring of joy.

Reform in Germany

Meanwhile in eighteenth- and nineteenth-century central and western Europe, the Jewish community underwent its own earth-shattering changes owing, first, to the French Revolution and, second, to the ensuing Emancipation from the ghettos in the major cities and from concomitant medieval disabilities Jews had suffered. While freedom from former restrictions was obviously a welcome turnaround, it was not without hazard. A goodly number of Jews felt ineluctably attracted to the cultural and religious values of the non-Jewish society to which they were newly exposed, and they began to sense that the traditions in which they had been reared paled by comparison. There were those who shucked their ancestral ways and opted for the way of the majority, while others knew that concessions of various kinds and varying degrees were going to have to be made, if Jewish identity was to be maintained and Judaism was to survive. Reform became the catchword of the day; and no segment of Jewry in either western or central Europe remained untouched; even Orthodoxy was profoundly affected.[22] Theology, prayer, and worship were thus enormously reshaped by historical and socioeconomic events from the close of the seventeenth century throughout all of the nineteenth.[23]

One of the byproducts of the Emancipation was the formation of liturgical scholarship in a new key. No longer were prayer texts to be commented upon solely with devotional or homiletical intent. Critical tools now came to be applied to the prayer book for the triple purpose of ascertaining the correct text, determining its historical background, and finding out the actual intended meaning of each prayer unit. At the forefront of such endeavors were the grammarians/copyists/expositors Wolf Heidenheim (1757–1832), Eliezer Landshuth (1817–1887), and Seligmann Baer (1825–1897). And the first to put liturgiology on a sure scientific footing was the luminary Leopold Zunz, whose path-blazing works are still very much in use.[24] In the meantime a small group of Jews in Hamburg took the initiative in introducing changes of public worship by (1) abridging prayers, particularly the medieval accretions (many of which were no longer understood anyway); (2) according a prominent place to the vernacular alongside (or occasionally in place of) the Hebrew; and (3) introducing the organ and choir, as part of a larger effort at transforming Jewish worship into a model of western decorum. The synagogue they established was the Hamburg Temple (1817), where they introduced what is generally referred to as the Hamburg Prayer Book (Hamburg, 1819).

The next generation, marked as it was by rabbis who had joined the laity in its Reform cause, was dissatisfied with on-the-spot, piecemeal, practical reforms and sought to revise the prayer book according to theologically consistent principles as well as contemporary aesthetic sensibilities. The deliberations of the progressively minded rabbinic conferences held in the mid-1840s on matters pertaining to liturgy and *halakhah* provided helpful guidelines to rabbis and congregations.[25] By now the lines were clearly drawn: (1) the extreme Reform position articulated by the *Reformgemeinde* in Berlin and its eventual pastor Samuel Holdheim; (2) the moderate, gradualist Reform—or, as the term came to be, Liberal—one formulated by the likes of Leopold Stein and Abraham Geiger; (3) the Conservative stance adhered to by Michael Sachs, Zacharias Frankel, Manuel Joel; and (4) Neo-Orthodoxy created by Samson Raphael Hirsch.

Reform in North America

In the middle of the nineteenth century the second major wave of Jewish immigration to the United States was comprised largely of those fleeing persecution from German-speaking lands. Many brought with them their reforming tendencies. Rabbis sought to implement the new ideas concerning worship that had sprouted on European soil. They ranged from moderate Reform (Leo Merzbacher, Adolph Huebsch, Isaac Mayer Wise) to traditionalist Reform, or, what I would call, proto-Conservative (Benjamin Szold, Marcus Jastrow, Alexander Kohut, and Aaron Wise) to enlightened Orthodox (Isaac Leeser and Sabato Morais). The bold, principled, and consistent David Einhorn was a notable exception to the near-

universal temperate tendency in American Jewish liturgy over
a hundred years ago. Believing that compromise would be
fatal to Judaism in the long run, Einhorn composed his bril-
liantly restructured prayer book, *Olath Tamid,* which blends
together the theology, ritual consensus, and aesthetics of Reform in a truly astonishing fashion. On the other hand, Isaac
M. Wise sought to mold and promote an agreed-upon uniform
prayer manual for all the American congregations; and to sig-
nal his hope and dream he named his mildly Reform rite *Minhag America.*

A generation later, in the 1890s, the time was ripe to ven-
ture a single liturgy for all the Reform congregations in the
United States. Isaac S. Moses, who in the course of his long
rabbinic career used a variety of revised prayer books, including those by Einhorn and Wise, laid the foundation for the new
amalgamated prayer book in the form of a draft. The scholarly
Kaufmann Kohler and others on an editorial commission
worked with Moses's proposed draft, combining the best features of *Olath Tamid* and *Minhag America* (and others as well)
into what became the *Union Prayer Book,* the longest-lasting
non-Orthodox rite anywhere in the world. Let us illustrate how
the two older prayer books left their imprint on their liturgical
offspring.

The first two influences we will examine are from the end
of the *Tefillah:* the prayer for peace (*Sim Shalom*) and the silent
meditation following (*Elohai Netsor*). All of the twentieth-
century editions of the *Union Prayer Book,* except for *Gates
of Prayer,* have appropriated Wise's slightly revised Hebrew
text of "Grant us peace" because it nicely modulated particu-
larism with universalism. As the Reconstructionist prayer
books have made a point of adopting the Wisean version and
translating it almost word for word, we can conveniently cite
their English rendition of Wise's Hebrew:

> Grant peace, welfare, blessing, grace, loving-kindness and
> mercy to us and to all who revere Thee. Bless us, O our Father,
> one and all, with the light of Thy countenance; for by the light

of Thy countenance Thou hast given us, O Lord our God, the
Torah of life, gracious love, charity, blessing, mercy, life and
peace; and may it be good in Thy sight to bless Thy people Israel
and all the other peoples with abundant strength and peace,
    Blessed be Thou, O Lord, Author of Peace.[26]

This prayer for peace as adapted by Wise entered the *Union
Prayer Book*. But the very next paragraph, the silent meditation which follows it, is basically a translation of David Einhorn's modification of a German paraphrase of *Elohai Netsor*
used by the radical Reform community of Berlin:

> O God, guard my tongue from evil and my lips from uttering
> deceit. Be my support when grief silences my voice, and my
> comfort when woe bends my spirit. Plant humility in my soul,
> and strengthen my heart with perfect faith in Thee. Help me to
> be strong when temptations and trials come, and to be meek
> when others wrong me, that I may readily forgive them. Guide
> me by the light of Thy counsel, and let me ever find rest in Thee,
> who art my strength and my redeemer.
>
> May the words of my mouth and the meditations of my heart
> be acceptable in Thy sight, O Lord, my strength and my
> redeemer.[27]

We conclude by citing one of five prayers that the *Union
Prayer Book* offers for Sabbath eve. Here too we see the
eclecticism of American Reform liturgy in the 1890s. Neither
by Wise nor by Einhorn, this prayer originated in a service
manual for Friday night designed by Kaufman Kohler,[28] premier theologian of the Reform movement at the turn of the
century, son-in-law of David Einhorn, and chief editor of the
1895 version of *The Union Prayer* I.[29] A touch grandiloquent
and rather *gemütlich*, the calming prayer is full of associations
with Sabbath eve observance in the home: the kindling of the
Sabbath lamp, the singing of *Shalom Aleikhem* ("Welcome,
Angels [Messengers] of Peace"), the parental blessing of the
children, and the *Kiddush* over a goblet of wine. Adding to the
overall effect are the citations from Scripture skillfully inter-
woven into the prayer: Malachi 3:20; Psalm 133:3; and

Malachi 3:24. Its message exemplifies nineteenth-century Reform optimism, spirituality, and universalism:

> Now that the daily task is laid aside and we are gathered in the house of God, the hush of solemnity comes over us; and we feel a refreshing rest in the holy quiet of the sanctuary. Softer than the twilight calm is that peace that comes to us here with healing on its wings. Like the dew of Mount Hermon falling upon the hills of Zion, it instills new vigor into the tired frame; and the soul, weary from life's stern combats, is refreshed out of the abundance of God's grace. Our daily work is blessed and hallowed by Sabbath-rest, and dignity is given to labor and to life by Sabbath-hours of worship.
>
> When the shades of night veil from our eyes the beauties of the earth, a world of holier splendor opens up before the mind. At eventide, behold, there is light. The brightness of the fireside shines forth to tell that a divine spirit of love holds sway. How solemn life with its joys and its trials appears in the light of the duties and affections of home, how greatly all blessings are enriched, how much all cares and sorrows are softened. It is at this hour, O God, that Thy messenger of peace descends from on high to turn the hearts of the parents to the children and the hearts of the children to the parents, strengthening the bonds of devotion in the household and making it a temple worthy of Thy presence.
>
> We thank Thee, O God, for the sanctity of this day which ever fostered moderation, purity and fidelity in the souls of Israel. The Sabbath light shone into the life of our fathers as a beacon across a storm-tossed sea; it sent its comforting rays into Judah's tents when they were wrapt in the darkness of persecution, and the iron had entered the souls of the martyred race.
>
> Let the day be no less welcome to us now that our lot has fallen in brighter times and pleasanter places. Children of happier lands may we nevertheless prize and preserve Israel's heritage that it bring comfort and joy to us and to future generations. May the Sabbath cup be to us a cup of salvation which we lift up calling upon the name of the Lord. And as this weekly day of rest and worship enjoined by Thy Law has brought blessing to many nations, may it at last unite all men in a covenant of peace and holy fellowship. Amen.

NOTES

1. See A. L. Frumkin, *Seder Rav Amram Hashalem* (Jerusalem, 1912); E. D. Goldschmidt, *Seder Rav Amram Gaon* (Jerusalem, 1971).

2. See Israel Davidson, Simchah Assaf, and B. I. Joel, eds., *Siddur Rav Saadja Gaon . . .* (Jerusalem, 1963).

3. See E. D. Goldschmidt, ed., *Seder Tefillah shel Harambam al pi Ketav-Yad Oxford,* from the seventh volume of the *Makhon Lecheker Hashirah Ha'ivrit* (Jerusalem, 5719 [1959]), pp. 158–213; Jacob I. Dienstag, "The Prayer Book of Moses Maimonides," in Menahem Kasher, ed., *The Leo Jung Jubilee Volume* (New York, 1962), pp. 53–63.

4. See Solomon Buber and J. Freimann, eds., *Siddur Raschi* (Berlin, 1911); reprint ed. (Jerusalem, 1963).

5. See Simchah ben Samuel, *Machzor Vitry,* ed. S. Hurwitz (Nuremberg, 1923); E. D. Goldschmidt, *"Nusach Hatefillot shel Machzor Vitry lefi Ketav-Yad Reggio,"* in *Mechkarei Tefillah Ufiyyut* (Jerusalem, 1979), pp. 66–79.

6. See Abraham Rosenfield, ed., *The Authorized Selichot for the Whole Year,* 2d ed. (London, 1957). It was of such heartfelt collective outpourings that Leopold Zunz remarked in his *Die synagogale Poesie des Mittelalters* (Berlin, 1855), as translated in the Conservative *Sabbath and Festival Prayer Book* (1946): "If there are ranks in suffering, Israel takes precedence of all the nations: if the duration of sorrows and the patience with which they are borne ennoble, the Jews can challenge the aristocracy of every land; if a literature is called rich in the possession of a few classic tragedies— what shall we say to a National Tragedy lasting fifteen hundred years, in which the poets and the actors were also the heroes?"

7. The prayer of the uneducated cowherd found in *Sefer Hasidim* may be found in Nahum N. Glatzer, *Language of Faith* (New York, 1967), pp. 72–73.

8. Isaiah Horowitz, *Shenei Luchot Haberit* I, p. 249b.

9. Jakob J. Petuchowski, "Speaking of God," *Theology and Poetry: Studies in Medieval Piyyut* (London, 1978), pp. 31–47.

10. The individual Hymns of Unity for Sunday through Friday may be found, with helpful explanation, in Seligmann Baer, *Avodat Yisrael* (Roedelheim, 1868), reprint ed. (1937), pp. 133–49. As yet

there is, regrettably, no complete English rendition of all of the *Shirei Hayichud,* perhaps because, practically speaking, there is so little time on regular workday mornings to give them the full devotional concentration they amply deserve. A continuing desideratum is a translation of all these wonderfully luminous/numinous hymns into an English that captures at least a fraction of the layered meaning contained in the Hebrew.

11. See Isaiah Tishby, ed., *Pirkei Zohar* II (Jerusalem, 1969), pp. 79–144.

12. The Aramaic prayer, *Berikh Shemeih,* has this rubric before it: "Rabbi Shimon said, 'When they take the Torah scroll out in the congregation for reading therein, the heavenly gates of compassion are opened and they arouse love above, and one is requested to say this: "Blessed be His name etc." until "for life and for peace"'" (*Zohar, parashat vayak'hel,* p. 369).

13. The translation here is by Philip Birnbaum, *Hasiddur Hashalem: The Daily Prayer Book* (New York, 1949). For a discussion of the indirect polemic concerning a major tenet of the Christian faith contained in *Berikh Shemeih,* see Daniel Chanan Matt, *Zohar: The Book of Enlightenment,* Classics of Western Spirituality (Mahwah, NJ, 1983), pp. 18–19.

14. Nosson Scherman, *Siddur Imrei Ephraim: The Complete ArtScroll Siddur* (New York, 1985), pp. 340–41. See the present-day Conservative *Siddur Sim Shalom* (New York, 1985), pp. 252–53, and the Reconstructionist *Kol Haneshamah: Shabbat Eve* (Wyncote, PA, 1989), pp. 8–11, for a mellisonant and perhaps more evocative if not quite so close English versification by Zalman Schachter-Shalomi. Cf. the bit more literal but degenderized rendition in the Reform *Gates of Prayer* (New York, 1975), p. 159.

15. Perhaps the best comprehensive scholarly treatment of the subject of prayer in Hasidism is Louis Jacobs, *Hasidic Prayer* (New York, 1973). For a summary of the differences between the prayer-centered Hasidim and the learning-centered Mitnaggedim ("Opponents," i.e., eastern European "mainline," nonsectarian Jewry), see Norman Lamm, "Study and Prayer: Their Relative Value in Hasidism and Misnagdism," in *Samuel K. Mirsky Memorial Volume* (Jerusalem and New York, 1970), pp. 37–52.

16. Martin Buber, "The Rung of Prayer," *Ten Rungs* (New York, 1947), pp. 27–33.

17. For the original rabbinic story, see *Pesikta Rabbati* 184b–185a; and one translation of it in Claude G. Montefiore and Herbert Loewe, eds., *A Rabbinic Anthology* (Cleveland, New York, and Philadelphia, 1963 [reprint]), p. 321, no. 835.

18. Shneur Zalman, *Likkutei Amarim [Tanya]*, trans. Nissan Mindel, I (New York, 1972), ch. 38, pp. 224–32, for example. The recovery of the intellectual strain should not by any means be taken to mean any outright rejection of feeling. It was, after all, the same Zalman who prayed, "My Lord and God, I do not desire Your paradise; I do not desire the bliss of the world to come; I desire only You Yourself."

19. Nathan of Nemirov, *Rabbi Nachman's Wisdom*, ed. Zvi Aryeh Rosenfeld, trans. Aryeh Kaplan (Brooklyn, NY, 1973), pp. 9–16, 179–82, 305–307.

20. E.g., the same entreaty for peace in *Gates of Prayer*, p. 694, and in *Siddur Sim Shalom*, pp. 416–17. All of the moving supplications by the Bratslaver *rebbe* in the present abovementioned American Reform and Conservative rites come from his *Likkutei Tefillot*, ed. Nathan Sternartz of Nemirov, via the British Liberal *Service of the Heart*, ed. John Rayner and Chaim Stern (London, 1967), p. 282; and Glatzer, *Language of Faith*, pp. 314–15.

21. Lionel Blue and Jonathan Magonet, eds., *Forms of Prayers for Jewish Worship* (London, 1977), p. 349.

22. Hardy protagonist of Orthodoxy as Hirsch was, he was scarcely immune to all the arguments of his Reform coevals. In his synagogues he introduced a choir (all male, as would be expected, and without musical instruments) and, provoking a good bit of controversy, did away with the sacrosanct *Kol Nidre* formula chanted on Yom Kippur eve. He strongly endorsed the classical Reform doctrine of the Mission of Israel to all humankind. See Noah H. Rosenbloom, *Tradition in an Age of Reform* (Philadelphia, 1976), pp. 69–70.

23. The authoritative history of Reform Judaism is Michael A. Meyer, *Response to Modernity* (New York and Oxford, 1988).

24. Leopold Zunz, *Die synagogale Poesie;* and idem, *Die Ritus des synagogalen Gottesdienstes* (Berlin, 1859), among others.

25. The best—and only—detailed survey of all the Reform, Liberal, and Progressive liturgies in Europe since their beginnings is Jakob J. Petuchowski, *Prayerbook Reform in Europe* (New York, 1968).

26. Isaac M. Wise et al., *Minhag America: Daily Prayers* (Cincinnati, 1857); *The [Reconstructionist] Sabbath Prayer Book* (New York, 1945).

27. David Einhorn, *Olath Tamid: Gebetbuch für Israelitische Reform-Gemeinden* (Baltimore, 1848); *Olath Tamid: Book of Prayers for Jewish Congregations,* trans. Emil G. Hirsch (Chicago, 1896).

28. Kaufmann Kohler, *Sabbath Eve Service* (New York, 1891).

29. Central Conference of American Rabbis, *The Union Prayer Book for Jewish Worship* I (New York, 1895), pp. 35–38; cf. the last edition of the Reform rite to carry Kohler's prayer—with some stylistic emendations—*The Union Prayer Book for Jewish Worship* I (New York, 1940), pp. 62–63.

Christian Worship
to the Eve of the Reformation

JOHN F. BALDOVIN

[Editors' note: John Baldovin, Associate Professor of Liturgy at the Jesuit School of Theology, Berkeley, California, describes what is known of early Christian liturgical practices and shows how these became gradually modified in the course of later history up to the time of western Christianity's great upheaval, the sixteenth-century Reformation.]

Christian worship developed in both continuity and discontinuity with the worship of Israel. It also interacted with the various cultures in which Christians were situated. From the very beginning, the complex cultural world of the late Roman Empire (and even beyond the boundaries of the empire) inspired a variety of approaches to Christian faith and to liturgical practice as well.[1] The constant element within the variety of expressions of faith and worship was the acknowledgment of the radical centrality of the person of Jesus of Nazareth.[2] The story of Christian worship can be understood as the development of this christocentric insight as well as the adaptation (or readaptation) of cultic forms, especially in terms of sacred times and sacred places, by people who called themselves Christians. In an era that did not know printing, much less telecommunications, the pace and nature of these adaptations could vary greatly. Only with the advent of printing would liturgies be standardized.[3] Before that, despite efforts to homogenize various rites, we always find a good deal of divergence.

The fourteen centuries surveyed here will be divided into three periods: ante-Nicene (i.e., up to the Council of Nicea, C.E. 325); classic (the fourth to sixth centuries—to the death of Pope Gregory the Great, C.E. 604, in the West and the century of the emperor Justinian in the East); and medieval (a broad designation for both East and West ending with the fall of Constantinople, 1453, in the East and the beginning of the Protestant Reformation, 1516, in the West). Periodization is always to some extent a falsification, especially when one deals with a popular phenomenon like worship. We will be able to discern, however, major shifts that enable us to speak of distinct eras in liturgical development. The other major distinction to be noted is that of East and West in Christianity, a distinction that will become clearer when we treat the classic and medieval periods.

ANTE-NICENE WORSHIP

General Characteristics

In the first three centuries of its existence, the Christian movement spread throughout the Mediterranean world and beyond the eastern frontier of the Roman Empire. Christians were to be found mainly in the cities: Christianity was an urban phenomenon.[4] Major conflicts—with the Jews, with gnostic brands of Christian faith, and with secular authorities—forced the movement to define itself, especially in the latter half of the second century, and thus to canonize its own Scripture (which now included what we know as the New Testament) and line of authoritative tradition, called apostolic succession. It is probable that in a large city like Rome, several Christian language groups with varying practices existed at least up until the end of the second century.[5] It is also probable that the diverse cultures in which Christians found themselves inspired different ways of ritualizing the Christian experience. Therefore, the attempt to find the original source of a liturgical form is often fruitless. However, certain common elements can be discerned, among them the necessity of water baptism for initiation and the celebration of a ritual meal called the eucharist.

It also seems that Christian worship was in the main a private affair. As Gregory Dix correctly pointed out, this does not mean that it was individualistic, for it seems to have been inherently corporate; rather, Christians as members of an illicit religion were constrained to meet in private houses rather than public temples or meeting halls.[6] Thus, ante-Nicene Christian worship was shaped by its domestic setting. Very few examples of places for Christian worship have been unearthed for this period, but those that have been found point to a private setting, even when walls have been removed to provide a larger meeting space.[7]

A third characteristic of Christian worship in the first three hundred years was its improvisational nature. We possess very few written texts for this period, perhaps because prayers were offered freely, though within a defined structure. Several early Christian writings attest to the fact that the eucharistic prayer was improvised.[8] Moreover, the texts that we do possess are not full liturgies in the modern sense of a liturgical text but rather collections of prayers without directions or with very few directions, for example, as are found in the early church orders.[9] Other sources for the study of early Christian liturgy include letters, Christian apologies, sermons, manuscript fragments, and archeological remains.

Initiation

The earliest attestation to Christian baptism outside the New Testament can be found in the proto–church order, called the *Didache,* a document whose provenance is most likely Syria at the end of the first century or the beginning of the second. Here Christians are instructed to baptize after instruction and one or two days of prayer and fasting for both the candidates and those who are to perform the baptism. The baptism is to be performed in cold running water, but if neither cold nor warm running water are available, then water may be poured over the head of the candidate while the trinitarian formula ("in the name of the Father and Son and Holy Spirit") is invoked.[10] Only the baptized are to be admitted to the eucharist. Basically the same information is provided by a mid-second-century Roman witness, Justin Martyr. He adds that baptism is called "enlightenment, because those who are experiencing these things have their minds enlightened," and makes it clear that the culmination of the initiatory rite is participation in the eucharistic meal.[11]

Up to this point we have no evidence of anointing or other auxiliary practices allied with the ritual of the baptismal act. Whether or not such additional rituals were performed has been the subject of much debate.[12] By the beginning of the third century, however, the *Apostolic Tradition,* attributed to Hippolytus of Rome,[13] witnesses an elaborate interrogation of the candidates (called *catechumens* from the Greek for "hearers"); a three-year process of preparation (the catechumenate) including prayer, fasting, and exorcisms; and baptism on the night between Saturday and Sunday.[14] The initiatory rite itself included a prebaptismal renunciation of Satan and an anointing of the body with the oil of exorcism, immersion in water three times accompanied by three credal questions, anointing of the body with the oil of thanksgiving, and (after being clothed and led into the assembly) a hand-laying by the bishop with prayer and a further anointing on the forehead.[15] The rite concluded with the exchange of a kiss with the bishop, common prayers, the kiss of peace with all, and the celebration of the eucharist. The elements of this structure are corroborated by the earliest Christian Latin writer from North Africa in the early third century, Tertullian.[16]

This pattern of baptism–anointing–eucharist is not the only one to be found in the ante-Nicene period. Evidence from Syria reveals a pattern of anointing–baptism–eucharist in which there is no postbaptismal anointing. Moreover, the prebaptismal anointing signifies not exorcism and purification but rather alliance with the royal-messianic anointing of Jesus at the Jordan.[17] Thus the ante-Nicene churches knew several theological models for Christian initiation.

Eucharist

The eucharist (= Greek "thanksgiving") is the ritual meal that served not only as the culmination of the initiatory process but also as the ongoing ritual focus of Christian assembly. It is impossible to tell with any certitude how frequently it was celebrated in the ante-Nicene period, for frequency seems to have varied from place to place.[18] Perhaps even as early as the late first century, ritual elements were distinguished from the ordinary communal meal.[19] At any rate by the mid-second century the eucharistic rite was definitively separated from the communal meal, which came to be called the *agape* (Greek, "love [feast]") and eventually died out. At the same time a service of readings was added to the beginning of the eucharistic rite itself. The latter consisted of a four-action shape: taking, blessing, breaking, giving—the offering of bread and wine, eucharistic prayer, breaking of the bread (fraction), and consumption of the bread and wine (communion)—as an imitation of Jesus' actions at the Last Supper.[20] Some ascetic groups, however, seem to have substituted water for wine.[21]

The first description of a liturgy that combined a ministry of the word with the eucharist is found in Justin Martyr (mid–second century).[22] Justin's report of the Sunday assembly reveals the following structure:

Readings
Preaching
Common Prayers
Kiss of Peace
Presentation of Bread and Wine
Eucharistic Prayer
(Fraction)
Communion
(Dismissal)

The readings were taken from both the Hebrew Scriptures and the "Memoirs of the Apostles" (presumably the writings that make up the New Testament). The "president"[23] extemporized the eucharistic prayer. Though no mention is made of the fraction and dismissal, they must have taken place, given their functional nature in the service, and they are witnessed a half-century later in a similar description given by Hippolytus.[24]

By far the greatest part of scholarly attention with regard to the ante-Nicene eucharist has centered on the origin, nature, and development of the eucharistic prayer or *anaphora* (Greek, "[prayer of] offering"). Most scholars are agreed today that its origins lie in Jewish prayers, but since the rabbinic sources postdate the New Testament writings, there is little agreement as to precisely how it developed out of the prayer tradition of Israel. For the greater part of the past century, attention centered on the *berakhah* (blessing) and more specifically on the *Birkat hamazon* (blessing of the meal = concluding grace after meals), but more recently the rabbinic prayer form whose operative verb is some form of the root *ydh* (as in *modim* or *nodeh*)—usually translated as "give thanks"—has been suggested as the more proximate ancestor of eucharistic prayers.[25]

One of the major questions with regard to the anaphora has been the function of the narrative of the institution of the eucharist, which in later western theological reckoning formed the central or consecratory part of the prayer. However, some of the earliest examples of the eucharistic prayer do not contain an institution narrative, but rather thanksgiving and praise to God for Christ are joined with petition for the coming of the kingdom. One must also keep in mind that for the ante-Nicene period we possess only a few witnesses to the anaphora and that these witnesses themselves stem from an era in which improvisation of the prayer was the norm.

From this rudimentary nucleus, as it were, a number of diverse and expanded forms developed, which included an initial thanksgiving series for God and the work of creation, the acclamation "Holy, Holy, Holy" (the Sanctus, which may have been derived from the *Kedushah* of the synagogue by way of Christian daily prayer),[26] an expanded anamnesis

(memorial) and (ultimately) consecratory epiclesis (or invocation of the Holy Spirit), and a series of intercessions for the
living and the dead.[27]

Feasts and Seasons

In several ways, the early calendar reflects Christianity's
origins in the faith of Israel. The major feasts of Pascha (Easter) and Pentecost are transformations of Jewish festivals. The
celebration of the Lord's Day (Sunday) correlates with the
septenary rhythm of the Sabbath. The fast days, Wednesday
and Friday, are consciously distinguished from the Jewish
fasts on Mondays and Thursdays.

The earliest Christian feast is Sunday, the first day of the
week, the Lord's Day. There is considerable debate on the
question of how long and which groups of primitive Christians
observed the Sabbath, but at least there are glimmers in the
New Testament (Acts 20:7ff.; 1 Cor. 16:2; Rev. 1:10) that
some Christians were observing Sunday in a special manner
in the first century.[28] In any case, the Sunday eucharistic observance of Jesus' death and resurrection, or the weekly
Pascha, was universal by the middle of the second century.[29]

The annual celebration of Jesus' death and resurrection took
place in conjunction with the Jewish Passover. The first groups
to celebrate this annual Pascha, most probably in Asia Minor,
did so on the night of the fourteenth of Nisan—hence their
designation as Quartodecimans. This meant, of course, that it
would be celebrated on whatever day of the week this date fell.
Eusebius relates a controversy late in the second century over
this observance that conflicted with the Roman practice of an
annual Pascha observed on Sunday. It is possible that Rome
and other churches observed only the weekly Pascha up to the
mid–second century and that the origins of the controversy
concerned whether or not to observe an annual Pascha at all.
Rome and most other churches settled on observing the Pascha
on a Sunday, but the final decision as to how this Sunday was
to be determined was not made until the Council of Nicea.[30]

The celebration of the paschal feast lasted fifty days in the ante-Nicene period, thus culminating with the fiftieth day (Greek, *Pentecoste*); i.e., the equivalent of the Jewish feast of Weeks.[31] The fifty days seem to have been a period of continuous joyful celebration in which neither fasting nor kneeling were allowed.

As we have seen it was customary to prepare for Christian initiation by fasting. At Rome in the ante-Nicene period this may have been three weeks. In any event, as Pascha became the occasion for the major annual celebration of initiation, this fast was added to the already existing fast related to Pascha, a fast that could last several days or even a week. Talley has argued that the forty-day Lenten fast preceding Pascha actually had it origins in an Alexandrian fast that began on January 7 (the day after Epiphany, January 6) and imitated the fast of Jesus in the wilderness according to the chronology of Mark's Gospel. This fast culminated in Christian initiation in mid-February, not at the annual Pascha. Further, he has suggested that the origins of the Christian calendar may be found in a course-reading of the Gospels beginning on Epiphany.[32]

Whether or not the birth of Christ was celebrated by a special feast in the ante-Nicene period has also been debated. Contrary to the older (still popular) hypothesis that both the western feast of Christmas (December 25) and the eastern feast of Epiphany (from the Greek, "manifestation"—January 6) originated in a post-Nicene adoption of pagan solar festivals, Talley has argued for an ante-Nicene origin of these feasts in the attempt of Christians to correlate Christ's birth chronologically with his death, in some traditions dated to March 25 and in others to April 6.[33] Whether ante- or post-Nicene, the earliest stage of both Christmas and Epiphany seems to have been a unitive celebration of Christ's incarnation rather than a feast focusing on one or another aspect such as his birth or baptism. The same can be said for the Pascha, which celebrated not only Christ's resurrection but his death and resurrection as a unified event.

Much of the current debate on the origins of the liturgical

year has turned on the theory of Gregory Dix that ante-Nicene
Christians had an eschatological view of time, wherein historical
dates and feasts were of minor importance, and that the new
situation brought about under Constantine, in which Christianity was made legitimate, inspired an historicized concept of
time that led to a multiplication of feasts.[34] Though there is
considerable merit to Dix's argument, it needs a great deal of
nuance. Concern with historical dates and facts was not new
to the post-Constantinian Christians of the fourth century.[35]

Another important element in the development of the Christian calendar was the observance of the memorials of the
saints. Closely tied to the general Christian cult of the dead,
but on a larger basis (that of the extended Christian family),
the martyrs were remembered with the celebration of the
eucharist at their graves on their yearly anniversary. Thus the
ante-Nicene origins of saints' days were strictly local, tied to
the possession of relics by their own Christian community.[36]

Liturgical Prayer

Very little can be said with certainty about the nature of
corporate Christian liturgical prayer in the ante-Nicene period.
Various set times for prayer are recommended in different
ante-Nicene Christian writers: on rising; at the third, sixth, and
ninth hours; on retiring; and at night. In addition, some writers
mention mealtimes and cockcrow.[37] Tertullian speaks of
prayer at morning and evening as *legitimae orationes* (official
or statutory prayers).[38]

It had been common to suppose that morning and evening
prayer were celebrated in common in the ante-Nicene Church.
Bradshaw and Taft have shown, however, that this puts too
much weight on Tertullian's "official prayers." In addition,
Taft has pointed to the eschatological nature of Christian
prayer, the likelihood that speaking of morning, noon, and
night was a way of saying "pray always," and the anachronism
of making the distinction between private and public prayer

for this period.[39] The extent to which Christian prayer was in continuity with Jewish daily prayer continues to be debated.[40]

THE CLASSIC PERIOD

General Characteristics

There can be little doubt that the fourth-century imperial acceptance of Christianity brought about profound changes in the way Christians worshiped. Though these changes have at times been exaggerated, as in Dix's theory of historicization, we can discern some major shifts in Christian liturgy that are attributable to the Constantinian revolution.

In the first place, the scale of Christian worship was transformed from the mainly domestic setting of the early Church to the great basilicas and shrines funded by the emperor and other wealthy benefactors. Christian basilicas were particularly important, for they signified the move of Christian worship into public space. The basic basilican form was that of a public meeting place—as imperial court, court of justice, assembly hall, etc. It was transformed on a longitudinal axis to meet the requirements of Christian processions, many of which began in outdoor public spaces.[41]

The new scale of Christian liturgy also encouraged the adoption of further ceremonialization, mostly drawn from the imperial court. The result was, at least in the major cities, what Aidan Kavanagh has called "liturgy on the town," the use of public streets and places as well as Christian shrines and basilicas for an open manifestation of Christianity as the major religious force in society.[42] In addition, different churches and shrines were employed for liturgy on different feast and fast days, creating systems that have been called stational liturgy.[43]

The second factor brought about in part by the changed political and social situation of the fourth century was the standardization of liturgical texts and forms. The influx of a

large number of people into the Church diluted the quality of
its leadership, and this, as well as growing concern over orthodox formulations of the Christian faith, especially the Arian
crisis and its aftermath, encouraged the writing down of set
texts for liturgical use.[44]

The new social climate was almost certainly also influential
in the creation of monasticism, the banding together of ascetics
who flourished in a kind of living martyrdom now that the age
of persecution had ended.[45] This Christian form of life, atten-
tive as it was to contemplation, resulted in attitudes toward
Christian worship and liturgical forms that were to be of permanent significance.

Another important factor in the development of Christian
liturgy in the fourth century is the origin of the Roman rite.
For the first time in the latter half of the century we find
Christian liturgical texts in Latin.[46] The use of this language
for worship was to mean the development in the West of a
liturgical ethos different from the Greek-speaking East. Moreover, in this period, one finds the gradual growth of various
centers for Christian worship, centers that consolidated local
practice and led to the creation of different rites.[47] In the fourth
century itself, however, one can still discern more similarities
than differences in the liturgical practice of major centers like
Antioch, Alexandria, Jerusalem, Rome, and Constantinople.
In subsequent centuries these centers were to create distinctive
liturgical rites, though not without some mutual dependence.

Initiation

The fourth to the sixth centuries offer a rich mine of information on the practice of Christian initiation. This is the era
of the great *mystagogiae* (explanations of the mysteries),
which provide both description of the ceremonies as well as
theological reflection on them. They were preached by bishops
or presbyters as expositions on the sacramental events either
before or after they took place. The four greatest mystagogical
collections of the late fourth century are those of Cyril (Jerusa-

lem), Ambrose (Milan), John Chrysostom (Antioch), and Theodore of Mopsuestia (Syria).[48] In addition, archeological evidence has aided the reconstruction of baptismal practice.[49]

A lengthy preparation for initiation (catechumenate) seems to have flourished in the fourth century. Its success, i.e., the conversion of the masses to Christianity, doomed it to extinction, since within a relatively short period infant, not adult, initiation predominated. We have no idea of whether the lengthy and elaborate catechumenate alluded to by the fourth-century writers was ever more than an ideal for a limited number of people, for we do have evidence of quick mass conversions and baptism.[50] In any case there seems to have been a stress on keeping the baptismal instructions as well as the rites themselves secret (the *disciplina arcani)* so as to increase their solemnity and importance. There can be little doubt that a certain air of mystification, seemingly absent in the ante-Nicene period, characterized the rites of initiation in the fourth century and afterward.[51]

From the fourth century on, we note increased attention given to the period of immediate preparation for the rites of initiation. The candidates give in their names and are examined at the beginning of Lent. The Lenten period serves as a time of intense preparation by prayer, fasting, and instruction, culminating in the rites of initiation at the Easter Vigil.

The classic period also witnesses an elaboration of the ceremonies of initiation themselves. Elements like the clothing with a new white garment after baptism and the giving of a lighted candle to the newly initiated become part of every liturgical tradition.[52] Even more important, the prebaptismal anointing, which we have seen had a royal-messianic tone in the Syrian tradition, now begins to take on a purificatory and exorcistic meaning as we found in the third-century *Apostolic Tradition* in the West. Gradually the Syrian rites adopt a post-baptismal anointing, which seems to take over the meaning of the old prebaptismal anointing.[53]

Perhaps even more significant than the development of the rites is the theological commentary found in writing of this period. The manner of explanation that predominates is typology, whereby images from the Hebrew Scriptures have found their authentic expression in Christian practice and also in which the Christian rites themselves act as symbols or reflections of Christ.[54] Moreover, in the fourth century we find a kind of renaissance in the Pauline theology of baptism, emphasizing the symbolic act of death and burial with Christ (Romans 6:3–9). The development of commentaries on the liturgical ceremonies also encouraged a certain identification of the meaning of each aspect of the rite. Thus the postbaptismal anointing and/or episcopal imposition of hands were related to the gift of the Holy Spirit.[55] In the medieval period the assigning of discrete meanings to various parts of the rite was to lead to a distinct theology of confirmation, especially in the West, where baptism and confirmation became separated in time.

Eucharist

Nowhere did the post-Constantinian transformation of the scale of worship have a greater impact than on the eucharist. Requirements of large spaces and a greater number of people led to expansion of this recurring ritual especially at the points where movement took place: the entrance, the presentation of the gifts, and communion. Robert Taft refers to these as the "soft points" of the liturgy, elements that had a tendency to expand with prayer and psalmody to cover the longer time required for liturgical actions.[56] Here we find the raison d'être for the expansion of psalmody and litanies in the eucharistic rites of both East and West.[57]

On the other hand, we find in this period that the service of readings begins to contract. Justin Martyr had reported that the Hebrew Scriptures and New Testament material were read at the Sunday assembly for as long as time permitted. In the fourth century, before the expansion at the soft points of the liturgy, there seem to have been several scriptural readings prior to the reading from the gospel, which always came last. With the exception of certain solemn occasions, most rites reduced the number of readings before the gospel to one, usually taken from the New Testament.[58]

In the classic period of liturgical development one can discern a certain settling in of the various traditions of the eucharistic prayer, even though most of the manuscripts were written later. In the East we find three major traditions: the Antiochene (West Syrian), Alexandrian, and East Syrian. Although all of these traditions exhibit common contents (i.e., praise of God, Sanctus, institution narrative, epiclesis, developed intercessions), they differ in structure. The Antiochene or West Syrian structure is similar to the anaphora of the *Apostolic Tradition* but is much expanded. Important examples are the Anaphora of St. Basil, whose earliest recension may even predate Nicea and was later expanded into the form still currently in use by the Byzantine churches,[59] the Anaphora of St. James (from Jerusalem), the Anaphora of book 8 of the *Apostolic Constitutions,* and the most commonly employed eucharistic prayer in the Byzantine churches, the Anaphora of St. John Chrysostom.

The Alexandrian tradition, represented most clearly by the Anaphora of St. Mark, places the intercessions within the first part of the anaphora (i.e., before the Sanctus) and provides a first epiclesis before the institution narrative. The East Syrian tradition has been the object of much recent scholarly attention, for its most important representative, the Anaphora of Addai and Mari, lacks an institution narrative.[60] This tradition is even more complex in that the address of the anaphora shifts from God to Christ and its structure is far less linear than that of the Antiochene prayers. Some scholars have found in Addai and Mari and in its "cousin," the third Maronite Anaphora of St. Peter, a link back to the Jewish Grace after Meals (*Birkat hamazon*).[61]

The western traditions of the eucharistic prayer are somewhat simpler to describe. The prayer in the Roman rite, whose origins can be traced back to the late fourth and fifth centuries, is characterized by a predominance of sacrificial vocabulary, a split in the intercessions, with those for the living coming after the Sanctus and those for the dead toward the end of the prayer, and a variable pre-Sanctus section (called the *pref-*

ace).[62] There are, however, two other traditions in the West: the Gallican (from the region of modern-day France, Belgium, and Germany) and the Mozarabic (more properly Visigothic, from the Iberian peninsula). Both of these traditions are similar in that they follow the Antiochene pattern and their three main sections are always variable. For the most part, both of these traditions were replaced by the Roman rite in the medieval period.

A number of questions about the eucharistic prayer are currently disputed, among them whether the anaphora described by Cyril of Jerusalem contained an institution narrative,[63] the nature of the consecratory epiclesis and a developed theology of a moment of consecration,[64] and the precise meaning of sacrificial language in the prayers.[65]

Feasts and Seasons

A full development of what we know as the Christian calendar came about during the classic period. The year became divided into two cycles: (1) Christmas, Epiphany, the feasts of the saints and all other feasts that depend on a fixed date; and (2) Easter and the feasts and seasons dependent upon it, which are arranged according to the moveable date of Easter itself.

In the fourth-century, Christmas (December 25, originally western) and Epiphany (January 6—originally eastern) are gradually adopted by churches of the other region. In the East, Epiphany, which had been a unitive feast celebrating the whole of the incarnation, now becomes a feast of the baptism of Christ, and Christmas celebrates his nativity. In the West, Epiphany became the celebration of the baptism of Christ and his manifestation to the nations (represented by the Magi story of Matthew chapter 2), though at Rome the celebration was limited to the appearance to the Magi.[66] In most places major feasts were accompanied by an octave—eight days of liturgical celebration, often employing different urban churches.

A forty-day period of preparation for Easter became standard in the course of the fourth century, though the forty days were reckoned in different ways by the various churches.[67] In its origin this forty-day Lent seems to have been a way for the entire church to participate in the preparation of the candidates for initiation by prayer, fasting, and good works. Especially involved were those members of the community who had been excluded from the eucharist because of their sins.[68] As adult initiation waned, the penitential practice of the greater community loomed larger in Lenten observance.

Another important development in the shape of the calendar was the increasing articulation of Pentecost, the originally unitive fifty-day period of rejoicing following Easter. By the late fourth century one finds a celebration of the Ascension of Christ according to the Lukan chronology, i.e., on the fortieth day after Easter. By the fifth century in the West one finds some churches including fast days between Ascension and the day of Pentecost. Even later, in the seventh century, one finds an octave attached to Pentecost.[69]

A final development of major significance for the liturgical year was the expansion of the cult of the saints to include nonmartyrs, i.e., bishops and others who had witnessed to the Christian faith in an exemplary manner. As was mentioned above, the cult of the saints was originally tied to their tombs, i.e., their relics. Gradually relics were transferred to other churches and so the anniversaries of the saints were celebrated by those churches as well. A final stage in the process was the universalization of saints' feasts. They were celebrated by churches whether or not they possessed relics. Up until the invention of printing, however, each church's calendar of the saints retained a local character.[70]

Liturgical Prayer

The fourth century signals the development of the history of public liturgical prayer. For the first time we have indisputable evidence that Christians were gathering corporately for daily liturgical services. In the past century an important distinction was made by Anton Baumstark between two original types of daily office, types which eventually became mixed.[71] The first type, commonly called *cathedral* prayer, is popular

prayer of the church assembled with its leadership, characterized by the use of psalms and hymns that correspond to the
hour of the day, attention to ceremonial and ritual details like
lights and incense, and the presence of the bishop as presider
over the prayer. The content of the cathedral office consisted
of praise and intercession with very little didactic reading of
Scripture. One of the clearest examples of this form of daily
office can be found in the diary of Egeria, a western pilgrim
in Jerusalem at the end of the fourth century.[72]

The second form of daily office has been called *monastic*.
Originating with the ascetics of Egypt, the ethos of this style
of prayer lent itself more to contemplation with very little
ritualization.[73] Here the content of the two main hours of
prayer, before retiring and upon rising, had little to do with
the hour of the day but rather consisted of the psalms and other
Scripture, an attempt to aid the ascetic in the goal of continuous prayer.

Most of the developed daily offices in both East and West
are of a type that mixes the monastic and cathedral traditions.
The primary example in the West is the office found in the
sixth-century Rule of Benedict, which was to become the fore-
most exemplar of monastic tradition in that part of Christen-
dom.[74] This mandates eight daily offices: matins (in the middle
of the night), lauds (upon rising), prime (shortly after lauds),
terce (at the third hour), sext (at noon), none (at the ninth
hour), vespers (in the early evening), and compline (before
retiring). It should be noted that the vast majority of nonscrip-
tural ecclesiastical compositions called hymns originate not in
the eucharist but rather with the daily office.

THE MEDIEVAL PERIOD

In the East

From the seventh century on, it is necessary to distinguish
between East and West in dealing with the history of Christian

worship. The new Rome, Constantinople, soon became preoc-
cupied with the threat of Islam, which from the middle of the
seventh century dominated the once-Christian Near East.
Moreover, in the wake of the Councils of Ephesus (431) and
Chalcedon (451), eastern Christianity had experienced a split
in its ranks with much of Syrian and Egyptian as well as
Armenian Christianity belonging to the party called Mono-
physite.[75] Here we shall focus on the Byzantine rite, i.e., the
rite dependent on the city of Constantinople. The Byzantine
Empire itself, it should be remembered, experienced a massive
struggle over iconoclasm in the eighth and ninth centuries, a
struggle that saw the monastic (or iconodule) party emerge
victorious.

The liturgy of the capital city of Constantinople had a major
influence on the medieval development of the Byzantine rite.
The city's local calendar, with its commemorations of special
events in civic life, such as earthquakes and sieges, and its
outdoor processional liturgy, centering on the forums and major avenues as well as Justinian's Great Church (Hagia Sophia)
and a number of important shrines, were adapted throughout
churches of the Byzantine rite.[76] After the eleventh century the
once-popular outdoor processions were in a sense miniatur-
ized, i.e., brought within the walls of the church, accounting
for a good deal of the processional activity in the liturgy as
we know it.

While the contemporary Byzantine eucharist reflects the
cathedral practice of Constantinople, the daily liturgical prayer
or Divine Office of the Byzantine rite owes more to the monastic
tradition. This tradition, stemming mainly from the Palestinian
monastery of St. Sabas, became the dominant form of liturgical
prayer after the Latin conquest of the Fourth Crusade (1204).[77]

Rich theological commentary accompanied the development of
the liturgy, particularly of the eucharist. These commentaries
tended to understand the liturgy as either a mirror of the interior or spiritual life (after the mode of Alexandrian theology)
or a representation of the mysteries of salvation in Christ (Antiochene mode). Among the more important Byzantine liturgi-

cal commentaries are those of Maximus the Confessor (mid–seventh century), Germanus of Constantinople (mid–eighth century), and Nicholas Cabasilas (mid-fourteenth century).[78]

In the West

The history of liturgical development in the West is ultimately the story of the dominance of the Roman rite. In the course of the Middle Ages the rite of the city of Rome won out over other local western rites because of the symbolic centrality and importance of the old capital of the Roman Empire. Several other rites, however, did flourish for a time. The major non-Roman western rites are Ambrosian (the rite of Milan, which in many respects was very similar to the Roman), Gallican (the rite of modern-day France, Germany, and Belgium, which was heavily influenced by the Eastern rites), and Mozarabic (the rite of the Visigothic Iberian peninsula).[79] The eighth-century liturgical reform of Pepin, king of the Franks, which was continued under his son, Charlemagne, included an attempt to romanize the Gallican liturgy. This movement, aided by the scholarly work of the monks Alcuin and Benedict of Aniane, was to some extent successful, but in the process a number of Gallican elements were mixed with the (pure) Roman liturgy, whose genius was "sobriety and sense."[80] A similar transformation of the Spanish liturgy was undertaken in the eleventh century in the wake of the Gregorian reform. Many of the elements once considered most characteristic of the Roman rite, like the ceremonial use of incense and the multiplication of private prayers (*apologiae*) of the priest, actually arose as features of the Gallican and Mozarabic rites.

As in the East, the texts of the western liturgical books were arranged for those who employed them during the liturgy. There were originally no complete prayer books containing all of the texts for a single type of celebration, but rather sacramentaries (containing the prayers said by the priest), lectionaries (sometimes subdivided for gospel and epistle readers), antiphonaries (for those who lead the chants), and *ordines*. An *ordo* contained the special directions for a particular liturgy.[81] As more and more of the ministerial functions of the eucharist were relegated to the officiating priest,[82] all these texts were collected in a book called the missal.

There were a number of other significant developments in medieval western liturgy, among them the retention of Latin as a liturgical language as the various national languages developed; the placement of the altar at the east wall of the church, with the priest facing the wall to pray; the elongation of the choir in Romanesque and Gothic churches, with the result that the people were farther away from the altar and the focus of liturgical action; and the silent recitation of the eucharistic prayer. Moreover, the shift of western Christian influence to the lands north of the Alps also corresponded with a significant transformation of Christian piety—from a more communally centered sense of divine presence to one that focused on the holiness of things, and hence a certain reification or objectification of worship.[83]

The central event of Christian worship, the eucharist, thus became an event celebrated in a foreign tongue, with less and less participation—at most masses the priest alone received communion and the people were silent. By the eleventh century the use of unleavened bread for the consecrated host had become widespread. Around the same time communion in the chalice was withdrawn from the faithful, perhaps out of an exaggerated fear of spilling the precious blood, with the result that the eucharist became a visual experience whose pinnacle was seeing the consecrated host. The practice of elevating the host began around the thirteenth century.[84]

Just as the eucharist became the property of the clergy, so too daily liturgical prayer became more and more the province of professionals—the clergy and the monks. One sign of the decline of popular participation in the liturgy of the hours can be found in the development in the thirteenth century of the breviary, a book containing all of the psalmody, prayers, and readings for the office. This book, which arose out of the needs of the Roman curia, was quickly adopted by the Franciscans and thus popularized.[85] At the same time shorter offices, like the Office of the Blessed Virgin Mary, were developed for lay people.[86]

In the course of the Middle Ages the classical integrity of the sacraments of initiation was dissolved in the West. While the eastern churches retained the traditional unity of the sacraments, with baptism and a postbaptismal chrismation followed by reception of the eucharist even when a bishop was not present to do the postbaptismal anointing,[87] the western churches opted to maintain the role of the bishop in postbaptismal chrismation. With the growth of the church and its expansion to rural areas, this meant that although infants were baptized soon after birth (because of the danger of dying in original sin), they had to wait for the bishop to come before they could be confirmed and receive the laying-on of hands. Thus confirmation developed in the West as a separate sacrament, which eventually received its own theological justification as a gift of the Holy Spirit for the strengthening of growth in the Christian life.[88]

Unlike the Christian East, where commentary on the liturgy was the major form of theological interpretation, the West developed two forms of theological reflection on worship. The first consisted of commentary on the liturgy similar to that found in Maximus the Confessor and Germanus of Constantinople. Its first representative was Amalarius of Metz (ninth century), who treated the liturgy in allegorical fashion, though not without opposition. Perhaps the most florid example of this type of commentary can be found in the work of the bishop Durandus of Mende (fourteenth century).[89] The ninth century also saw the beginnings of theological treatises and controversies about the eucharist in the debate between Paschasius Radbertus and Ratramnus, both monks of Corbie in northern France. With the rise of scholastic theology in the twelfth century came further development of technical reflection on the sacraments that was increasingly distanced from their liturgical celebration and focused on their interior meaning.[90]

NOTES

1. See, for example, J. G. Dunn, *Unity and Diversity in the New Testament* (Philadelphia, 1977).

2. See Robert F. Taft, *The Liturgy of the Hours in East and West* (Collegeville, 1986), pp. 334–40; Ferdinand Hahn, *The Worship of the Early Church* (Philadelphia, 1973), pp. 12–31.

3. On the impact of printing on liturgy, see Aidan Kavanagh, *On Liturgical Theology* (New York, 1984), pp. 103–6, 114, 119.

4. See Wayne A. Meeks, *The First Urban Christians* (New Haven, 1983); John F. Baldovin, *The Urban Character of Christian Worship* (Rome, 1987), pp. 253–59.

5. See George La Piana, "The Roman Church at the End of the Second Century," *HTR* 18 (1925): 201–77.

6. Gregory Dix, *The Shape of the Liturgy* (Westminster, 1945), pp. 12–35. Christians were subject to sporadic rather than continuous persecution, but they remained officially illicit up to Constantine (313 C.E.): see W. H. C. Frend, *Martyrdom and Persecution in Early Christianity* (Oxford, 1965).

7. See Robert Milburn, *Early Christian Art and Architecture* (Berkeley, 1988), pp. 8–18.

8. For example, *Didache* 11; Justin Martyr, *I Apol.* 67; Hippolytus, *Apostolic Tradition* 9. For a convenient collection of early liturgical texts in English translation, see Lucien Deiss, ed., *Springtime of the Liturgy* (Collegeville, 1979). On the improvisational nature of the eucharistic prayer, see Allan Bouley, *From Freedom to Formula* (Washington, DC, 1981).

9. As Paul F. Bradshaw points out in his essay above these church orders are not necessarily examples of liturgies that were actually celebrated.

10. *Didache* 7. The most useful collection in English translation of texts on initiation is E. C. Whitaker, *Documents of the Baptismal Liturgy,* 2d ed. (London, 1970).

11. Justin Martyr, *I Apol.* 61.

12. See, e.g., L. L. Mitchell, *Baptismal Anointing* (London, 1966); G. H. Lampe, *The Seal of the Spirit* (London, 1967); for a survey of opinions, see Aidan Kavanagh, *The Shape of Baptism* (New York, 1978); Gerard Austin, *Anointing with the Spirit* (New York, 1985), pp. 3–37.

13. On the problems of authorship and provenance, see G. J. Cuming, *Hippolytus: A Text for Students,* GLS 8 (Bramcote, Notts., 1976).

14. Hippolytus, *Apostolic Tradition* 20–23.

15. Some modern authors consider this hand-laying, prayer, and anointing to be the equivalent of the sacrament of confirmation: see Austin, *Anointing with the Spirit;* pp. 11–15. For a more radical suggestion, see Aidan Kavanagh *Confirmation: Origins and Reform* (New York, 1988), pp. 39–51.

16. See Whitaker, *Documents of the Baptismal Liturgy,* pp. 7–10.

17. See Gabriele Winkler, "The Original Meaning of the Pre-baptismal Anointing and Its Implications," *Worship* 52 (1978): 39–45; Georg Kretschmar, "Recent Research on Christian Initiation," *SL* 12 (1977): 87–106; Ruth Meyers, "The Structure of the Syrian Baptismal Rite," in Paul F. Bradshaw, ed., *Essays in Early Eastern Initiation,* JLS 8 (Bramcote, Notts., 1988), pp. 31–43.

18. See Robert F. Taft, *Beyond East and West* (Washington, DC, 1984), pp. 61–62.

19. Cf. 1 Cor. 11:17–26; *Didache* 9–10. The nature of the eucharist in the *Didache* is a matter of debate: see Willy Rordorf, "Didache," in Rordorf et al., *The Eucharist of the Early Christians* (New York, 1978), pp. 1–18.

20. See Dix, *Shape of the Liturgy,* pp. 48–82; recently, Dix's insistence on the importance of the first action—"taking"—has come under some fire: see Richard Buxton, "The Shape of the Eucharist: A Survey and Appraisal," in Kenneth Stevenson, ed. *Liturgy Reshaped* (London, 1982), pp. 83–93.

21. Cyprian of Carthage (mid–third century), *Letter* 63, in Daniel J. Sheerin, *The Eucharist,* Message of the Fathers of the Church (Wilmington, DE, 1986), pp. 256–68. On the the possibility that in some primitive churches the meal consisted only of the breaking of bread, see Hans Lietzmann, *Mass and Lord's Supper* (Leiden, 1953–1979). Today few scholars accept Lietzmann's radical distinction between a Palestinian Jewish-Christian joyful breaking of

bread and a Hellenistic death-memorial.

22. Justin Martyr, *I Apol.* 65–67. In addition to Deiss, *Springtime of the Liturgy,* a useful collection of texts on the eucharist (especially the eucharistic prayer) is R. C. D. Jasper and G. J. Cuming, *Prayers of the Eucharist: Early and Reformed,* 3d ed. (New York, 1987), here at pp. 28–30.

23. On the question of who presided at the ante-Nicene eucharist, see Paul F. Bradshaw, *Liturgical Presidency in the Early Church,* GLS 36 (Bramcote, Notts., 1983).

24. *Apostolic Tradition* 4, 9, 21: Jasper and Cuming, *Prayers of the Eucharist,* pp. 34–38. For an elegant description of the ante-Nicene eucharist (but without the reading synaxis), see Dix, *Shape of the Liturgy,* pp. 142–44.

25. See Thomas J. Talley, "The Literary Structure of the Eucharistic Prayer," *Worship* 58 (1984): 404–20.

26. See Bryan Spinks, "The Jewish Sources for the Sanctus," *Heythrop Journal* 21 (1980): 161–79.

27. See Talley, "Literary Structure"; idem, "From Berakah to Eucharistia: A Re-opening Question," *Worship* 50 (1976): 115–37; Bryan Spinks, "Beware the Liturgical Horses," *Worship* 59 (1985): 211–19.

28. For the debate on the origin and nature of Sunday observance, see Willy Rordorf, *Sunday* (Philadelphia, 1968); Samuele Bacchiocchi, *From Sabbath to Sunday* (Rome, 1977).

29. See, e.g., Justin Martyr, *I Apol.* 67.

30. Eusebius of Caesarea, *Ecclesiastical History* V. 23–25. On the Quartodeciman controversy, see Thomas J. Talley, *The Origins of the Liturgical Year* (New York, 1986), pp. 5–27.

31. On the dating of Pentecost, see Talley, *Origins,* pp. 57–60.

32. Talley, *Origins,* pp. 129–34, 163–214.

33. Ibid., pp. 79–155; for an overview, see A. G. Martimort, ed., *The Church at Prayer* IV (Collegeville, 1986), pp. 77–82.

34. Dix, *Shape of the Liturgy,* pp. 303–19.

35. See Taft, *Beyond East and West,* pp. 15–29; Baldovin, *Urban Character,* pp. 102–4.

36. See Martimort, *Church at Prayer* IV, pp. 108–11.

37. See Taft, *Liturgy of the Hours,* pp. 13–29.

38. Tertullian, *De Oratione,* in Taft, *Liturgy of the Hours,* pp. 17–18.

39. Paul F. Bradshaw, *Daily Prayer in the Early Church* (Lon-

don, 1981/New York, 1982), pp. 50–51; Taft, *Liturgy of the Hours,* pp. 27–29.

40. See Roger Beckwith, *Daily and Weekly Worship: Jewish and Christian,* JLS 1 (Bramcote, Notts., 1987).

41. Richard Krautheimer, "The Constantinian Basilica," *Dumbarton Oaks Papers* 21 (1967): 117ff.; idem, *Three Christian Capitals* (Berkeley, 1983).

42. Kavanagh, *On Liturgical Theology,* p. 65.

43. Baldovin, *Urban Character,* pp. 35–38. The *statio* was the meeting place of the assembly.

44. See Bouley, *From Freedom to Formula,* pp. 255–64.

45. For the origins of monasticism, see Derwas Chitty, *The Desert A City* (Oxford, 1966). On the social situation in general, see Peter Brown, *The World of Late Antiquity* (London, 1971), pp. 34–114.

46. See Theodor Klauser, *A Short History of Western Liturgy* (New York, 1969).

47. See Taft, *Beyond East and West,* pp. 167–68.

48. For a collection of *mystagogiae* in English translation, see Edward Yarnold, *The Awe-Inspiring Rites of Initiation* (Slough, England, 1971); for a thorough analysis and comparison, see Hugh Riley, *Christian Initiation* (Washington, DC, 1974).

49. See Milburn, *Early Christian Art,* pp. 131–38, 144–45.

50. See Ramsey McMullen, *Christianizing the Roman Empire* (New Haven, 1984), pp. 1–5.

51. See Alexander Schmemann, *Introduction to Liturgical Theology* (Crestwood, NY, 1986), pp. 91–110.

52. For a charming, if conflated, narrative picture of the rites of initiation in this period, see Aidan Kavanagh, "A Rite of Passage," in Gabe Huck, *The Three Days* (Chicago, 1981).

53. Cyril of Jerusalem and Theodore of Mopsuestia report post-baptismal anointings, whereas their contemporary John Chrysostom (in Antioch) does not.

54. On typology, see Jean Daniélou, *The Bible and the Liturgy* (Notre Dame, 1956); Yarnold, *Awe-Inspiring Rites,* p. 93, n. 23.

55. One can already find this in the third-century treatise of Tertullian, *De Baptismo* 8.

56. See Taft, *Beyond East and West,* pp. 151–92, esp. 151–54, 167–68; for a detailed analysis of this development of the presentation of the gifts in the Byzantine rite, see idem, *The Great Entrance*

(Rome, 1975).

57. For the Byzantine rite, see Juan Mateos, *La Célébration de la parole dans la liturgie byzantine* (Rome, 1971); for the Roman rite, John F. Baldovin, "Kyrie Eleison and the Entrance Rite of the Roman Eucharist," *Worship* 60 (1986): 334–47; Peter Jeffery, "The Introduction of Psalmody into the Roman Mass by Pope Celestine I," *Archiv für Liturgiewissenschaft* 26 (1984): 147–65. For a comparative study, see Baldovin, *Urban Character*, pp. 241–47.

58. See Mateos, *Célébration de la parole;* Josef A. Jungmann, *The Mass of the Roman Rite* I (New York, 1950), pp. 391–419.

59. On the development of the Anaphora of St. Basil and its relations with that of St. James, see John Fenwick, *Fourth-Century Anaphoral Construction Techniques,* GLS 45 (Bramcote, Notts., 1986).

60. For the state of the question, see Bryan Spinks, *Addai and Mari—the Anaphora of the Apostles: A Text for Students,* GLS 24 (Bramcote, Notts., 1980).

61. See Talley, "From Berakah to Eucharistia," pp. 129–37.

62. See Enrico Mazza, *The Eucharistic Prayers of the Roman Rite* (New York, 1986); Martimort, *Church at Prayer* II, pp. 88–106.

63. See John F. Baldovin, *Liturgy in Ancient Jerusalem,* JLS 9 (Bramcote, Notts., 1989), pp. 25–28.

64. See Dix, *Shape of the Liturgy,* pp. 268–302; Bryan Spinks, "The Consecratory Epiclesis in the Anaphora of St. James," *SL* 11 (1976): 19–32.

65. See Kenneth Stevenson, *Eucharist and Offering* (New York, 1986).

66. See Talley, *Origins,* pp. 134–47.

67. Ibid., pp. 214–25; Martimort, *Church at Prayer* IV, pp. 66–72.

68. On the development of the liturgy of penance, see Joseph Favazza, *The Order of Penitents* (Collegeville, 1988).

69. See Talley, *Origins,* pp. 62–70; Martimort, *Church at Prayer* IV, pp. 58–61.

70. See Martimort, *Church at Prayer* IV, pp. 108–50; Peter Brown, *The Cult of the Saints* (Chicago, 1981).

71. See Taft, *Liturgy of the Hours,* p. 32.

72. See John Wilkinson, *Egeria's Travels* (London, 1971, Warminster, 1981), pp. 123–26; Taft, *Liturgy of the Hours,* pp.

48–56; Bradshaw, *Daily Prayer*, pp. 77ff.; for a less technical commentary and description, see George Guiver, *Company of Voices* (New York, 1988), pp. 59–64.

73. See Taft, *Liturgy of the Hours*, pp. 57–73; Nathan Mitchell, "The Liturgical Code in the Rule of Benedict," in Timothy Fry et al., eds., *RB 1980: The Rule of Benedict in Latin and English with Notes* (Collegeville, 1981), pp. 379–414.

74. See Taft, *Liturgy of the Hours*, pp. 121–40.

75. See Peter Brown, "Eastern and Western Christianity in Late Antiquity: A Parting of the Ways," in idem, *Society and the Holy in Late Antiquity* (Berkeley, 1983), pp. 115–88; Robert F. Taft, "Liturgy and Eucharist I: East," in Jill Raitt, ed., *Christian Spirituality II: High Middle Ages and Reformation* (New York, 1987), p. 415.

76. See Baldovin, *Urban Character*, pp. 205–26; for a description of the Byzantine books and a helpful glossary, see Herman Wegman, *Christian Worship in East and West* (New York, 1985), pp. 250–72.

77. Taft, "Liturgy and Eucharist," p. 415.

78. See Robert F. Taft, "The Liturgy of the Great Church: An Initial Synthesis of Structure and Interpretation on the Eve of Iconoclasm," *Dumbarton Oaks Papers* 34–35 (1980–1981): 45–75. For a detailed analysis of the correspondence of the iconography or decoration of the churches with the liturgy, see Hans-Joachim Schulz, *The Byzantine Liturgy* (New York, 1986).

79. For a description of these rites, see Martimort, *Church at Prayer* I. On several other local western rites, see Archdale King, *Liturgies of the Primatial Sees* (London, 1957); and idem, *Liturgies of the Past* (London, 1959).

80. See Edmund Bishop, "The Genius of the Roman Rite," in idem, *Liturgica Historica* (Oxford, 1918), pp. 1–19.

81. See Wegman, *Christian Worship,* pp. 150–70; for more detail and comprehensive bibliography, see Cyrille Vogel, *Medieval Liturgy* (Washington, DC, 1986).

82. On the introduction of the private mass, see Cyrille Vogel, "La Multiplication des messes solitaires au moyen-âge: Essai de statistique," *Révue des sciences religieuses* 55 (1981): 206–13; idem, "Une mutation cultuelle inexpliquée: Le Passage de l'eucharistie communautaire à la messe privée," *Révue des sciences religieuses* 54 (1980): 231–50.

83. See Albert Mirgeler, *Mutations in Western Christianity* (New York, 1964); Alexander Gerken, *Theologie der Eucharistie* (Münster, 1973), pp. 97–102.

84. On these changes and the development of eucharistic piety, see Martimort, *Church at Prayer* II, pp. 130–42; Wegman, *Christian Worship*, pp. 229–33; Nathan Mitchell, *Cult and Controversy* (New York, 1982), pp. 163–84.

85. Taft, *Liturgy of the Hours*, pp. 308–10; S. J. P. van Dijk and J. H. Walker, *The Origins of the Modern Roman Liturgy* (Westminster, MD, 1960).

86. See Guiver, *Company of Voices*, pp. 104–14.

87. Thus a presbyter could perform the anointing with chrism that had been consecrated by the bishop.

88. See Nathan Mitchell, "Dissolution of the Rite of Christian Initiation," in *Made not Born* (Notre Dame, 1976), pp. 50–82; J. D. C. Fisher, *Christian Initiation: Baptism in the Medieval West* (London, 1965); Austin, *Anointing with the Spirit*, pp. 17–20.

89. See Jungmann, *Mass of the Roman Rite*, I, pp. 74–92.

90. See Joseph M. Powers, *Eucharistic Theology* (New York, 1967), pp. 22–31; Mitchell, *Cult and Controversy*, pp. 76–96.

Christian Worship
since the Reformation

SUSAN J. WHITE

[Editors' note: Susan White, Lecturer and Tutor in Liturgy and Worship at Westcott House, Cambridge, England, carefully delineates the complex diversity of styles of worship that issued out of the divisions within western Christianity caused by the sixteenth-century Reformation, many of which still continue to characterize the various Christian denominations down to the present day.]

There is a strong temptation among liturgical scholars to divide the history of Christian worship neatly into two major periods—pre-Reformation and post-Reformation—and in the present volume we have indeed yielded to that temptation. But in so doing we do not mean to suggest that such division is without serious difficulties. To be sure, during the early years of the sixteenth century a liturgical fragmentation occurred that permanently altered the landscape of Christianity. But to concentrate on these sixteenth-century divisions tends to mask the diversity in practice of the previous centuries. Such a radical dissection of history also suggests that nothing of the reformers' medieval past was carried over into the renewed Christian worship that they implemented. However, recent scholarship has made us increasingly aware of the very real continuity that existed between the medieval and Reformation liturgical mindset.[1] Since nearly all of the leaders of the earliest phase of the Reformation were Roman Catholic clergy[2] deeply embedded in the theological world of the Middle Ages, it is not surprising to find in post-Reformation worship a variety of medieval structures and presuppositions.

The Origins of Liturgical Reformation

But all of this being said, certain specific events around the turn of the sixteenth century spawned an organized movement toward religious purification, and Christian worship became the most visible indicator of theological and ecclesiastical change. Papal prestige had been seriously eroded during the previous century, and successive political and financial crises in the Vatican had precipitated the rise in influence of national governments. At the same time, however, popular piety was thriving, especially in northern Europe. Even though participation in the official liturgy had become increasingly monopolized by clergy, organized, paraliturgical popular devotions had sprung up throughout the late Middle Ages, giving lay people a variety of opportunities for the exercise of their faith.[3] Printing had made manuals of prayer more widely available, and vernacular hymnody had undergone a revival, especially in Poland and the Low Countries. But there were serious abuses of the official liturgy,[4] and in the end this combination of liturgical abuse and liturgical piety set the stage for the radical reevaluation of Christian worship by those in the sixteenth century who sought the reformation of the Church.

The Lutheran Tradition in the Sixteenth Century

With its nationalist tendencies and its remoteness from the source of papal authority, northern Europe became the laboratory for liturgical reform. It was Martin Luther (1483–1546), an Augustinian monk and professor of Scripture at the University of Wittenberg, whose passionate belief in the centrality of the Word of God and of faith led to a direct confrontation between the forces of stability and the forces of reform.[5] Beginning in 1517, Luther not only argued for a reduction of abuses related to the Christian liturgy,[6] but also put forth his own solutions in the form of revised services of public worship. All of these solutions had at their center Luther's firm conviction that many of the prevailing practices were based on a notion that one's salvation could be earned through good works rather than coming by God's grace through faith alone. Masses for the dead, the celibacy of the clergy, the monastic life, pilgrimages, the withholding of the eucharistic wine from the laity, the mediatorial role of the ordained ministry, and the belief that in the eucharist the sacrifice of Christ was repeated and could be applied to the forgiveness of sins all fell under Luther's condemnation. Having searched the Scriptures to find explicit warrants in the words of Jesus for the Church's various sacramental actions, Luther found that only baptism and the eucharist qualified. But although baptism and the Lord's Supper were important, it was the public proclamation and preaching of the Word of God that were the liturgical center of Luther's revisions.

The first of Luther's reformed services, the *Formula Missae et Communionis* of 1523,[7] was a truncated version of the existing medieval rite. While it remained in Latin and retained many of the features of traditional practice, revised rubrics and prayer texts were aimed at repudiating "everything that smacks of sacrifice."[8] The reading of Scripture and preaching, the receiving of the communion bread and wine by all the people (instead of by clergy only), and the communal recitation of the Lord's Prayer were indispensable additions to the traditional mass. The *Formula Missae* has been called Luther's greatest liturgical writing.[9]

By 1526, however, Luther had become convinced that a more radical revision of worship was necessary, and in that year he produced a vernacular service[10] with only the words of institution to introduce communion. German hymns were composed for this service (many by Luther himself), and ever since, the Lutheran worship tradition has nourished a treasured musical heritage.[11] Few adaptations in medieval church buildings were needed to accommodate Lutheran worship, but since the presider at communion was enjoined to face the people over the altar, it would have been necessary to remove it from its customary location against the wall.[12]

Luther also revised the rites of Christian initiation. His 1526

Order of Baptism Revised eliminated various medieval baptismal ceremonies, including the giving of the lighted candle and of salt, the breathing on the child, and the first exorcism. Luther emphasized that the rites of initiation should be conducted during the ordinary Sunday gathering of the community; he declared that confirmation, for which no specific warrant in the pages of Scripture had been found, was no longer to be considered a sacrament. Each local pastor, however, was urged to examine the faith of the children of responsible age and to lay hands on them.[13]

The Beginnings of the Reformed Tradition of Worship

Others of the period, however, desired a more thoroughgoing reformation of Christian worship. Swiss reformers Ulrich Zwingli (1484–1531), Martin Bucer (1491–1551), and John Oecolampadius (1482–1531) found that Luther's retention of certain medieval elements in his theology and practice left too much room for abuse, and they argued especially against his view of the carnal presence of the body and blood of Jesus Christ in the eucharistic elements of bread and wine. The failure of Luther and the Swiss reformers to come to any agreement on this matter at the Marburg Colloquy (1529) marked the fracture of the Reformation into several distinct theological (and, thus, liturgical) camps.[14]

Reformed worship of this early period is marked by a more radical move away from its medieval precursors, aiming always to approximate what was understood to be the practice of the primitive Church. Although each of the early Swiss reformers produced his own services for public use, it was John Calvin's *Form of Church Prayers ... According to the Custom of the Ancient Church* (1542) that became the liturgical inspiration for subsequent forms of Reformed worship. Calvin (1509–1564) was convinced of the absolute sovereignty of God in all matters, and the tone of all of his services is didactic, with long exhortations and instructive prayer texts throughout.[15] At the eucharist, the Roman canon was replaced by the words of institution alone, with instructions for the examination of conscience following, and those who were deemed unworthy were prohibited from participating in the Lord's Supper.[16] Calvin valued liturgical music[17] and saw to it that metrical versions of the psalms were composed for inclusion in public worship as a way for the Christian people to sing the Scriptures. But he disapproved of the use of musical instruments, including organs, which he thought were designed "only [to] amuse people in their vanities."[18] Calvin also insisted that stone altars be replaced by wooden communion tables, in order that no suggestion of the sacrifice of the mass remain.

Like the Lutheran reformers, the Swiss argued strongly for the retention of the baptism of infants, in order that they might be "reckoned among God's children."[19] Calvin's rites of initiation were, like Luther's, greatly simplified versions of their medieval predecessors, and all ceremonies that might "prevent the people from coming directly to Jesus Christ" were abolished. Calvin required that baptismal fonts should be placed in the front of church and that baptism always be a public act. (It was this fear of secrecy that led him to inveigh against the baptism of newborns by midwives, a common practice when illness threatened the life of the child.)[20]

The Sixteenth-Century Anabaptists

For most of the Reformers, baptism was less a subject of debate than was the eucharist. But one group, seeking a more thorough purification of the Christian Church, saw the prevailing practice of infant baptism (paedobaptism) as something that undercut their progress toward reform. Because of their refusal to accept the validity of infant baptism (whether administered by Roman Catholics or by reformers), these so-called Anabaptists began rebaptizing those adults who made a public confession of faith. Often on occasions of baptism, a milk pail was brought into the church building so that water could be poured over the heads of believers.[21]

Many Anabaptist groups also emphasized pacifism, the restriction of the Lord's Supper to those demonstrating purity of life, the rejection of civil government, and the communal ownership of property, seeking always to achieve an undefiled community of faith. As a result of their radical liturgical and social practices, Anabaptists were denounced by Protestants and Roman Catholics alike, and under severe persecution many thousands of believers were martyred. Although several subgroups of sixteenth-century Anabaptists can be distinguished,[22] all are marked by the desire to integrate worship, society, and government into a pure and seamless whole.

The Sixteenth-Century Roman Catholic Reformation

At the same time the Catholic Reformation (often called the Counterreformation) left its own mark on liturgical practice and piety. A council convened at Trent (1545–1563) sought to curb abuses and to settle matters that had been thrown into question by the success of Protestantism; several sessions dealt directly with Christian worship.[23] The institution by Jesus Christ of all seven of the traditional sacraments, the sacrificial character of the mass, the doctrine of transubstantiation, and the denial of the chalice to the laity were reemphasized, and baptism, confirmation, and matrimony were given special treatment during the council, as were popular, paraliturgical devotions, particularly the invocation of saints in prayer and the place of relics and images.

One of the most important results of the council's deliberations was the establishment of the Congregation of Sacred Rites. Aiming at a standardization of public worship according to the council's official decrees and with a uniform liturgy for all of Roman Catholicism as the ultimate goal, the Congregation immediately undertook the reform of the medieval liturgical books. In most of these revisions, the liturgical practice current in the city of Rome was the norm, and the diverse, local worship heritages of the rest of the Church were essentially ignored. Although some of these local rites (and especially those in France) survived the council's efforts toward uniformity, most did not, and the liturgical books produced at the behest of the Congregation of Sacred Rites formed the official liturgy of the Roman Catholic church until the Second Vatican Council authorized a new round of revisions nearly four centuries later.

The Second Generation of Sixteenth-Century Protestant Reformers

Meanwhile a second generation of reformers was establishing Protestant liturgical practice in the British Isles, Holland, and Scandinavia. As the Reformation spread west, its worship generally became more eclectic in character, choosing from and combining previously isolated strands of theological thinking, and shaping itself according to the particular political situation in which it developed. Thomas Cranmer (1489–1556), for example, gave lasting shape to the worship of the reformed Church of England in two successive editions of the *Book of Common Prayer* (1549 and 1552).[24] Lutheran, Zwinglian, and Calvinist theological tendencies in Cranmer's sacramental theology and practice make his vernacular re-workings of the medieval rites controversial to this day.[25]

Like his continental predecessors, Cranmer was concerned that there be no hint of adoration of the bread and wine at the eucharist,[26] that baptism be a public event, that participation of the laity in worship be increased, and that liturgical emphasis be placed on the proclamation of Scripture. Although the continental reformers had made some attempts at instituting a daily office in parishes, it was Cranmer who made the practice workable. He not only revised the medieval daily offices (matins, lauds, and prime, which were customarily said as one office for morning; and sext, none, vespers, and compline said together for evening), with the whole Psalter to be read through monthly at the two offices, but he also directed that all parish clergy say morning and evening prayer daily in public. (John Knox [c. 1505–1572], Cranmer's counterpart in Scotland, was less ambiguous in his liturgical and theological leanings and framed the services in the *Book of Common Order* according to strict Calvinist principles.)[27]

The musical requirements of various editions of the *Book of Common Prayer* also shaped the whole course of English (and, hence, American) church music.[28] Because music was seen as a part of the ministry of the Word, it was necessary to insure that appropriate texts were chosen and that the music served to make those texts clear and audible so that every word might be "plainly understood."[29] Throughout the last half of the century, anthems, metrical psalms,[30] and hymns began to be composed for inclusion in the Prayer Book services, and *The Book of Common Prayer Noted* (1550) by John Merbecke set the congregational parts of the liturgy to easily sung unison melodies designed to be performed without accompaniment. Cathedral music was generally more elaborate than that intended for parishes, and well-known composers such as Thomas Tallis (1505–1585) and William Byrd (1543–1623) lent their talents to music for cathedral choirs.

During the eighty years between 1520 and 1600, the liturgical scene in Europe had undergone as massive a change as the political scene. Vernacular worship had been established by all of the various Protestant groups, with service books and Bibles cheaply available,[31] and church music was beginning to find a reformed voice. At the same time, new Roman Catholic texts in Latin had been authorized by the Congregation of Sacred Rites and mandated for use by all those parishes that had remained within the fold. One of the main Protestant objections to Roman practice had been celebration of the mass without communicants. But although frequent communion of the laity was desired, the reformers had found it impossible to achieve, since people were accustomed to infrequent communion (once a year had been common) and resisted change. In the end, four times per year was the usual practice among the Reformation churches. But the penitential tone that had pervaded pre-Reformation piety persisted in both Protestantism and Roman Catholicism; Protestants insisted on long, didactic exhortations, the barring of the unworthy from the communion table, and repeated examinations of conscience, and Roman Catholics continued to pursue penitential disciplines of various sorts.

Christian Worship in the Seventeenth Century

During the next century, those desiring a more thorough reformation of the Church began to gain influence, and worship again came under scrutiny. Although renewal movements affected most of the established Protestant churches,[32] the most influential of these was English Puritanism. Fear of idolatry led to the renewed demand for the abandonment of many rites and ceremonies, and each detail of public worship was to be guided by the authority of Scripture. The abolition of ecclesiastical vestments, musical instruments, feast days, the sign of the cross at baptism, kneeling at communion, the use of the term *priest,* and any suggestion that the communion table was an altar were all points on which these Puritans stood fast.[33] Eventually the Puritan desire to establish a pure commonwealth with full congregational autonomy in matters of church government led to a constitutional crisis in England. With the political success of the Puritan forces, services from the *Book of Common Prayer* were discontinued from 1645 to 1660, and the *Directory for the Public Worship of God* (1645), which incorporated Presbyterian liturgical principles, was imposed throughout England and Scotland.[34]

The most extreme example of this effort toward ecclesiastical purification is found in the worship of the Society of Friends (Quakers). Under the leadership of George Fox (1624–1691), the Quakers believed that the "Inner Light" of Christ was available to all Christian believers who waited for it in silence. As a result, the experience of baptism and the Lord's Supper became wholly spiritualized, with the physical elements of bread, wine, and water abandoned in favor of an inward "feeding on Christ" and cleansing from sin; silent meetings became the typical form of worship. This is the reformation of Christian liturgy at its most radical, and among many Quakers it continues to this day with little change.[35]

During the seventeenth century, the New World began to be explored and divided according to religious as well as temporal authority, and this had its own impact on the liturgy. Among Roman Catholics, preaching came to be more important to the task of evangelization, and under the influence of religious communities dedicated to this task, especially the Society of Jesus and the Franciscans, the seventeenth century has been called the golden age of Roman Catholic preaching. Among Protestants, the New World provided the laboratory in which the order of worship was made to mirror the ordering of the state, with a pure theocracy the ultimate goal in many places. The exposition of Scripture was central to this vision of the unified Christian life, and long, didactic sermons and exhortations formed the heart of every service of worship.

The seventeenth century was also a golden age for Protestant Church music, and the works of Heinrich Schütz, Henry Purcell, and Orlando Gibbons remain monuments to the reformed ideal of the marriage of Scripture and music.[36] In addition, Psalters such as the *Bay Psalm Book* (1640) in America and *Rous's Version* (1650) in Scotland gave expression to the Puritan insistence that only the words of Scripture were fit for the voices of Christian people. At the same time, Baroque art and architecture gave Roman Catholicism a form it could call its own. With their rich ornamentation and playful interplay of decorative motifs, Baroque interiors stood in sharp contrast to the simple and unadorned worship spaces of most of seventeenth-century Protestantism.[37]

By the end of the century, the intense religious controversies (as well as the religious enthusiasm) that had been the hallmark of most of this period had abated. Prayer Book worship had been reestablished in England, Puritan worship had found a comfortable home in America, and even marginalized groups, such as Quakers and Anabaptists, had generally found relief from persecution. Among continental Lutherans, where an active Pietist movement had sought to infuse new life into faith and worship by emphasizing hymnody, personal prayer, and the study of Scripture, Lutheran orthodoxy was beginning to reassert itself. Although nearly all Calvinist churches had abandoned service books by the end of the century, worship had generally ossified all across their European range, with services dominated by lengthy and didactic explications of scriptural texts and by a penitential and confessional tone.[38] Even though Protestants and Roman Catholics continued to be interested in advancing their own religious and political interests, active debate on liturgical and theological matters had settled into routine diatribes, without any real innovations in substance or tone.

Enlightenment and Enthusiasm in the Eighteenth Century

The lack of religious enthusiasm that marked the late 1600s would have important consequences for Christian worship during the century that followed. On the one hand, it provided fertile ground for rationalism to take root; on the other hand, it encouraged the flowering of independent renewal movements across the breadth of Christianity. The dialogue between these two forces—rationalism and renewal—would continue to play itself out well into the nineteenth century.

The eighteenth-century Enlightenment made a clear impact on the liturgical practice and piety of all of the churches that traced their origins to the Reformation, but it also had a strong influence on Roman Catholicism. Because of its exaltation of human reason, Enlightenment rationalism put any form of the supernatural under suspicion, and preaching and the informed study of Scripture, as activities of the enlightened mind, came to dominate Protestant worship in an even more emphatic way than before. Baptism and the Lord's Supper, valued primarily for their impact on the human mind and their usefulness as a method of recalling the virtues of Christ, were considered a duty of those who took the scriptural mandates of Jesus seriously. This emphasis on the memorial aspect of the sacraments led to a further decline of sacramental piety in much of Protestantism, with both the eucharist and baptism generally pushed to the margins of Christian experience.[39]

During the later years of the eighteenth century we begin to see concrete evidence of the reevaluation of Roman Catholic worship in the light of the prevailing rationalism. Since it was believed that the individual human mind was capable of direct apprehension of truth, there came to be an increasing emphasis on personal and local autonomy. The decrees of the Synod of Pistoia (1786), for example, encouraged local practices, forbade the placement of more than one altar in a single church building, and condemned the liturgical use of Latin, the multiplication of masses, and certain extraliturgical devotions. Although the council decrees aroused both popular and official opposition and were never put into effect, they stand as testimony to the interplay between Roman Catholicism and the Enlightenment.[40]

But at the same time, a number of movements developed that sought to revitalize Christian faith and practice and to move away from a strictly rationalist approach to religion. John Wesley (1703–1791), a devout and scholarly priest of the Church of England, sought a practical religion to serve the needs of the increasing masses of urban poor. His study of the worship practices of the early Church led him to reevaluate the prevailing apathy in the matter of the sacraments and also to restore certain liturgical elements lost since the Reformation. An ardent and successful preacher, Wesley encouraged weekly celebration of the eucharist and the establishment of "classes" and "bands," small groups of believers that met weekly for prayer and examination of conscience and that were designed to nurture sacramental piety. Wesley's brother Charles (1707–1788), an indefatigable composer, contributed over fifty-five hundred hymns to the cause of Christian renewal.[41] Although John Wesley hoped that his movement would lead to a revival of lively sacramental practice in the Church of England, the intense rationalism of eighteenth-century Anglicanism made a rupture inevitable, and Wesleyan Methodism spread independently to all parts of the globe. After Wesley's death, however,

Methodist interest in the sacraments was never as strong as he would have wished.[42]

Responding to many of the same rationalist intellectual forces in religion, the Great Awakening, which spread throughout the American colonies from 1720 until after the Revolutionary War, hoped to restore spiritual vigor to the Christian faith and used various worship techniques in doing so. As ideological descendants of the Dutch Pietist movement, the various strains of the Great Awakening were all founded upon the necessity for personal conversion, giving rise to the individualism that would mark much of nineteenth- and twentieth-century Christianity.

The doctrinal and practical underpinnings of the Great Awakening movement were provided by the renowned American theologian Jonathan Edwards (1703–1758). Edwards, who combined an interest in the empirical scientific method of Newton and Locke with a desire for a new reformation of the Christian life, sought an "experimental religion" that could give believers a due sense of the relationship between divine truth and human existence. And Christian worship became the laboratory in which these religious experiments were undertaken. Public repentance, public forgiveness of sin, and preaching for conversion were aimed at arousing the "religious affections" through well-directed sense experience.[43] At the time, the Great Awakening affected all Christian denominations in America but was met with serious resistance on the part of those of a more thoroughly rationalist persuasion, who were suspicious of the emotional and enthusiastic quality of the new religion. But even within renewed communities, there was dissension and schism over the degree to which renewal must be effected, and by the end of the eighteenth century, Enlightenment rationalism had reestablished its dominance in Christian theology and worship.

Romanticism and Revivalism in the Nineteenth Century

The nineteenth-century reaction to the excesses of Enlightenment rationalism took two forms, both of which had significant impact on liturgical piety and practice. The first of these is generally termed *romanticism,* which could trace its roots to late eighteenth-century Germany,[44] and which sought to recapture the religious experience of an idealized past. Many figures in both the Protestant and Roman Catholic Romantic movements looked to the medieval period as the golden age of Christianity, an era when work, religion, and society were thought to have formed a cohesive whole, and even those groups such as Lutherans and Anglicans that had so decisively rejected medieval piety in the sixteenth century hoped for the restoration of certain medieval worship practices.[45]

Several liturgical trends related to romanticism can be identified. The Oxford movement in Anglicanism, Mercersberg theology in the American Calvinist churches, the work of Johann Loehe (1808–1872) in Lutheranism and of Prosper Guéranger (1805–1875) in Roman Catholicism each sought in a different way to restore the eucharist to the center of religious experience. As a result, in those segments of the Church that were affected by the romantic movement, eucharistic devotion and frequency of communion increased dramatically.[46] At the same time, the translation of medieval hymns by composers such as John Mason Neale (1818–1866) and the reproduction of medieval church buildings by such architects as A. W. N. Pugin (in England) and Ralph Adams Cram (in the United States) gave audible and visible expression to this medieval nostalgia.[47] Concomitant with this nostalgic approach to the experience of worship, however, was a rise in religious sentimentality and the privatization of liturgical piety, with some Protestant groups moving close to the idolatry so greatly feared by the sixteenth-century reformers.

The second major influence on Protestant worship in the nineteenth century, particularly in American Protestantism, was the rise of frontier revivalism.[48] With a vast land area being settled rapidly, practical measures were necessary to serve the religious needs of an increasingly unchurched rural population, and the pattern of worship developed to meet this need has persisted in many segments of American Protestantism to this day. Charles Grandison Finney (1792–1875), a

Presbyterian lawyer and church leader, began conducting
revivals in the mid-1820s after a profound conversion experience during which he received, as he put it, "a mighty baptism of the Holy Ghost."[49] During these open-air gatherings
(which were often called "camp meetings" and which usually
lasted several days), fiery preaching for conversion, subjective
and sentimental hymn texts set to simple, easily learned tunes,
and emotional prayer and responses all led to the baptism of
those who had repented of their sins and to the celebration of
the Lord's Supper.[50] (Although for most groups affected by
revivalism in the nineteenth century the tendency toward infrequent communion prevailed, at least one group born on the
frontier, the Christian Church [Disciples of Christ], believed
that Scripture commanded a weekly celebration of the Lord's
Supper presided over by a lay elder, a practice that persists to
this day.)[51]

By the turn of the twentieth century, Protestant Christianity
had once again divided, this time not along denominational
or confessional lines but, rather, over the question of where
authentic religious experience was to be found. In the Church
of England, for example, evangelicals concentrated on the
necessity of conversion and on a Scripture-based form of ecclesiastical and liturgical life, while those affected by the Oxford movement sought a return to an idealized past. In the
United States, the worship life of those American Presbyterians and Methodists influenced by frontier styles came closer
together, while believers on the East Coast retained their individual liturgical identities. And all across the denominational
spectrum, those groups in which the Enlightenment attitude
toward the supernatural persisted had pushed the sacraments
to the margins of liturgical life, while those steeped in medieval nostalgia drew them toward the center. In a very real
sense, the divisions in worship were incarnated in the church
buildings the various subgroups occupied. The brightly lit,
auditorium-like churches, dominated by platform stages and
huge central pulpits and inspired by the frontier camp meeting,
stand in sharp contrast to the dim and lofty altar-centered

imitations of Gothic churches that expressed the new sacramentalism.[52]

Christian Worship in the Twentieth Century

With new liturgical lines drawn and the old ones dissolved, a certain degree of liturgical flexibility and freedom was established. The dawn of the twentieth century witnessed the birth of Pentecostalism, which saw itself as the restoration of authentic apostolic faith and emphasized the necessity of "baptism of the Spirit" as distinct from water baptism.[53] Marked by spontaneous, ecstatic utterances, speaking in tongues (glossolalia),[54] and revivalist-style preaching, Pentecostal worship presupposes the constant possibility that God may break into the service, which moves Pentecostalism decisively away from the Enlightenment suspicion of the supernatural. While Pentecostalist worship is most closely associated with the Churches of God, the Assemblies of God, and the Foursquare Gospel Churches, charismatic spontaneity has begun to influence the worship of mainline Protestants and Roman Catholics as well.[55]

At the same time, the search for the Christian liturgical past which had occupied the time of so many nineteenth-century romanticists had set the stage for modern liturgical scholarship, which would come to maturity in the twentieth century as the liturgical movement.[56] In Roman Catholicism, historical studies explored the Jewish prehistory of Christian worship, uncovered the earlier variety of liturgical practice, and documented the accumulation of various devotional adjuncts. The stripping away of extraneous liturgical material in the various rites, the simplification of rubrics, the recovery of ancient signs and symbols, the attempts at cultural indigenization of liturgical practice, and what the Second Vatican Council (1962–1965) referred to as "full, conscious, and active participation" of the laity were all aimed at revitalizing forms of worship that had undergone little change in nearly four hundred years.[57] In response to the council decrees, worship in the vernacular was allowed in place of Latin, and new liturgical texts were developed for all rites.

By the middle of the twentieth century, the Roman Catholic liturgical movement had begun to affect the worship life of many Protestant churches as well. The scholarly analysis of documentary evidence from the earliest period of Christian worship led groups that had been divided from one another since the Reformation to a common liturgical ground. During the theologically and politically turbulent 1960s, Anglicans, Lutherans, Methodists, and Presbyterians each underwent their own versions of a liturgical revival, resulting in a new generation of revised service materials, including hymnals. Many of these groups have sought to restore the sacraments of baptism and the eucharist to the center of their worship, having found evidence of the importance of these actions in both early Christian and Reformation sources. At the same time, a great deal of liturgical experimentation took place throughout the Christian Church,[58] and such matters as the adequacy of liturgical language came under intense scrutiny. But other Protestant groups, especially those with strong ties to rationalist or revivalist worship patterns, have remained relatively untouched by these trends, and their worship continues to be centered on exhortation, prayer, and the reading and preaching of Scripture. Even though the worship of these groups is remarkably similar, most actively resist set liturgical texts and service books.

The Future of Christian Worship

The future of Christian worship will undoubtedly be shaped by a number of forces already at work in the modern world. Since the birth of the World Council of Churches in 1948, concern with ecumenical convergence among separated Christian bodies has taken on a more formal aspect. Important bilateral dialogues resulted in the 1982 consensus document entitled *Baptism, Eucharist, and Ministry*, which highlights many points of agreement on liturgical matters.[59] In addition to ecumenism, the adaptation of liturgical practice to diverse cultural circumstances should also have a significant impact on the future of Christian worship, especially with the Christian churches in the Third World growing at such an astonishing rate. But at the same time, a strong conservative backlash has also appeared in a number of different segments of the Church, largely as a reaction to the rapid changes in liturgical practice and piety in recent years. Many groups calling themselves "traditionalists" have taken their stand on the restoration of the worship practices and service books of the era just prior to the latest round of revisions.

Finally, the impact of what has been termed the "Religious Right," and its communications vehicle "televangelism," cannot be underestimated. With over 1 billion television sets currently in operation throughout the world, evangelical services of worship come into almost every home, subtly shaping the liturgical expectations of large numbers of people. The ultimate impact of the largely neo-Enlightenment and individualist understanding of Christian worship that is presented to viewers has yet to be thoroughly analyzed. It is quite possible, however, that to the extent that this form of televised worship replaces worship in local parish churches, it may tend to work against current trends in liturgical renewal.

NOTES

1. See, for example, James F. White, *Protestant Worship: Traditions in Transition* (Louisville, 1989).

2. The major exceptions to this rule are John Calvin and Philipp Melanchthon.

3. Associated with the flourishing of various sorts of lay devotions is the rise in popularity of pious confraternities, the cult of relics and of the Virgin Mary, pilgrimages, the rosary prayers, various feasts such as Corpus Christi, and the endowment of chantry masses by craft guilds.

4. The most notable of these abuses was the subsidization of various liturgical activities in order to produce temporal and spiritual benefits for individuals and groups.

5. A standard, if slightly dated, biography of Martin Luther is Roland Bainton, *Here I Stand* (New York, 1951). The standard English edition of the reformer's writings is *Luther's Works,* 55 volumes (Philadelphia, 1955–1986).

6. See *An Open Letter to the Christian Nobility of the German Nation* (1520) and the *Babylonian Captivity of the Church* (1520) for details of Luther's critique of the prevailing sacramental theology and liturgical practice.

7. For a convenient English translation, see R. C. D. Jasper and G. Cuming, *Prayers of the Eucharist: Early and Reformed,* 3d ed. (New York, 1987), pp. 191–95. Luther Reed, *The Lutheran Liturgy* (Philadelphia, 1947), provides a good overview of the whole phe tnomenon of Lutheran worship.

8. From the introductory exhortation to the *Formula Missae,* in Jasper and Cuming, *Prayers of the Eucharist,* p. 192.

9. Reed, *Lutheran Liturgy,* p. 72.

10. The *Deutche Messe.* For the German text, see Irmgard Pahl, ed., *Coena Domini I* (Freiburg, 1983), p. 27.

11. See Frederich Blume, *Protestant Church Music* (New York, 1974), pp. 1–125.

12. For details of the architectural implications of the various liturgical traditions, see James F. White, *Protestant Worship and Church Architecture* (Oxford, 1964).

13. See Reed, *Lutheran Liturgy,* pp. 38–39.

14. For a conservative analysis of the eucharistic debates that took place at the Marburg Colloquy, see Hermann Sasse, *This Is My Body* (Minneapolis, 1959).

15. For biographical information on John Calvin, see William Bouwsma, *John Calvin: A Sixteenth-Century Portrait* (Oxford, 1988); and for Calvin's sacramental and liturgical thinking, see Ronald S. Wallace, *Calvin's Doctrine of Word and Sacrament* (Edinburgh, 1953); Killian McDonnell, *John Calvin and the Church* (Princeton, 1967).

16. See *Pahl, Coena Domini I,* p. 347, and the English translation in Jasper and Cuming, *Prayers of the Eucharist,* pp. 213–18.

17. "Among other things fit to recreate man and give him plea-

sure, music is either first or one of the principal; and we must value it as a gift of God" (from his "Epistle on the Geneva Service Book of 1542," Bouwsma, *John Calvin*, p. 135).

18. Bouwsma, *John Calvin*, p. 225.

19. From the rubrics in Calvin's *Form of Prayers*.

20. John Calvin, *Institutes* VI.15:19.

21. Rollin Stely Armour, *Anabaptist Baptism* (Scottsdale, PA, 1966).

22. For example, the Hutterites, Melchiorites, Swiss Brethren, Mennonites, and the Zwickau Prophets. See George H. Williams, *The Radical Reformation* (Philadelphia, 1962).

23. See *The Canons and Decrees of the Council of Trent*, trans. H. J. Schroeder (Rockford, IL, 1978); Reinhold Theissen, *Mass, Liturgy, and the Council of Trent* (Collegeville, 1965).

24. See Geoffrey Bromiley, *Thomas Cranmer, Theologian* (New York, 1956); Geoffrey Cuming, *A History of Anglican Liturgy*, 2d ed. (London, 1982); and Horton Davies, *Worship and Theology in England*, 5 vols. (London/Princeton, 1961–1975). For the mutual influence between sixteenth-century English and the *Book of Common Prayer*, see Stella Brook, *The Language of the Book of Common Prayer* (London, 1965).

25. One famous debate was carried on after Gregory Dix (*The Shape of the Liturgy*, Westminster, 1945), asserted that Cranmer's eucharistic theology was thoroughly Zwinglian in character. The challenge to that statement was picked up by G. B. Timms in *Dixit Cranmer et non Timuit* (London, 1947) and Cyril Richardson in *Cranmer and Zwingli on the Eucharist* (Evanston, IL, 1949).

26. The so-called Black Rubric ("Declaration on Kneeling"), which was printed at the end of the communion service in the 1552 edition of the *Book of Common Prayer*, was designed to avoid the suggestion of devotional attachment to the eucharistic bread and wine by forbidding kneeling at communion.

27. See William D. Maxwell, *The Liturgical Portions of the Genevan Service Book* (Westminster, 1965).

28. See Blume, *Protestant Church Music;* Louis F. Benson, *The English Hymn* (Philadelphia, 1915 = Richmond, VA, 1962).

29. From Article 49 of the Royal Injunctions, 1569. The principle of one note per syllable of text was operative.

30. The most famous of those in the sixteenth century who trans-

lated the psalms into metrical verse were Thomas Sternhold (d. 1549) and John Hopkins (d. 1570).

31. By law, the *Book of Common Prayer* could not be sold for more than 2 shillings unbound (or 3 shillings and 4 pence bound).

32. For example, the Pietists among Lutherans in Germany, and the rise of Quakerism and the Baptist Churches in England.

33. For an overall view of this topic, see Horton Davies, *The Worship of the English Puritans* (Westminster, MD, 1948); Stephen Mayor, *The Lord's Supper in Early English Dissent* (London, 1972).

34. For a convenient text, see Ian Breward, ed., *The Westminster Directory,* GLS 21 (Bramcote, Notts., 1980).

35. For the theological underpinnings of Quakerism, see the work of its great apologist, Robert Barclay (1648–1690), and especially his *An Apology for the True Christian Divinity as the Same Is Held Forth and Preached by the People, in Scorn, Called Quakers* (1678). See also n. 52 below.

36. See Blume, *Protestant Church Music.*

37. See Rudolf Wittkower and Irma Jaffe, eds., *Baroque Art: The Jesuit Contribution* (New York, 1972).

38. Exceptions to the generalized religious lethargy in this period are provided by the Moravians, and by Dutch precisianism, both of which would have some influence on eighteenth-century renewal movements.

39. See Davies, *Worship and Theology.*

40. See, for a brief discussion of this topic, Enrico Catteneo, *Il culto cristiano in Occidente* (Rome, 1978).

41. See J. Ernest Rattenbury, *The Eucharistic Hymns of John and Charles Wesley* (London, 1964); Eric Routley, *The Musical Wesleys* (New York, 1968).

42. See Ole Borgen, *John Wesley on the Sacraments* (Nashville, 1972); John Bowmer, *The Sacrament of the Lord's Supper in Early Methodism* (Westminster, MD, 1951).

43. See Jonathan Edwards, *A Treatise Concerning the Religious Affections* (1746).

44. For an analysis of the effect of nineteenth-century romanticism on Roman Catholic theology, especially in Germany, see Thomas F. O'Meara, *Romantic Idealism and Roman Catholicism* (Notre Dame, 1982).

45. See Marvin O'Connell, *The Oxford Conspirators* (New

York, 1969); James F. White, *The Cambridge Movement* (Cambridge, 1979).

46. At the same time as this medieval romanticism was going on, a romanticism of the Reformation period was also at work and is expressed in the work of N. F. S. Grundvig in Denmark and Catherine Winkworth in England.

47. See Phoebe Stanton, *Pugin* (New York, 1971), and Ralph Adams Cram, *The Substance of Gothic* (Boston, 1917), for the philosophical and historical context of Gothic revivalist architecture.

48. See Whitney R. Cross, *The Burned-over District* (New York, 1965); William G. McLoughlin, *Revivals, Awakenings, and Reform* (Chicago, 1978).

49. Charles G. Finney, *Lectures on the Revivals of Religion*, ed. William G. McLoughlin (Cambridge, MA, 1960).

50. See Charles A. Johnson, *The Frontier Camp Meeting* (Dallas, 1955).

51. Another factor that shaped eucharistic practice in this period was the American Temperance movement, which, in seeking to ban the production and consumption of alcohol, managed to introduce grape juice in place of communion wine in large segments of American Protestantism.

52. Even the Society of Friends (Quakers) underwent divisions during this period, with Joseph Gurney promoting evangelical trends in England and Elias Hicks (1748–1830) resisting those same trends in the United States, so that in some places Quaker worship looks very much like its mainline counterparts, with set texts and an ordained ministry.

53. See Walter J. Hollenweger, *The Pentecostals* (Minneapolis, 1972).

54. The biblical texts most often cited in support of this practice are Acts 2:4 and 1 Cor. 12:10.

55. See Killian McDonnell, *Charismatic Renewal and the Churches* (New York, 1976).

56. See Ernest B. Koenker, *The Liturgical Renaissance in the Roman Catholic Church* (Chicago, 1954).

57. For the English translation of the decrees of the Second Vatican Council, see Austin Flannery, ed., *Vatican Council II: The Conciliar and Post-Conciliar Decrees* (Collegeville, 1975).

58. At times this liturgical experimentation took rather extreme forms, with carbonated drinks and potato chips substituted for the

bread and wine at communion, and with avant-garde poetry and prose replacing more traditional prayer texts.

59. World Council of Churches, *Baptism, Eucharist, and Ministry*, Faith and Order Paper 111 (Geneva, 1982).

Index

Addai and Mari, anaphora of, 31, 169
Akiba, 59
Alcuin, 174
Alenu, 119
Alexandria, 11, 163, 166, 169, 173
Amalarius of Metz, 176
Ambrose of Milan, 167
Ambrosian rite, 174
amoraim, 110, 120
Amram Gaon, 36–37, 138
Anabaptists, 188–89, 193
Anglican worship, 190–91, 195, 197–98, 200; *see also Book of Common Prayer*
anointing, 11, 159, 167–68, 176
Antioch, 166–67, 169–70, 173–74
Apostolic Constitutions, 16, 169
Apostolic Tradition of Hippolytus, 13, 15, 159, 161, 167, 169
Ari: *see* Isaac Luria
aron hakodesh, 70–71, 74
Ashkenazic rite, 138–39, 141
Augustine of Hippo, 14
Austin, J. L., 38
Avi-Yonah, Michael, 72

Babylonia, 23, 36–37, 112, 114, 116–19, 123, 125–26, 128, 130; *see also* Talmud, Babylonian
Baer, Seligmann, 147
baptism, 4, 11, 13, 16–17, 32, 83, 87–88, 157–59, 163, 166–68, 170–71, 176, 186–90, 192, 194–95, 198–201
Bar Kokhba, 50, 59
Baumstark, Anton, 171

Ben Baboi, 36
Benedict of Aniane, 174
Benedict, Rule of, 172
Benjamin of Tudela, 119
Besht: *see* Israel Ba'al Shem Tov
Bethlehem, 86, 104
Bible reading in worship, 112, 115, 119–20, 123, 125, 160, 163, 168–69, 172, 174–76, 186, 190, 193–94, 198, 200; *see also* Torah
Bickermann, Elias, 55–58
birkat hamazon: see grace after meals, Jewish
bishops, 8, 9, 11–13, 83, 87, 159, 166, 171–72, 176
Black, Matthew, 50
Book of Common Order, 191
Book of Common Prayer, 29, 190–93
Bradshaw, Paul F., 36–37, 164
Braga, Council of, 10
Buber, Martin, 144
Bucer, Martin, 187
Byrd, William, 191
Byzantine, 71–73, 75–76, 80, 139; Byzantine rite, 169, 172–74

Cabasilas, Nicholas, 174
Cairo Genizah, 23–24, 31, 110, 124–27, 129
Calvin, John, 187–88, 190
Calvinist churches, 194, 197
Chalcedon, Council of, 173
Charlemagne, 174
chrism: *see* anointing
Christian Church (Disciples of Christ), 198

207

Chrysostom, John, 11, 167; anaphora of, 169
Church of England: *see* Anglican worship
church orders, 3, 12–14, 16–17, 158
Clement of Rome, 8
Cohen, Shaye, 73
Comte, August, 33
confirmation (Christian rite), 168, 176, 187, 189
Congregation of Sacred Rites, 189–91
Constantine, 6–7, 81–82, 84–88, 164–65, 168, 173
Constantinople, 157, 166, 173–74
Cram, Ralph Adams, 197
Cranmer, Thomas, 190
Cross, F. L., 14
Cyril of Jerusalem, 166, 170

Darwin, Charles, 25–26, 31
Dead Sea Scrolls, 23; *see also* Qumran
Decalogue, 115
Deichmann, Friedrich Wilhelm, 81
Didache, 31, 158
Didascalia, 83
Directory for the Public Worship of God, 192
Disciples of Christ: *see* Christian Church (Disciples of Christ)
Dix, Gregory, 158, 164–65
Douglas, Mary, 39
Dura-Europos, 31, 72, 73–76, 83, 93, 101
Durandus of Mende, 176
Durkheim, Emil, 25–26

Ecumenism, 200–201
Edwards, Jonathan, 196
Egeria, 172
Einhorn, David, 148–50
Einstein, Albert, 26
Elazar ben Moses Azikri, 143
Elbogen, Ismar, 23–25, 30
Eleazar ben Azariah, 59–60
Eleazar ben Judah of Worms, 139

Elvira, Council of, 88
Ephesus, Council of, 173
eucharist, 4, 11, 13, 16–17, 33, 83, 85, 87–88, 157, 159, 160–62, 164, 168–77, 186–92, 194–95, 197–98, 200–201; eucharistic prayer, 158, 160–62, 169–70, 175
Eusebius of Caesarea, 162

fast, 114–15, 118, 158–59, 162–63, 165, 167
feasts, 8, 54, 58, 114–16, 118, 142, 162–65, 170–71, 192
Finney, Charles Grandison, 197–98
Fox, George, 192
Franciscans, 76, 176, 193
Frankel, Zacharias, 148
Friends, Society of: *see* Quakers

Galilee, 51, 70–73, 76, 77–78
Gallican rite, 170, 174
Gamaliel, 23–24, 49, 53, 55, 57, 59–60, 62
Geertz, Clifford, 39
Geiger, Abraham, 148
geonim, 117, 122–28, 130
Germanus of Constantinople, 173–74, 176
Gibbons, Orlando, 193
Goldenberg, Robert, 60–61
Goodenough, E. R., 72
grace after meals, Jewish, 38, 116, 161, 169
Great Awakening, 196
Gregory the Great, 157
Guéranger, Prosper, 197
Gutmann, Joseph, 75

Hasidism, German, 139–40; Polish, 143–46
Havdalah, 119–26
Heidenheim, Wolf, 147
Heiler, F., 49
Heinemann, Joseph, 46–47, 114, 116
Heisenberg, Werner, 26
Hillel, House of, 51, 58

Hiller, E., 70
Hippolytus: *see Apostolic Tradition*
Hirsch, Samson Raphael, 148
Hoffman, Lawrence A., 45–47, 80, 128
Holdenheim, Samuel, 148
Horsely, Richard, 49
Huebsch, Adolph, 148
Hugh of St. Victor, 29
hymnody, 15, 142–43, 172, 185–86, 191, 194–95, 197–98, 200

Ignatius of Antioch, 8
initiation, Christian: *see* baptism; confirmation; eucharist
Isaac Luria (= Ari), 142
Islam, 128, 144, 173
Israel Ba'al Shem Tov (= Besht), 144

Janowitz, Naomi, 32
Jastrow, Marcus, 148
Jeremias, Joachim, 17
Jerusalem, 24, 51–53, 55–57, 59, 70–72, 74, 77–79, 82, 86, 97, 105, 111–13, 115, 166, 169–70, 172
Joel, Manuel, 148
Judah ben Samuel Hechasid, 139
Jungmann, Joseph, 30
Justin Martyr, 159–60, 168
Justinian, 157, 173

Kabbalah, 141–45
Kaddish, 119
Karaism, 182
Kavanagh, Aidan, 165
Kedusha: see trishagion
Kiddush, 119, 126, 150
Kilmartin, Edward J., 29, 32–33
Knox, John, 190
Kohl, Heinrich, 70–72, 76
Kohler, Kaufmann, 149–50
Kohut, Alexander, 148
Kraabel, A. Thomas, 73, 80
Krautheimer, Richard, 81, 84, 87
Kuhn, Thomas, 25–28

Lakatos, Imre, 27–28
Landshuth, Eliezer, 147
Langer, Suzanne, 38
Lardner, Gerald, 38
lectionary: *see* Bible reading in worship
Leeser, Isaac, 184
Levine, Lee, 47
Levi-Strauss, Claude, 32, 39
Loehe, Johann, 197
Lord's Supper: *see* eucharist
Luther, Martin, 185–87, 190
Lutheran worship, 193–94, 197, 200

Maimonides, Moses, 125, 138, 145
Marburg Colloquy, 187
Mass: *see* eucharist
Mathews, Thomas, 81
Maximus the Confessor, 173–74, 176
Meeks, Wayne, 32
Merbecke, John, 191
Merzbacher, Leo, 148
Methodist Worship, 195–96, 198, 200
Meyers, Eric, 72–73, 80
Minhag America, 149
Mishnah, 35–36, 52–53, 70, 112
monasticism, 7, 10, 17–18, 166, 172–73, 186
Moore, G. F., 70, 72
Morais, Sabato, 148
Moses, Isaac S., 149
Moses de Leon, 141
Mozarabic rite, 170, 174

Nachman of Bratslav, 145–46
Nathan of Nemirov, 146
Neale, John Mason, 197
Neusner, Jacob, 32, 47, 79–80
Nicea, Council of, 156, 162, 169
Nisbet, Robert, 25–26

Oecolampadius, John, 187
Olath Tamid, 149

paganism, 6, 73
Palestine, 35–38, 50, 61, 70–73, 75–80, 110, 112, 116, 119, 123, 125–26, 139; *see also* Talmud, Palestinian
Passover, 36, 54–55, 116, 126
Pentecostal worship, 199
Pepin, 174
persecution, 7, 139, 166, 189, 193
Petuchowski, Jacob, 58
Pistoia, Synod of, 195
piyyutim, 117, 123, 127, 129, 138–39
Prell, Riv-Ellen, 39
Presbyterian worship, 192, 197–98, 200
priesthood, 44, 48, 50, 52–62, 78, 88, 175, 192
psalmody, 7, 9–10, 17, 115, 119, 168, 172, 176, 188, 190–91, 193
Pugin, A. W. N., 197
Purcell, Henry, 193
Puritan worship, 192–93
Putnam, Hilary, 26

Quakers, 192–93
Qumran, 44, 51

Radbertus, Paschasius, 176
Rashi: *see* Solomon ben Isaac of Troyes
Ratramnus, 176
Reform Judaism, 146–51
Reif, Stefan, 47, 61
revivalist worship, 197–98, 200
Roman Catholic worship, 188–91, 193–95, 197, 199–200
Roman Empire, 38, 44, 50, 52, 60, 156–57
Roman rite, 30, 166, 169–70, 174, 176, 187, 189
Rome, 73–77, 80, 83–87, 102–3, 106, 162–63, 173

Saadiah, 126, 128, 138
Sabbath, 58, 114–16, 118, 126, 142–43, 150–51, 162

Sachs, Michael, 148
sacrifice, 44, 54–55, 57–58, 169–70, 186, 188–89
Saldarini, Anthony, 47, 50–51
Sanctus, 161, 169–70
Sarason, Richard, 45–47
Schechter, Solomon, 24
Scherman, Nosson, 29–30
Schütz, Heinrich, 193
scribes, 44, 48, 50–55, 57–62
Sephardic rite, 138, 141
Shakers, 144
Shammai, House of, 51, 58
Shema, 48, 50–55, 57, 59–62, 114, 126
siddur, 33, 118, 121, 123, 129
Simchah ben Samuel of Vitry, 138
Simeon Hapakoli, 59
Society of Jesus, 193
Solomon ben Isaac of Troyes (=Rashi), 138
Stein, Leopold, 148
Sukenik, E. L., 71
Sunday, 159–60, 162, 168, 187
Syria, 12, 74, 83, 93, 158–59, 167, 169, 173
Szold, Benjamin, 148

Taft, Robert F., 5, 16, 164, 168
Talley, Thomas J., 163
Tallis, Thomas, 191
Talmon, S., 44
Talmud, 35, 49, 70–71, 77, 110, 112, 117, 122, 129; Babylonian, 23–24, 60, 118; Palestinian, 24, 58–59, 114
talmudic, 77, 111–17, 119–20, 122–29
tannaitic, 32, 110
Tefillah, 23–24, 48, 49–50, 52–53, 55–62, 114, 149
Temple, 43, 46, 48, 50–59, 61, 78–79, 81, 97, 110–13, 115
Tertullian, 159, 164
Theodore of Mopsuestia, 167
Theophilus, patriarch of Alexandria, 11, 18
Torah, 51, 53–54, 56, 58, 70–71,

75–78, 111, 115–16, 119, 125,
    141–42, 146, 150–51; *see also*
    Bible reading in worship
Tosefta, 53
Trent, Council of, 189
trishagion, 116–17, 126, 161
Turner, Victor, 35, 38

Union Prayer Book, 149–51

Vaison, Council of, 10
Vatican Council, Second, 190, 199–
    200
Vitry: *see* Simchah ben Samuel of
    Vitry

Watzinger, Carl, 70–72, 76
Wesley, Charles, 195
Wesley, John, 195
Wise, Aaron, 148
Wise, Isaac Mayer, 148–50

Yavneh, 49, 58, 59
year, liturgical: *see* feasts
Yehudai Gaon, 36

Zahavy, Tzvee, 80
Zalman, Schneur, 145
Zohar, 141–42
Zunz, Leopold, 23, 25, 147
Zwingli, Ulrich, 187, 190